# Praise for *Containing Community*

"In this book, Greg Bird identifies and radically conceptualizes being-with as the problematic node that connects thinkers who in other respects are quite diverse such as Agamben, Esposito, and Nancy. His interpretation, acute and rigorous, illuminates in an admirable fashion a decisive passage of contemporary thought."

— Roberto Esposito, author of *Communitas: The Origin and Destiny of Community*

"In this exceptional book, Greg Bird offers for the first time in English a rigorous account of the common philosophical origins of Nancy, Agamben and Esposito's work on community. By emphasizing the centrality of the proper in the ontology of being in common and tracing it back to Heidegger, Bird places Nancy, Agamben, and Esposito at the center of contemporary economico-political philosophical debates."

— María del Rosario Acosta López,
DePaul University

# Containing Community

**SUNY series in Contemporary Italian Philosophy**

Silvia Benso and Brian Schroeder, editors

# Containing Community

## From Political Economy to Ontology in Agamben, Esposito, and Nancy

Greg Bird

SUNY PRESS

Published by State University of New York Press, Albany



Printed in the United States of America



For information, contact State University of New York Press, Albany, NY
www.sunypress.edu

Production, Ryan Morris
Marketing, Fran Keneston

Library of Congress Cataloging-in-Publication Data
Names: Bird, Greg, 1978- author.
Title: Containing community : from political economy to ontology in Agamben, Esposito, and Nancy / Greg Bird.
Description: Albany : State University of New York Press, 2016. | Series: SUNY series in contemporary Italian philosophy | Includes bibliographical references and index. | Description based on print version record and CIP data provided by publisher; resource not viewed.
Identifiers: LCCN 2016030427 (print) | LCCN 2015042620 (ebook)
ISBN 9781438461854 (hardcover : alk. paper)
ISBN 9781438461861 (pbk : alk.paper)
ISBN 9781438461878 (e-book)
Subjects: LCSH: Communities—Philosophy. | Agamben, Giorgio, 1942– comunitàe viene. | Esposito, Roberto, 1950- Communitas. | Nancy, Jean-Luc. Être singulier pluriel.
Classification: LCC B105.C46 (print) | LCC B105.C46 B57 2016 (ebook) | DDC 320.01/1—dc23
LC record available at https://lccn.loc.gov/2016030427

10 9 8 7 6 5 4 3 2 1

To Kevin my love

# Contents

# Acknowledgments

Sections of chapters 1 and 5 appeared in my essay, "Roberto Esposito's Deontological Communal Contract," and parts of chapter 5 appeared in "Community, Immunity, and the Proper: An Introduction to the Political Theory of Roberto Esposito" which I co-wrote with Jon Short. Both were published in *Angelaki: Journal of the Theoretical Humanities* (18.3). I am a grateful to Jon for allowing me to use our co-written material in this chapter.

I must begin by thanking Roberto Esposito for not only inviting me to spend two summers in Napoli and Pisa, but for his mentorship and for introducing me to the Italian Theory circle. I am grateful for all the conferences, seminars, and dinners I have had with many friends in this circle, including Stefania Achella, Daniela Calabrò, Diego Ferrante, Dario Gentili, Dario Giugliano, Enrica Lisciani Petrini, Valentina Mascia, Marco Spina, Elettra Stimilli, Davide Tarrizo, and Marco Spina. Thank you to the staff at *SUM* in Napoli, Antimo Chiariello, Federica Dura, Giovanne Ideale, and Ivana Orefice, for making me feel at home and for being patient with my Italian. Although I still can't say that *agg parlat tropp napulitan*, I now feel as if I have found *una casa lontano da casa*.

Back in Toronto, I owe many thanks. To Brian Singer, Kathy Bischoping, Anne O'Byrne, Philip Walsh, and Lorna Weir; without your intellectual and personal mentorship, this book would never have been written. My department and Wilfrid Laurier University, provided me with the time and means to complete this book. To my close peers, Jon Short, Kristin Hole, James Overboe, Mihnea Panu, Raluca Parvu, and Kristin

Shaw, thank you for helping me work through the process of writing and many of the ideas presented in this work. To my many friends in Toronto, thank you for being who you are. To my mother Kathryn Wells, David, Alison and Tony, in-laws Candice and Bob and the rest of the Hegges, and, of course, Kevin, thank you for your love, support, and patience. Finally, thank you to my acquisitions editor, Andrew Kenyon, for your timely responses, encouragement, and patience; to the blind reviewers for your thoughtful feedback; to my copy editor Daniel Otis; to my editorial assistant Jessica Kirschner; to my senior production editor Ryan Morris; and to everyone else who has contributed to printing this book at SUNY Press. Although this book is attributed to a single author, it is not the work of single person.

# Introduction

The focus of this book is three key texts that were products of the turn-of-the-century debate about community in continental philosophy: Giorgio Agamben's *Coming Community*, Roberto Esposito's *Communitas*, and Jean-Luc Nancy's *Being Singular Plural.* What follows is not an introductory text that provides a comprehensive, synthetic, and categorical summary of this debate. I engage in a politically grounded philosophical elaboration of how the exigency of community has been addressed by each philosopher. I aim to underline and draw attention to the critical insights each makes in regard to the prospect of rethinking community in our globalized world.

The first wave of this debate took place in France. In his original essay "The Inoperative Community," Nancy explicitly formulated community in Heideggerian terms, with a Bataillian inflection, around the problem of death and finitude. Blanchot's Lévinasian rejoinder, with an alternative Bataillian inflection, in *The Unavowable Community* helped Nancy to revamp his original statements. The final result was a redrafted publication as *The Inoperative Community.* In this work, Nancy drew a line between negative formulations of community based on the Other and his Heidegger-inspired notion of a plural ontology grounded in the existential analytic of being-with. Nancy is quite clear about these distinctions in his introduction to the Italian edition of Blanchot's book, later published as *La communauté affrontée*, and in his extensive reflections on Blanchot in his recently published *La communauté désavouée.*

The texts produced by Nancy and Blanchot in the 1980s revived, emboldened, and updated Bataille's project of overhauling how community had traditionally been understood in the West. But these texts are only of secondary concern for this book. My main interest is the three subsequent texts that were written in the 1990s. They represent a second wave of this debate. Each expands and further develops the terms laid out by the earlier debate. They helped to elevate the problem of the commons to a position of prominence not only in the rethinking-communism discussion, but also within continental philosophy itself.

*The Coming Community*, *Communitas*, and *Being Singular Plural* play a monumental role in their authors' larger body of work. These three texts also helped elevate each author to prominent positions in philosophy both on the continent and abroad. They have become, with Esposito arriving on the scene a little later, core references for those interested in a whole series of questions and problematics they address. Surprisingly, very little has been written in English that considers them as a group of thinkers. Although this debate took place in the 1990s, many of the insights made in these texts are directly relevant for contemporary social and political theory. Not only has each philosopher carried the ideas he develops in his text on community forward in his subsequent writings, but many of the insights he makes in these texts are critical for those who remain skeptical of, yet committed to, to the exigency of community—especially those of us who continue to identify as unorthodox communists.

If we were to try to summarize the collective efforts of Agamben, Esposito, and Nancy, we might say that each strives to conceive of community in a way where being is no longer dominated by having. Community can only occur in an ontological ethos or form-of-life where we can use things without appropriating them, or in a deontological modality where the sharing and division that define our being-in-common are no longer conceived in proprietary ways, or, for Nancy, in a coexistential modality of sharing where we no longer attempt to appropriate that which divides and shares us out. Put differently, what might a community look like when our being together is no longer defined by what we have or can have, by what only a few can and do have and the majority can't or doesn't have? Moreover, what if community is no longer constituted through the collective appropriation and redistribution of property—that is, if being included and ultimately belonging are no longer determined by one's possession of common property?

This is a problem of philosophy as much as of political economy. The first two chapters aim to make this clear. The first chapter examines various problems that have arisen in the dispositif of the proper in modern political economy that has come to dominate how we conceive of politics, and ultimately community. My main reference in this chapter is Pierre Joseph Proudhon's critique of the property prejudice. The second chapter consists of an examination of Heidegger's thinking on the proper, especially his later formulations of the Ereignis. In the final three substantive chapters, I examine how Agamben, Esposito, and Nancy address the dispositif of the proper from the perspective of both political economy and ontology.[1]

# 1

# Political Economy and the Proper

> The distinguishing feature of Communism is not the abolition of property generally, but the abolition of bourgeois property. But modern bourgeois private property is the final and most complete expression of the system of producing and appropriating products that is based on class antagonisms, on the exploitation of the many by the few. In this sense, the theory of Communists may be summed up in the single sentence: Abolition of private property.
>
> —*The Communist Manifesto*, 223

> [S]ystematic community, the deliberate negation of property, is conceived under the direct influence of the property prejudice; and it is property that is to be found at the root of all communist theories. . . . The members of a community, it is true, have no property, but the community is the proprietor, and proprietor not only of goods but of persons and wills. It is because of this principle of sovereign property, that labor, which should be imposed on man only by nature, becomes a human commandment.
>
> —*QP*, 203; *WP*, 196

Although the recent texts on community cannot be reduced to the classical debate between Anarchists and Marxists, it would be wrong to overlook it. To varying degrees each philosopher appeals to the spirit of the anarchic aphorism—no gods, no masters, *and* no property. In fact, each has taken up and pushed this mantra well beyond simply reversing and opposing gods, masters, and property. Nancy continues to search for ways to deconstruct Christianity, Agamben has written several archaeological expositions of economic theology, and since the 1980s Esposito has sought to elaborate on various impolitical fissures that will disrupt the enclosure caused by political theology. The second precept is largely, but not exclusively, addressed through their critiques of metaphysical philosophy, especially the notion of the subject. In the substantive chapters on each of them, I return to the first two tenets repeatedly, but for the purposes of the opening chapter of this book, I want to focus on the third, which is at the forefront of each of their texts on community. Each attempts to conceive of community beyond the dispositif of the proper. Over the course of this chapter, I provide a rough outline of the rise of this political economy in the West, starting with Locke.

I have chosen to start with political economy before turning to Heidegger's ontology of the proper in the second chapter to demonstrate how significant this tradition is for the texts on community, especially Esposito's and Nancy's.

One cannot ignore the large shadow cast by Heidegger on the texts about community, as his work serves as the primary philosophical resource each draws from, especially Nancy and Agamben, but to commence with Heidegger would lead us down a treacherous path. For starters, we would have to deal with his retrograde politics, a problem that has proven to be a source of great consternation in the secondary literature on each of the three philosophers.[1] Heidegger's critics also charge him with obscurantism, a charge that has also been laid on our three main philosophers. Étienne Balibar, for example, praises Esposito and Nancy for their rigorous deconstruction of the role of property in the constitution political borders in an essay called "Citizenship without Community" in *We, The People of Europe* (2004). Elsewhere, however, he takes issue with those who seek to deconstruct the proper, notably Derrida. Such efforts, he argues, represent a shallow, postmodern, and, by implication, ideological defense of the liberal archetype of the possessive individual. What else can come from Derrida's call for "ex-appropriation" than Heideggerian wordplay, such as that between "*Eigen, Eigentum, Eigenschaft,* and *Ereignis*" (2002, 313)? Heideggerian eschatology, he continues, may lead to "an *Enteignung* [dispossession], a depropriation or disappropriation of the subject, of what is 'proper' to the subject (*Eigen*)," but, he asks, how formidable is political resistance when its source is etymology? To oppose appropriation as the lever for revolutionary social changes, he concludes, is a de facto promotion of a radical form of alienation, *abyssal alienation*, by which he means a radicalization of difference (2002, 315).

It is precisely the terms of this critique that Agamben, Esposito, and Nancy address, not solely in the so-called "jargon of authenticity," but in their political and economic horizons. Balibar's critique goes beyond simply indicting them for being Heideggerians, because it presses up against a much broader problem that each philosopher has struggled with: trying to formulate a type of politics that avoids, rather than counters, the trappings of the dispositif of the proper. Nancy's and Agamben's vehement opposition to formulating political prescriptions and ascribing to any operative type political practice, for example, has become a sticking point among their critics.[2] We might even call theses critiques updated versions of the longstanding dogma held by Marxists that the anarchic refusal to combine economic appropriation with political appropriation (i.e., the state must be seized along with the factories), leads to an utterly impotent form of politics. Each of the three main philosophers we examine in this book, however, has provided a litany of tools for rethinking precisely how the dogmatic call for appropriation, or worse, re-appropriation, represents nothing more than an ideological defense of the dispositif of the proper. What if politics are no longer conceived in the aporetic dialectic of alienation and appropriation? Moreover, what if community itself is no longer constituted as something that is proper to those who belong and thus improper to those who don't?

Before we get to these questions, much context must be provided. Over the course of this and the next chapter I have selected a handful of themes that must be covered before I turn to the substantive investigations of the three philosophers. What follows is not a comprehensive overview of the broader problematic of proper, but rather a rough sketch. In this chapter, I provide a brief account of the role of the political economy in modern Western political theory. Then I examine, in broad strokes, the three authors' general critique of the role of the proper in formulating community. I end by addressing their common goal of dis-containing community. In the second chapter, I return to each of these issues, explicitly addressing them in relation to Heidegger's ontological philosophy.

## I. The Proprietary Confusion

If we were to pinpoint a central moment in the genealogy of this dispositif, we would have to begin when the West set out to colonize the rest of the world. Pope Alexander VI's Papal Bull of 1493, the enclosure movement in England, and the social contract tradition epitomized by John Locke's theory of property, are three formative moments in what is now an unrelenting and all-encompassing process. Today, we are well beyond the point of "primitive accumulation" as the relentless drive to appropriate things has engulfed everything that has stood in its path. In our contemporary neoliberal era, we are running out of objects to convert into property.[3] Very few are immune to the proper, as conservatives, liberals, and communists alike are dogmatically committed to this now hegemonic dispositif. At its core rests the modern model of the proprietary subject. Although Hugo Groitus was the first to articulate this subject, Locke's version became the archetype that we still employ today.[4] In paragraph 27 of his *Second Treatise on Government*, Locke famously claimed:

> Though the earth, and all inferior creatures, be common to all men, yet every man has a *property* in his own *person*: this no body has any right to but himself. The *labour* of his body and the *work* of his hands, we may say are properly his. Whatsoever then he removes out of the state of nature hath provided, and left it in, he hath mixed his *labour* with, and joined to it something that is his own, and thereby makes it his *property*. It being by him removed from the common state of nature hath placed it in, it hath by this *labour* something annexed to it, that excludes the common right of other men: for this *labour* being the unquestionable property of the labourer, no man but he can have a right to what that is once joined to, at least where there is enough, and as good, left in common for others.

Locke's liberal doctrine of property represented a radical break from the two conventional doctrines of his time—"acquisition"/"conquest" and "legal division" (Arendt 1998, 110). Property and ownership had been viewed as human inventions that were supported by human laws, but Locke argued that the human is by nature a proprietary being. There are two essential elements in this new model of the subject, which has had drastic effects on modern thought: he elevated the personal as the principle domain of property, and he created a stark division between the proper and the common.

First, above and beyond the *animal laborans* or *Homo faber*, Locke's human is a *Homo approprians*. She is not just an owner of herself, but also of all that she produces through her labor. This formulation established a modern paradigm of property, which grounded ownership in the idiom. Second, *Homo approprians* is also an anticommunal model of the human. Prior to his reversal, the natural world was largely viewed as a common world. In the commons there were no distinctions between things held or not held because everything stood in its preappropriated and natural state. Everything could be shared and put to common use. In Locke's formulation, however, the proper is constituted through the very negation of the common as uncommon. This uncommon orientation rests at the very core, perhaps the essence of the proper.

Both these elements are present in the central activity of the appropriating human: *taking* things and rendering them one's own. Locke claims, for example, that property begins with the act of "taking any part of what is common, and removing it out of the state nature leaves it in" (1980, §28). Taking a good from the common, however, is not enough to constitute it as private property, for this can only occur when laborers "add" to it. This appropriative action therefore consists of two moments—first, taking something from the commons, and second, converting it into a fabricating thing. In the process, part of the subject is transferred into the thing, which according to Locke is enough to claim the thing as an extension of one's own private sphere. The thing becomes a part of that person, and therefore the appropriator should be entitled to exclusive ownership and enjoyment of the thing, with the proviso that one should never accumulate excessive amounts of property. The act of appropriation not only "inclose[s] it [the appropriated thing] from the common" (1980, §32), he argues, but it also creates a private boundary that "excludes the common right of other men" (1980, §27). It constitutes an "enclosure," "boundary," or "distinct territory" that shields the private proprietor from the commons (1980, §37). The liberal state, therefore, has a duty to protect the "private rights" of those who bear "private property," and not just the commons (1980, §28). The state, he famously announces, must serve the "mutual *preservation* of the lives, liberties and estates, which I call by the general name, *property*" (1980,

§123) or simply "*the preservation of their property*" (1980, §124). It is this very extension of property to include not just estates (belongings) but also lives and liberties that becomes the *raison d'état* of the modern liberal state. Locke's invasive model of property is, of course, formulated as a late defense of the enclosure movement. It would take a few more centuries for the idiom to completely appropriate the proper and the proper the idiom, but Locke set the wheels of this proprietary confusion in motion.[5]

* * *

In *The Human Condition* Hannah Arendt claims that when Locke extended property to include the personal, he created a menacing confusion that continues to confound modern political thought and politics. He gave the modern state a contradictory mandate: to protect a person's right to invade and to protect a person's right to an exclusive domain. On the one hand, the state was elevated as the guardian of private property. It was charged with the role of preventing the commons from further intruding into the public sphere (1998: 111). On the other hand, he failed to distinguish between political and economic rights because his notion of property is all-encompassing. Thus, the state was tasked with defending private property in general.

From Arendt's republican perspective, Locke's economization of politics created a major impasse. To become a genuine *zoon politikon*, there must be a clear separation between the *idios kosmos* and the *koinos kosmos*. The *oikos* is supposed to shield the *idios kosmos* from the common, and political beings must have their own personal space to reflect and develop on their own accord. In capitalism, however, the private is completely exaggerated. Property over things is confused with property over one's person, and the state is obligated to preserve private property in general. The net result is a pervasion of privacy. Modern states, she contends, privilege the "privative trait of privacy," mere privation, which is a kind of privacy that the Greeks attributed to "idiots" (ibid.). This is a far cry from the positive sense of the private, which the Greeks referred to as "the privacy of 'one's own' [*idion*]" (1998, 38). This is her famous thesis that in modern societies the blending of the public and the private spheres leads to an erosion of both. When the *koinos* is mixed with the *idios*, neither performs its proper function. If everything is property, we no longer have a common world, but a social world. Put in Fenichel Pitkin's terms, the big "blob" of the social destroys the common (1998).

What is striking about Arendt's critique of the conflation of the proper with the idiom is her subtle reflection on the modern paradigm of political economy. When the political is dominated by the economic, the result is mass political privation. Moreover, when property is retranslated into political terms—the possession of the fundamental democratic right to individual autonomy—the political subject represents a mirror image of the economic private proprietor. Beyond Locke's appeal to the *animal laborans* as the source of property, the central political conflict for *Homo approprians* is based on property and, of course, its central political-economic activity is appropriation. The conflict between the bourgeoisie and the proletarians is one between bad versus good forms of appropriation. If the private appropriation of the bourgeoisie is simultaneously economic and political, the only way the collective form of appropriation by the proletarians can be truly revolutionary is if their appropriative response is likewise economic and political. Either way, appropriation becomes the medium of human relations. "The body," she argues, "becomes indeed the quintessence of all property because it is the only thing one could not share even if one wanted to" (1998, 112). Yet, she argues that the body is ideally a private entity that cannot be divided or shared (*koinos*). When the state regulates appropriation, the economic and political senses of property are confused, and the idiom is confused with the proper. This confusion between the economic and the political is addressed by Agamben and Esposito in their biopolitical writings, which I return to in later chapters, but for now it is necessary to focus on the classical accounts of this problem. Although it is not possible to cover the entire literature concerning Locke's conflation of the proper with the idiom, or, to put it differently, his proprietary confusion, it is necessary to address a few introjections that will help set the stage for the three substantive chapters in this book. I briefly examine the early critiques of this confusion raised by Marx and Proudhon. Then I will briefly turn to C. B. Macpherson's and Étienne Balibar's writings on this problem.

* * *

Marx and Proudhon actually held very similar positions on the proprietary confusion. Both were critical of Antoine Destutt de Tracey's sensualist reading of Locke. In a rarely cited passage in the second part of the first book of *The German Ideology*, Marx and Engels consider the distinction between property (*Eigentum*) and personal peculiarity (*persönlichen Eigentümlichkeit*) (1998, 245–48; 1954, 210–12). They criticize Destutt de Tracey and Max Stirner for reducing personal peculiarity to property. Such an etymological reduction, they contend, represents an ideological defense of private property. Destutt de Tracey, they argue, serves the interests of private property when he treats "individuality" as an "inalienable property." By holding that "*propriété, individualité* and *personnalité*" are "identical," they claim, the "the me [*moi* in French] includes the mine [*mein* in German]" (1998, 245; 1954, 210). Personality (the me) is confused with private property (the mine). Marx and Engels dismiss this simple *jeu de mots* of *propriété* and *personnalité* as a "liberal" interpretation of socialism. They also accost Stirner for his *Wortspiel*, which is really a *Wortverdrehung* (twisting, distortion of words) of *Eigentum* (property) and *Eigenheit* (peculiarity or character). Stirner carries this "theoretical nonsense" to the extreme point when he "declares" that the *Eigen* (proper), which he reduces "to the concept of property," is "an eternal truth." He thus provides an ideological defense of private property when he exploits "the etymological connection between the words *Eigentum* and *Eigen*" (1998, 246–47; 1954, 211). Such etymological nonsense, they note with a berating tone, leads Stirner to reduce the indispensable "to have" to private property. Could one not "have a stomach ache" in a communist society, they ask, without reducing it to the register of property (1998, 246; 1954, 211)?

Marx and Engels argue that those who reduce the person to property weaken the communist cause. Private property would be enlisted to defend the personal against the forces of communal property, but in "reality" the personal cannot be reduced to property because "I only have property insofar as I have something vendible, whereas what is peculiar to me [*meine Eigenheit*] may not be vendible at all" (1998, 247; 1954, 211). Although "private property" has "alienated [*entfremdet*] the individuality, not only of people, but also of things" in capitalism, the distinction between property and personal peculiarity is not erased (ibid.). They are only indistinguishable in the worldview of the bourgeoisie, where the "sphere of synonymy" between "*propriété Eigentum und Eigenschaft*" and "*property Eigentum und Eigentümlichkeit*" appears to be a reality (1998, 248; 1954, 212).[6] Private property becomes the common measure, that is, commodification in a double sense, of everything.[7] Derrida cites this passage in *Specters of Marx* and in *Margins of Philosophy*. In the earlier work, he argues that this "critique of etymologism" raises the question about "the history and value of the proper—*idion, proprium, eigen*," which is found not only in Marx and Engels, but in "several others (Plato, Leibniz, Rousseau, etc.)" (1982, 216, fn. 13). It is not without significance, he remarks, that Marx and Engels chose to use "the proper" as their "example" in this passage.

Five years before Marx and Engels started writing *The German Ideology*, Pierre Joseph Proudhon's *What Is Property?* was published. Proudhon argues that Destutt de Tracey made a "puerile confusion" by reproducing the metaphysical prejudice that "everything which man could call his own was identified in his mind with his person" (*QP*, 50; *WP*, 52). This "false analogy" led him to equate "possession of things" with "property in the powers of the mind and body" (*QP*, 50; *WP*, 53). It created a tautological characterization of property as "the property of the property of being a proprietor" (*QP*, 50; *WP*, 52).[8]

Destutt de Tracey's confusion is based on a defense of the modern liberal reading of "sovereignty." Proudhon claims that the democratic notion of sovereignty replaces the monarchic model of the grand Master with multiple self-mastering individuals. To justify self-mastery, individuals have to be conceived of as private proprietors and as sovereign masters. Liberals such as Destutt de Tracey confuse the economic with the political in order to constitute a sovereign subject. A sovereign man is treated as if he is a "proprietor even of his own faculties," deplores Proudhon (*QP*, 50; *WP*, 53). Proudhon has two problems with this reduction.

First, the traditional concept of sovereignty as "'*the power to make laws*'" is a "relic of despotism" (*QP*, 28; *WP*, 30).[9] In reference to the nineteenth-century distinction between reason and passions, he argues that democratic sovereignty is based on a simple shift in the rule of passions from one person to several (*QP*, 27; *WP*, 29). As the mere "expression of the will," sovereignty is inseparable from the passions. It is not based on justice, which appeals to "law" as the "rule of reason." Therefore, he concludes, the events of 1789 were merely a slight "progress[ion]" in sovereignty, not a "revolution," and Rousseau's social contract, based on the general will, represents a continuation of the antiquated sovereign paradigm (*QP*, 28–29; *WP*, 29–30).

Second, by failing to distinguish between "acquired" things and "innate" qualities, the "right of property" is generalized to include the "right of [personal] domain" (*QP*, 49–51; *WP*, 52–53). Idiomatic qualities are thus reduced to the judicial "right of domain over a thing" (*QP*, 49; *WP*, 52).[10] Beyond the linguistic confusion of property qua quality and property qua economic thing, he is also troubled by how this operation draws from the metaphor of the self-mastering subject. He dismisses this by raising the aporia of self-reflection to argue that one cannot "own," "dominate," even "control" one's faculties as a "sovereign master"; rather, one can only make "use of them" (*QP*, 50; *WP*, 53). Moreover, since a despot is satiated by self-satisfaction, she is dominated by her senses rather than intellectually in control of them. Therefore democratic political economy represents a pluralization of despotism.[11]

There is a second strain in Proudhon's critique of the property prejudice that brings us back to Locke's *Homo approprians*. In his proclamation that "*la propriété, c'est le vol!* ["property is theft!"]," he does not just challenge the bad form of appropriation, like Marx, but he also questions how property itself is constituted. In a subsection of chapter 5 called "Characteristics of Community and Property," Proudhon argues that the social contract represents nothing more than an ideological tool devised by conspiring thieves who aim to enhance their private interests at the expense of the commons (*QP*, 1867; *WP*, 2005). This critique has been repeated many times by social and political theorists. Rousseau, for example, admitted that the social contract served as a weak substitute for communal relationships.[12] Proudhon's critique is based on a distinction he makes between classical and modern notions of property. He argues that the modern notion of property creates a particular type of prejudice that is antagonistic to community. With romantic undertones, he appears to be advocating for a resurrection of the classical model. Classically, he argues, property was viewed as something that was *held back* from others. To appropriate and convert something into property was an exclusionary act. It blocked others from having direct access to the good. Property thus was conceived as an exclusive enclosure that was antagonistic to the commons. On the flip side, the commons was conceived as a place that was open and inclusive. It was a place where everyone was expected to unreservedly share with each other. In the commons, people were less inclined to hold things back to be used exclusively for themselves.

This is, of course, an exaggerated reading that paints a picture of the commons as the place where sharing happens in absolute terms, which is a romanticized and problematic image of community. Yet Proudhon does appear to insinuate that the commons is the place where sharing occurs without reservations. This ideal, he claims, is present in the eighth commandment, "Thou shall not steal" (*QP* 205, *WP* 198). "The Hebrews,"[13] he continues, understood *lo thi-gnob* as "'Thou shall not steal,' that is, thou shall not hold back/retain [*tu ne retiendras*], thou shall not put anything aside for thyself." To be openly received into the commons, then, one must openly "bring all that he has" without "secretly" holding back a portion for himself. In other words, nothing is set apart, withdrawn, hidden, or concealed because the commons is ideally an open place. To enter the commons, one must *let go* of possessions and proceed with open hands. Letting go in this formulation is an activity that releases one's grasp over the good, which is different than making a gift of one's goods as if they were things that could be offered as a contribution, like a tax.

Proudhon's main concern in this passage is the possession of goods or objects. He did not carry this analysis as far as contemporary theorists of community have by extending the opening to include individual identity. Agamben, Esposito, and Nancy summon the powers of dis-containment to the fullest extent possible to thoroughly disrupt the appropriative disposition of the modern subject, whereas Proudhon was merely concerned with highlighting the privative orientation of the modern model of property. The three contemporary theorists also have Heidegger's distinction between the primary modalities of holding and letting go to draw from, which I will discuss in detail in the next chapter. Nevertheless, Proudhon's critique of the property prejudice provides an interesting opening for challenging the standard model of *Homo approprians* as the creature who is defined by its *capacity to take things.*

The classical model of exclusionary property oscillated between holding and letting go, and only the modern model treats property as invasive. It oscillates between the modalities of taking and giving. Proudhon argues that the primary source of this particular conception of private property is thievery. His proof for this claim is etymologically based. In Latin, he claims, theft (*le vol*) is either referred to as *fur* ("I carry away"/"*j'emporte*") or *latro* ("I conceal myself"/"*je me cache*") (*QP*, 205; *WP*, 198). His reference to carrying away is consistent with most Indo-European languages, which treat theft as an action that carries away (*deferre* is the root of "differ" and "defer") something from the commons. In this thieving sense of property, property is no longer constituted as holding something back from the commons in an exclusionary manner, but as taking something from the commons for oneself. It is an invasive action. This sense is also present in the second term. *Latro* translates as "robber" or "bandit." It stems from the Ancient Greek *latron*, who was a hired, noncitizen mercenary or anyone else who provided a service for pay. In legal terminology, "conceal" (*concelare*) is synonymous, but only indirectly connected, with *latitare*, which is an act of hiding away from creditors, that is, to lie hidden (*latere* or "latent" in English). Like the differing act, larceny is an act that separates a good from the commons, carries it away, and converts it into a private good. The *latro* is an economic entity without political identity. A "robber," Proudhon argues, "is a man who conceals, carries away, and diverts a thing which does not appertain [*appartient*] to him in any manner whatsoever" (*QP*, 205; *WP*, 198).[14] In this act, the thief separates, conceals, and ultimately closes herself off from the commons. Thus, in both senses the thief rips and tears the commons apart, deprives it, and then hides the stolen object in her own private *oikos*.

Proudhon even proclaims in sheer hyperbole that this modern conception of property took hold when the "*argot* of thieves" was standardized in the French language and then codified in French Law (*QP*, 205; *WP*, 198). His primary evidence is based in his misreading of the etymology of "the thief" (*le voleur*). *Voler*, he claims, derives from "*faire la vol*, from the Latin *vola*, palm of the hand, means to take [*prend*] all the tricks in a game of cards, so that the *voleur*, the thief, is the beneficiary who takes all, who gets the lion's share" (*QP*, 205; *WP*, 198).[15]

Although Proudhon's scholarship is wanting, he does provide an interesting interpretation of how property is conceived by modern liberal philosophy. He argues that the property prejudice leads us to treat property as something that is invasive and thus constituted through the modality of taking. The invasive model of property creates a new image of the commons. In the classical model, ownership derives from holding things back from the commons. The commons was not conceived of as the container of property, but as a place without property that was open and inclusive. But with the modern property prejudice and the invasive activity of *Homo approprians*, we end up with a perverted image of the commons. Common property is perpetually in conflict with private property. To protect or even enhance common property, it must invade and appropriate the private. But this is a proprietary, thus privative, notion of the commons, which is closed, exclusionary, and in the end uncommon.[16]

Today we really cannot speak of a commons, but of a public. In neoliberal discourse, the state steals from private owners to enhance the public. Nowhere is this reversal more apparent than in the neoliberal discourse of "taxpayers." A taxpayer, as opposed to a citizen, must pay a tribute on behalf of the public. Since private property reigns, the tribute is taken from the taxpayer. Politicians employ this rhetoric to continue their attack on the public sector and public property. But even mainstream left-wing political parties have succumbed to this reversal. When they demurely speak of taking taxes from the taxpayers, they justify it on the grounds that the taxes will be used in the interest of the public; in other words, they will be given back to the public. It is received not as a gift, but as a return on the investment.

* * *

Notable social democratic interpreter of Locke, C. B. Macpherson, sheds additional light on the proprietary confusion. In *The Political Theory of Individualism*, he argues that seventeenth-century liberal democratic theory was based on the notion that an individual has a "possessive quality." The individual was conceived "as essentially the *proprietor* of his own *person* or *capacities*, owing nothing to society for them. The individual was seen neither as a moral whole, nor as a part of a larger social whole, but as an owner of himself. The relation of ownership, having become for more and more men the critically important relation determining their actual freedom and actual prospect of realizing their full potential, was read back into the nature of the individual. The individual, it was thought, is free inasmuch as he is *proprietor* of his *person* and *capacities*" (italics added, 1962: 3). As the "possessive market society" expanded, humans were not only defined by property, but their personal property was further divided between "labour products" and "possession of personality" (1962, 48). Personal freedom and autonomy now had two new preconditions: one must be in possession of and have control over oneself, and one must own the things in one's immediate world. This formulation resonates with Proudhon's reading of the proprietary confusion. For Macpherson it resulted in a complementary system of rights based on property. The right to possess private property in things could only be secured when complemented by the right to possess one's own person. In advanced capitalism, this confusion is nearly complete, because now the possessive individual is conceived solely in the narrow sense of economic property (1978). Like Arendt, he partially attributes this reduction to how labor is treated as if it is one's "own" and exclusive property (1975, 97).

As a representative of the New Left discourse of the 1960s and '70s, Macpherson sought a revised solution for socialism. He argued that this could only be accomplished by reversing the liberal framework of property. Property must be treated as a "right to not be excluded"; thus, the "means of labour" should become a "non-exclusive right" (1975, 98–99). Macpherson's claim rests on a distinction between property over things and property over oneself. Things should be distributed and shared across the community in a fair and just manner. Individual capacities, however, are personal and separate. They should not be confused with property over things.

Macpherson's solution falls within the "technological determinism thesis" Marx employed in the *Grundrisse* when he speculated that automated production could put an end to hard labor. Many in the New Left advanced this position in their euphoric celebration of the postindustrial society.[17] Advances in industry gave rise, some thought, to a postscarcity era where the basic necessities for life could be provided to everyone. Industrial production could be fully "automated" and hard labor was no longer required to meet our basic needs. Humanity could be released from the shackles of labor, we could restrict the division of labor, and human capacities would no longer be converted into property. Thus, human capacities could be placed on the proper side of the political-economic scale and legally protected by the political right to individual autonomy.

Macpherson's thesis is situated in the discourses of the 1960s and '70s. We know that the utopian dream of a fully automated, utopian society where everyone was freed from the realm of necessities, the so-called knowledge economy, has not only failed to produce a liberated humanity, but it is been marked by even further economic polarization, environmental degradation, and global conflict. In Italy, the reception of the postindustrial thesis has been remarkably different than in North America. From the *Lotta Femminista* wages for housework campaign, to the broader post-*operaismo* campaign, radical Italian theorists have sought to rethink the revolutionary formula beyond the trappings of workerism (*operaismo*), and even beyond economism. Instead of conceiving of "immaterial labour" as liberating, many have argued that today most knowledge and emotional workers make up the growing masses of the precariat. If there is to be a liberating element in this type of work, it is the liberation from the machines and the *operativity* of capitalism. This frees people from the slavery of the factories and opens new possibilities for thinking about a global movement in very different terms than the traditional theories of revolution. Hardt and Negri's "multitude," for example, represents a postworkerist model of the revolutionary subject. I mention this here because both Agamben and Nancy draw from this alternative reading of operativity in their work, only both do so while trying to radically disrupt the property prejudice.

* * *

In the article I mentioned in the introduction to this chapter, Balibar interrogates the "reversal" of possessive individualism (2002). He also seeks to rectify the division of the possessive individual into economic and political property. He begins with a lengthy exegesis on Locke's model. At the core of this model, he argues, the possessive individual is defined as the "individual-*qua*-owner" (2002, 300). He then uses this model as a template to distinguish between three popular "reversals" of the "bourgeois worldview": Marx, Derrida, and Rousseau. I will focus only on the first two analyses.

The template of the possessive individual, Balibar argues, acts as an ideological front that distracts us from the exigency of the "collective subject." Since it is cut from the image of a private proprietor, we are less inclined to communal property, and thus to community. This explains why Marx appeals to "collective appropriation" to overturn private property (2002, 311). Marx's "speculative formulation," Balibar argues, is contingent on a "dialectical reversal": "the expropriation of the expropriators [as] an 'appropriation' by society and individuals in it of the very means and forms of the conditions of appropriation—an 'appropriation of appropriation'" (2002, 310).[18] Translated, this means that when the appropriative apparatuses of capitalism—means of production, state, etc.—are collectively appropriated, and the expropriating class is itself expropriated, a new template is established for the proper. What "appropriation of appropriation" means, however, only makes sense in light of his critique of Derrida.

Balibar situates Derrida's "eschatological reversal" on the other end of the scale. Derrida's "ex-appropriation" merely deconstructs the proper. Balibar's argument rests on the same logic Marx used against Destutt de Tracy and Stirner. Derridean philosophy, he argues, is unsuitable for politics because it merely engages in the Heideggerian game of word association (2002, 313). Like Marx, he questions "the doublet of *property* and *propriety*" that results in a "more fundamental notion which is neither ap-propriation nor ex-propriation, but simply 'propriation'" (ibid.). This fits with "Heideggerian speculative etymology," which reads the "'event'" as "forever to come, unpredictable and incalculable" (Ibid., fn. 26).

Balibar strategically formulates this argument to deliver the normative claim that to oppose appropriation as the lever for radical transformation is to promote a radicalization of "alienation," by which he means a radicalization of difference (2002, 315). That is, without appropriation, subjects are left in the conditions where their identities are heteronymously determined. But is either Balibar's call for the collective appropriation of the appropriated or Derrida's ex-propriating propriation a solution for the *Homo approprians* of modern political economy?

Proponents of political economy usually, and often unintentionally, confuse personal identity and personal property when dealing with the difference between alienation and appropriation. This is evident in the various interpretations of Marx's essay on alienation. In *Lectures on Ideology and Utopia*, for example, Paul Ricoeur argues that mediated identity can only be realized through an "objectification" (*Vergegenständlichung*) process (1986, 36–39). A subject must first exteriorize its interior before it can re-interiorize it and realize its capacities. If this process is fluid and without external interruptions, the subject experiences it as "estrangement" (*Entäußerung*). Estrangement, he argues, is unavoidable given that the process takes place within our plural conditions. It only becomes "alienation" (*Entfremdung*) when an other takes a subject's externalization, appropriates it, and then treats it as if it were their own property.[19]

Ricoeur exaggerates the autonomous exigency in this dialectic. A laborer becomes alienated when she internalizes the heteronymous and falsely identifies with it as if it is her own, which prevents her from asserting herself as a species-being (1986, 41–43). Here species-being, especially in Marx's manuscript, represents the human capacity to objectify and appropriate. To develop one's capacities, cognitive and bodily, one must first objectify oneself and then, in the second instance, appropriate this objectification. When difference intervenes between the first and second instances, alienation takes place. When one's capacities are appropriated and made to serve another's interests, yet one still identifies with them as if they are one's own, one is no longer capable of autonomously asserting oneself—even if it is just "relatively autonomous," a catch phrase signifying the aporia of the theory of autonomy. One becomes deferential, even subservient. Many labor process theorists, ranging from Gramsci's early critique of Fordism to Harry Braverman's critique of Taylorism, have pointed to the alienating effects of capitalist division of labor between those who conceptualize and those that execute tasks. One's capacities, which form the very basis of one's species-being, become heteronymous and objectification becomes alienation. To appropriate appropriation, in this sense, would mean to appropriate the structures of authorization in order to allow for people to be in control of their own capabilities, to render them proper to themselves and nonalienating.

## II. The Dialectic of Alienation and Appropriation

In their political writings on community and the proper, Agamben, Esposito, and Nancy do not give Proudhon the attention he deserves. His early and crude ruminations on the property prejudice helped to establish a critical discourse on the role of property in mainstream political thinking that spans from the left to the right. We might even call Proudhon the progenitor of this critique. After over a 160 years, what Proudhon viewed as a mere prejudice has metamorphized into the comprehensive, axiomatic, and hegemonic dispositif of the proper. Each of the three contemporary philosophers challenges this dispositif on multiple fronts. It is based in the metaphysics of the subject, it reduces difference to sameness (or identity), it is trapped in the ontotheological search for an original foundation, it creates an inclusion/exclusion framework, and so on. Each likewise arrives at the same conclusion: because the dispositif of the proper creates a series of enclosures, it prevents us from thinking about relationships and thus community.

A predominant feature of the dispositif of the proper is the dialectic of alienation and appropriation. When community is conceived as the product of this dialectic, community is constituted through the collective act of negating, overcoming, and appropriating alienating conditions. This formula of negating the negation, the lack, is repeated in most theories of collective emancipation, including anti-imperialist, national liberation, feminist, queer, antiracist, and communist politics. Today, the target of appropriation carries well beyond concrete forms of economic property. The proper now extends into such abstracted forms as personal identity (rights discourse, theories of recognition, or other forms of identity politics), ideas (self-determination, autonomy, or intellectual property rights), bodies (birth control, euthanasia, or aesthetic freedom), and collective identities (strategic essentialism, national identities, or cultural patents). Even theories that openly concede that the subject, collective or individual, can never be rendered whole continue to work within the parameters set out by this dispositif. Appropriation continues to act as the horizon through which salvation can be obtained.

When community is conceptualized as the finished product of the dialectic of alienation and appropriation, it is reified. Traditionally, Esposito argues, community is treated as "the thing itself that is opposed to its own annihilation [*proprio annientamento*]" (*CI*, 146; *CE*, 136). As something that is realizable, the realness of community works to immunize us from the "explosion (or implosion) of the nothing," that is, from nihilism. Esposito argues this immunization imperative actually results in a nihilistic model of community. His argument, which is similar to Nancy's, is astute. When community is hypostatized and subjected to the dialectic of alienation and appropriation, we are expected to commit a twofold act of appropriation to qualify as proper members of a community. By characterizing community as a thing, and not just a simple nomination for relationships, each is expected to appropriate not only property but the community itself. This second appropriation constitutes the right, even privilege, to claim partial ownership over the community. Without this second appropriative act—possibly the symbolic appropriation that completes the productive appropriation in Nancy's analysis—each would be merely engaged in an individualistic act of appropriation, which is the commonplace characterization of nihilism.

Nowhere is this collective nihilism more apparent than in the tautology of participation and sharing that factors in most revolutionary formulas: each revolutionary member must participate *in* the taking while simultaneously taking part *of* the participative activity. The former requirement is easier to comprehend: each must be a participant in the taking of expropriated materials, alienated identity, the state, and so on. Each takes her share of, appropriates, what had previously been taken away from her. As an end in itself, this activity is not conducive to community because it is primarily conducted for private, and often disparate and antithetical, purposes; that is, if it serves a purpose at all. For example, during riots participants engage in fleeting appropriative acts that are not translated into a properly communal action. They seek neither to transform their relationships with each other into communal relations, nor to transform their broader circumstances of shared privation into communal conditions. They merely invert the dispositif of the proper and dramatize it on a collective scale. The resulting mayhem simply reconfigures the already divisive conditions that are a byproduct of the collective nihilism that marks our times.

In the standard narrative, nihilism is contained when taking occurs on a communal scale. Each participant must appropriate the collective activity and make it proper to herself, that is, to appropriate her relationships, to take ownership over them, and to become a coproprietor of her relationships with others. Everyone must have a share in the participative activity itself. Sharing is the modality, the basis, and the bond of communal relationships. Without this shared element—sharing out, sharing in, and ultimately sharing with—appropriation remains uncommon. Without sharing, each participant engages in a negative act of appropriation that is private, individualistic, and antisocial. Esposito claims this merely amounts to a "division without sharing" (*CI*, 13; *CE*, 28).

The question these philosophers force us to address is: Doesn't this twofold appropriation absorb and nullify the division that defines our commonality? That is, doesn't it produce a condition of sharing without division? This raises another question. How can each participant appropriate the community without annihilating it, or, conversely, how can each participant be appropriated by community without being completely absorbed, and thus annihilated, by it? Either way, containing community or being contained by community creates a serious aporia for the dialectic of alienation and appropriation. This aporia is found in all zero-sum formulations of this problematic that are promoted by those who appeal to *Homo approprians*. Jean-Paul Sartre's exhaustive, yet failed, efforts in the *Critique of Dialectical Reason* testify to this aporia (1991). To appropriate relationships, to make them each and everyone's own, to make them proper to one's person and every other person involved, to qualify them as "ours," yet simultaneously "yours" and "mine," to depart from the "me" and become the "we," is to negate the exteriority that is necessary to be in—not have—a relationship with another in the first place. Appropriating their relationships renders their relations nonrelational, which is why Esposito calls Sartre's work a "great communitarian failure" (*CI*, 138; *CE*, 133). The dispositif of the proper provides but two alternatives to this dilemma: private individuals such as those found in the social contract tradition (division without sharing) or a hypostatized community that absorbs its subjects (sharing without division). Neither is a relational condition.

Jargon aside, this strain is of paramount importance for our neoliberal era. Today, the political is not just defined within the horizon of the economic, because the economic is simultaneously defined with the horizon of the political. The two have collapsed into each other such that it is nearly impossible to speak of one without enlisting categories originally belonging to the other. The traditional critique of political economy, that private interests dominate the public sphere, no longer carries the semantic breadth to adequately cover what has actually happened. It stands today as a naïve victim of its own accomplishments. Any solution it can proffer is immediately circumvented and recalibrated as yet another dimension of the dispositif of the proper. Regardless of where one is situated along the mainstream political spectrum, from left to right, when one speaks of politics one is forced to enlist economic categories. In our time, it is not just the public, or politics, that have been fused with the economic, but the political itself. To be clear, I am not claiming that the economic dominates the political, but that the political and the economic are now indiscernible. Although this general problematic originates in Aristotle's politics, its modern rendition has its theoretical basis in Locke's early formulation of *Homo approprians*.

Rights-based discourse is a key, yet bewildering, site for the implosion of the political and the economic. Whether the issue is the power that transnational corporations have over states in the global south or the ever-expanding powers that a shrinking group of global elites hold over the global economy as a whole, we find the same discourse at play. Real, substantial political rights are vertically allocated on the basis of private economic ownership. I have no issues with this critique. Where the problem arises is with the mainstream solution to this implosion. To counter this movement, human rights advocates conceptualize political rights as a form of property. Whenever human rights activists appeal to the formal processes of liberal democracy, or even to the informal categories supporting the notion of a rights-bearing human, the human that they are representing is the private proprietor. To make a rights-based claim in the name of another person or a collection of persons, the claim must be staked on the grounds of the fundamental and universal right to self-ownership. Since their humanity has been alienated, it is the state's or a global institution's duty to rectify this injustice. To not recognize this right not only alienates them from the quality that renders them legal persons, it fundamentally undermines the founding principles of liberal democracy. Whether the horizon of the human has been exhausted is a question explored in greater detail in the chapters that follow. I mention it here to highlight how important it is for each of our three main philosophers. It also marks the point where the dispositif of the proper becomes an issue for biopolitics and ontology.

* * *

In "The Compearance," Nancy argues that when our nexus is conceptualized in terms of a lack, the solution appears to be appropriation (*LC*, 1991; *TC*, 1992). In proprietary readings of communism, the community is constituted through the collective appropriation of property, which becomes common property. But given the problems caused by this formulation, it would be better for us to treat our nexus, our very relationships, as "inappropriable." In a different essay, he states,"'Alienation' has been represented as the dispossession of an original authenticity, which ought to be preserved or restored. The very critique of this determination—of an original propriety, authentic plenitude or reserve—has played a large part in contributing to the elimination of the alienation motif, insofar as a motif of loss of man's original self-production" (*UPF*, 37–38; *AFT*, 20). Proudhon complements this position by arguing that we must let go of the hold that the property prejudice has over us. If capitalism is constituted through the primary activity of taking, which appropriates and then converts that which is taken into private property, how can appropriation be an anticapitalist activity? Does this not reaffirm, rather than contest, the expansion of property? Why not attempt to traverse the property prejudice altogether? The call for re-appropriation retroactively legitimates the very basis of bourgeois property.

One of the fundamental flaws with Marx's theory of transformation, and even more so in some of its more simplistic interpretations, is this practical strain. A small group of leaders, for instance, must act as the private ambassadors of the new system because it cannot be fully comprehended by the masses. Dictatorship is required because the people will revolt because they are, at their core, *Homo approprians*. But is this a realistic solution or merely the most readily available solution? Furthermore, since the way has been paved by appropriation, why would we pursue the same path if we seek more fundamental changes? We need to pursue a transversal, rather than a reversal, of appropriation where belonging occurs in being-a-part-of the act of letting go. This has nothing to do with participation and its underlying logic of taking. It is merely the act of letting go together; where being-in-common is defined not by taking but by releasing. It is the very emancipative activity that occurs in the place where the interception was thought to have taken place. Marx would of course be critical of this model, which he dismissed as a "rebellion" (*Empörung*) rather than a "revolution" (*Revolution*) (1998, 361; 1954, 400). Yet he reinforces the contained model of community and the dispositif of the proper.

How one interprets the dialectic of alienation and appropriation is a first-order problem in more classical accounts of Marxism. To establish a communist order where alienation is abolished, proletarians must engage in revolutionary collective appropriation. Yet because this model is grounded in a notion of subject as *Homo approprians*, it too often slides into deterministic, even teleological, formulations. The destiny of *Homo approprians* can only be fulfilled when everyone's appropriative capacities are realized. And we know this is a dead end because the proper is private, not common. If we were, however, to view property for what it really is, a historically contingent product, then it would no longer be necessary to appeal to the appropriative model of revolutionary transformation. Appropriation is not an absolute and historically necessary lever for revolutionary transformation, but a mere option among many.

## III. Dis-Containing Community

Despite their political differences, one an anarchist and the other a romantic conservative, Proudhon and Heidegger were more troubled by the presence of the proper than anyone else in their fields of inquiry. Neither wanted to wholly annihilate the proper, but to deconstruct how the proper was framed by either political economy or metaphysical philosophy. For Heidegger, the metaphysical framework led to a closure of Being. For Proudhon, mainstream political economy led to a closure of the commons. How each sought to methodologically overcome these closures provides a telling blueprint for analyzing how Agamben, Esposito, and Nancy approach the proper in their work.

One way of examining this common strain in Heidegger and Proudhon is to turn to the notion of handiness. The motif of the hand is well rehearsed in Heideggerian scholarship. In *Of Spirit*, Derrida argues that Heidegger's primary "axiomatic" is grounded in the "domain of the hand," that is, *vorhandene* (presence-to-hand) and *zuhandene* (ready-to-hand), which he claims reduce the *proper* to a "very problematical opposition . . . between *giving* and *taking*" (1989 11). Giving and taking are primary modalities of the gift economy, which creates a proprietary orientation. It leads to a conception of Being as something that can be appropriated for Heidegger or of property as something that is the product of an appropriative action for Proudhon. When appropriation is the primary activity, however, sacrifice becomes the only means for preventing the enclosure from taking place. Ontologically, to put an end to the accumulative appropriation of Being, which will eventually lead to a total implosion, we must make an offering of our being. Being becomes a gift that we hand over. Politically, to stop the cyclical accumulation of appropriated goods, we must offer these goods to the commons. Property becomes a gift that we offer. Making a gift, whether of goods or of one's being, however, is not an ideal way to disrupt the activity of the *Homo approprians*.

When we read Heidegger alongside Proudhon, we find a subtle argument that the predominance of the giving-and-taking modality in modern thought eclipses the fundamental modality of holding-and-letting. If we want to disrupt the closure of the commons or of Being, then the sequencing of these modalities must be reversed. Heidegger employs this argument to deconstruct the metaphysical closure of ontology and Proudhon to overturn the property prejudice. Letting interferes with the appropriative gesture because it does not make a gift or offering of something as if it was ours to give in the first place. To let something go is to free the thing from our grasp, to no longer claim it as our property. This notion, and its wide array of etymological connotations, is central to all three of our thinkers' efforts to dis-contain community.

Heidegger's "turn" away from metaphysics can be read as effort to dis-contain the proper. In his writings on the problem of ontological difference, the proper ceases to be a noun and is used more like a qualifying adverb. Heidegger searches for a solution that opens up a new relationship to ontological difference where Being is no longer determined by being. Part of his solution is to dis-contain the hold this world has over us to ready us to properly belong to Being. The *Ereignis*, for example, acts as an extensive anarchic event that sends us along this path. In "Time and Being," he claims that the *Ereignis* is "what lets two things belong to each other, what brings the two things not only in their properness but keeps and holds them in their belonging-together, the containment of the two, the thing-contained (fact of the matter), is the *Ereignis*" (*TB*, 1972, 19; *ZD*, 1969, 20).[20] Heidegger draws our attention to the relationship between the framework and holding. This relationship was also emphasized in his early writings, such as his famous passage on the "breakdown" in *Being and Time* (*BT*, 1962, §16). The breakdown disrupts and reverses traditional phenomenological methods because it does not open unto something, that is, "discovering" or "uncovering," but seeks "*to let* that which shows itself be seen from itself in the very way in which it shows itself from itself" (*BT*, §7). Existentialism, he argues, must "let" the "phenomenon" "show itself in itself, the manifest" (*das Offenbar*).

Letting shifts our attention away from the thing in itself and reorients us to the framework. This schema was present in two additional strains in this text. First, it was present in his three modalities of proper disclosedness (*Eigentlich Erschlossenheit*): reticence or keeping silent for the modality of telling, unsettledness or uncanniness for the modality of understanding, and anxiety for the modality of affect (*BT*, §59). The "call to conscience," he claims, "is not to be tied up with an expectation of anything like a communication" (*BT*, §56). If the call is properly disclosed, rather than enclosed, then Dasein can be properly open to becoming a decisive/resolute (*entschlossen*) existent according to Nancy (*BP*). It was also present in his distinction between the "hermeneutical as" and the "apophantic as" (*BT*, §7, §33, and §44). Because a pure apophantic assertion is impossible, that is, the intellectualist equation of intellect with the thing, he argues, we have to redirect out attention away from that which is asserted and focus on how the thing can be conceived as something that can be asserted in the first place. Since the search for the "meaning of Being" hypostatizes Being, our first order of business is to reconsider how we have posited the meaning of Being.[21]

In his later writings, the *Ereignis* performs the same function. The *Ereignis* draws our attention away from Being toward something like the *insofar as* Being. In a direct attack on Husserlian phenomenology, Heidegger insists that we have to stay our course and remain focused on the pathway through which Being is manifested, not the thing in itself. By focusing on what holds us back from accessing Being, which is the framework that contains the tension and frames how we intend upon everything, he compels us to search for an *extension* (from *Ausdehnung* and *erstrecken*) rather than an *intention*.

The *frame* is an apparatus (or dispositif) that *works* by holding its parts together. It is a framework that operates by letting things be, in the double sense of granting permission (the may) and making possible (the can).[22] It is an apparatus that determines, limits, and bounds how things are conceptualized, conceived, and grasped. That is, it leads us to conceive of everything in terms of *taking*. For example, when a revolution is conceptualized through this framework, revolutionary activity is reduced to taking, that is, revolutionary appropriation. Heidegger's method allows us to disrupt the framework so that we can focus on the hold it has over us. In ontological terminology, claims John Caputo, focusing on the framework teaches us that "Being is not something that human thinking can conceive . . . but something which thinking can only be granted" (1993, 179). In other words, we are responsible for finding a passageway that lets Being be granted, rather than taken, held, or appropriated.

Methodologically, Heidegger claims that we must be attentive to "the path of thought rather than its content. To dwell rightly upon the content would simply block the progress" (*ID*, 23; *SI*, 85).[23] The con-tent (*com-tenere*) is that which is held together, that is, the thing held is an ensemble produced by a synthetic process. We must focus on the holding-together (containing), while holding back (*epochē*) from emphasizing the held-together (the thing contained or the content).[24] The held-together is framed by the holding-together, so to focus on the held-together would be to submit oneself to the economy that defines the held-together in the first place and to re-enforce the orientation of the framework.

Ultimately, Heidegger and Proudhon were concerned with the fundamental opposition between *holding* and *taking*, which are actions conducted by the hand. Proudhon's archetypical hand is that of the card shark, whereas for Heidegger it remains the romanticized handyman-artesian. Yet neither is content with the proprietary reading of the modern hand. It is not the place of the hand to present a gift from that which it has taken, but for the hand to let go of that which its has held onto. This, I shall contend throughout this book, is the correct reading of emancipation. *Emancipatus* is a composite word that combines the prefix *ex-* (out, away) and the noun *mancipum* (ownership). *Mancipum* is itself a composite word that combines *manus* (hand) and *capere* (take). If we are to emancipate humanity from *Homo approprians*, we must dis-contain, expose and render inoperative, the framework that holds the content together. This lesson comes to the fore when Heidegger is read alongside Proudhon. It cannot be ignored if we are to understand how Agamben, Esposito, and Nancy turn to the modality of *letting go* in order to dis-contain community.

* * *

The impasse caused by the dialectic of alienation and appropriation can also be discussed in more strictly methodological terms. When community is conceived as a substantial, consistent, or static thing, it is conceptualized as something that has been covered over and thus requires discovery. This gesture leads to an aporia because communal archaeologists project their own preconceptions into their work, such that the "community in itself" remains undiscoverable. Regardless, if community is based in the romanticized past perfect or in the mystical, utopian, or eschatological future perfect tense, community becomes an unobtainable and thus never realizable entity. Whenever a concerted effort is made to bring this unrealizable model into reality, the results are violence, bloodshed, and destruction.

Heidegger's dis-containment method provides an opening for

rethinking the impasse of community. Rather than continue to search for something that signifies community, community happens in the very process, in the pathway, of dis-containment. Methodologically, to dis-contain something is to disrupt how the content is held together. When the pathway is infused with content it is converted and henceforth blocked. The pathway does not lead to anything in particular because there is nothing to look forward toward and nothing to guide us. Community is nothing, not-a-thing, such that it cannot be grasped, held, appropriated, and contained. The traditional pathways are so cluttered with biases, prejudices, and presuppositions that each of the three main philosophers set out to readdress the exigency of community with a, relatively speaking, tabula rasa, or as a *rasum tabulae* (*PI*, 2005; *PE*, 1998).

How this is accomplished and how much of the slate must be wiped clean, however, is where disagreement arises. Some resort to a negative procedure, while others develop a transversal procedure. Commentators often confuse these two procedures. Part of this confusion stems from each philosopher's unwillingness to articulate their approach in strictly methodological terms. But another part of this confusion stems from the various readings of Heidegger that commentators have projected into their interpretations. Both approaches emerge from the critique of intentional phenomenology. Intentional phenomenology holds that a phenomenon can be discovered or uncovered. Husserl's famous rallying call for phenomenologists "to go back to the things in themselves" in the first volume of the *Logical Investigations* is the quintessential formula of this brand of phenomenology (2001, 168). Heidegger's dis-containment method partially derives from his critique of Husserl. To intend toward something and to positively identify it ("it, that *one*") is to negate the phenomenality of the phenomenon. After Heidegger's critique, second- and third-generation phenomenologists started to look for alternative methods. Most of the approaches in the literature on community, whether phenomenological or not, stem from this movement. The negative procedure represents a reversal of the intentional procedure. Negative phenomenologists contend that the positive approach destroys the essence of a phenomenon when it attempts to uncover and expose it, that is, to make it evident. If the phenomenon in question is truly a transcendental phenomenon, then how would it be possible to devise a method that will enable us to contain it? Beyond the question of size and scope, at issue here is the matter of perspective. A genuine phenomenon must be phenomenal; that is, it can only come forth and present itself on it its own terms. Despite the various ways the phenomenological *epochē* has been tinkered with, in the end, the intentional procedure remains too subjective.

Negative phenomenologists attempt to reverse the orientation. They appeal to a type of *epochē* that forces us to let go of ourselves, our ways of thinking, and in the end, our appropriative inclinations. This approach, however, draws many parallels with the eschatological tradition of negative theology. It carries the idea of dis-containment to its logical ends. If the phenomenon were to be absolutely dis-contained, such that it can freely come forth on its own right, to announce itself as the phenomenon, it will be exposed. Most proponents of the *via negativa* fear that an exposed phenomenon will be captured by our appropriative inclinations. They conduct themselves as guardians of the proper. Since the world is composed of thieves and many other types of mis-appropriators, they strive to entertain and distract us by devising elaborate labyrinths, composed of riddles and tangential passageways, which are supposed to lead us astray. Negative phenomenologists struggle to differentiate between the moral imperative that one *should not* intend toward the phenomenon, often conceived as an idiom/proper, and the practical imperative that one *cannot* intend toward the ______. Emmanuel Lévinas's "trace of the Other," which is implied in an "incision that does not bleed," is a good example (1996, 59). The phenomenality of the phenomenon is preserved because the incision is merely inferred, yet it is not identifiable; in theological terms; the reference performs divine rather than mystical violence.[25] A parallel formula is present in the Christian notion of an immaculate (unstained, unblemished) conception (*concipere*, to take in and hold), which is an inception that takes place without an identifiable trace of the Father. To remain transcendental, a phenomenon must be hidden, concealed, and sheltered. Only the other, mostly likely the Other, can initiate such a relationship. When the moment arrives, the initiation will come without warning or premonition. The suddenness of the arrival, the sheer uncanniness of the moment and the message, will be so disruptive that the self will lose itself in the moment and have no choice but to submit. In this typical formulation, difference is prioritized over sameness, transcendence over immanence, and the other over the self.

Critics of Agamben, Esposito, and Nancy often contend that their theories of community are constituted in this negative vein. Each is charged with replicating Heidegger's radically passive model. When translated into community, such a model becomes inherently conservative, altruistic, and alienating. This criticism, however, only directly holds for Maurice Blanchot's Lévinasian model of the "unavowable community" (*CU*, *UC*). It also holds some value, albeit of a lesser coin, when drawn against Agamben's coming community (*CV*, *CC*). Since Blanchot's little book serves as an important benchmark for the subsequent texts, I will use it to demonstrate how the negative procedure is used to conceptual community here. When translated into community, the negative approach causes an ethical and a political dilemma because its theological residues are combined with the phenomenological prejudice against the everyday world. To render the community unavowable or even incommunicable is to silence the community. If such a community were to remain incomprehensible to commonplace sensibilities, orientations, and speech, it could only be constituted by a disruption and movement away from the everyday world. It is hard to read Blanchot's notion of the "unavowable community," for example, without thinking about a group of elected brethren, who escape society to form their own ascetic community on the fringes of society. Despite their vow of silence, they still commune among themselves through a silent form of communication that unifies them in an abstracted and unspeakable deity. This secretive model of community is not a tangible political solution because it has few trickle-down effects for the rest of us who remain unelected and shut out of the from the rituals and traditions held by the ascetic clan. This community is completely submissive and pacified. I return to this problem in chapter 4, where I examine Agamben's affirmative accounts of the common habitus in the form-of-life of Franciscan monks.

The transversal procedure slightly reformulates the dis-containment method. Ultimately it is a method of radical admission, rather than submission. Instead of formulating community in relation to the alterity of the Other or other, Esposito and Nancy, for example, attempt to conceive of the relational aspects in the opening itself. This approach neither positively identifies community nor negatively shelters community; rather, it positively exposes the traditional models of community. It does not attempt to dis-contain that which is held together by the framework, to set it free as either a discoverable thing or a mysterious essence; instead, it traverses—works through and turns—the very framework to disrupt the formerly contained versions of community. Methodologically, the role of emphasizing is important. To emphasize the framework is to expose it, to weaken it, and to put us in a position to let it go. In Agamben's terms, this exposure renders it inoperative. This procedure clears the pathway so that we can conceive of an absolutely alternative type of community.

Perhaps the single motif that brings their dis-containment methodologies together is the notion of *division/sharing* (*partage* in Nancy, *condivisione* in Esposito, and possibly *comunicazione* in Agamben). This motif resonates with the traditional accounts of community where communal members are said to share a whole array of things that are divided among them, such as goods, decisions, symbols, and identity. How, each asks, can we reconceptualize the shared dimensions of community without containing that which is shared out? Moreover, how can we avoid conceiving of division without containing it? These questions are not just directed at the dispositif of the proper because they are equally concerned with Heidegger's characterization of the ontological event as definitively divisive. Put in less ontological terms, our conditions, our relations, ourselves—in short, our world is definitively divisive. There is no absolute difference, such as in the transcendental thing-in-itself implied in negative theology—just division. Heraclitus's famous testimony "*ēthos anthrōpō daímōn*," does not mean "character is fate," or at least should not be translated as such, because for each and in his own particular way, it signals that *humanity dwells in division.*

This change of perspective has profound consequences for how we have traditionally conceived of community. When proponents and adversaries of community raise the problem of difference, they reduce this problem to absolute terms. Community is both celebrated and demonized as a fortress that shelters and defends the same from being exposed to difference. Communitarians and cosmopolitans, to cite one of the more recent manifestations of this debate, forget that difference is essential to community. Difference is just as ubiquitous to community as sameness. In fact, it would be better to speak of differentiation than difference when reflecting on traditional notions of community. Communal identity is constituted through a differentiation process where sameness internalizes, but never annuls, differences. Internal homogeneity, even if just a myth, requires the constant threat of alienation. Without difference and differentiation, there is no identity. This narrative has reached the point of exhaustion. Since the grounds on which we relate with each other, neighbors and strangers alike, are divisive from the start, it no longer makes sense—or as Nancy might say, it makes too much sense—to think about difference and sameness in absolute terms.

In a community, each is so extensively divided up and shared out that no one is capable of grasping, holding, appropriating, and thus containing, the relationships that put us in common. What does this say about the prospects of escape? How can we absolve (loosen, unbind, or free) ourselves from our divisive nexus? What sword can sever this Gordian knot?[26] Most Heideggerians repeat this important question. It raises an obvious, yet difficult, question: If our conditions are *definitively divisive*, why do we seek to contain division? What happens, historically speaking, when a concerted effort is made to contain division? Heidegger speaks of atomic bombs, Agamben of concentration and death camps, Arendt of totalitarianism, Nancy of identity wars, and Esposito of thanatopolitics. Community thus must be rethought again. It has to be open, rather than closed, to division. Put differently, the task is not to dis-contain community, but to reconceive of community as the relationship that occurs in the movement of dis-containment. How each of the three main philosophers conceptualizes this task, and whether their solutions are adequately political and ethical, are the questions I pursue in the last three chapters of this book.

# 2

# Ontology and the Proper

Unfortunately, analyses of the dispositif of the proper continue to remain peripheral at best. Proudhon's challenge to the property prejudice represents an early critique, but it wasn't until Heidegger set out to reconfigure how ontological philosophy was conceptualized within the semantics of the proper, property, propriety, and even authenticity (all covered in his writings on *das Eigen*) and Derrida carried this project forward in his multivolume analysis of the proper that the hegemony of this political, and for some theological, economy began to be seriously challenged. Agamben, Esposito, and Nancy combine these two strains in their writings. Their interrogation of the proper covers a wide range of issues, from political economy (private and public property), biopolitics (proper and improper life), morality (appropriate and inappropriate behavior), epistemology (authentic and inauthentic representation), ontology (ontic and ontological inquiries), even to the problem of thinking about ethics and ontology. How Heidegger formulated and addressed the proper has profoundly influenced each of our three main philosophers.

The focus of this chapter is the proprietarian confusion. In the preceding chapter, I examined this confusion through the lens of political economy. Locke's *Homo approprians* gave rise to a model of the modern political-economic subject whose fundamental action is defined by appropriation. In this chapter, I turn to Heidegger's writings on the proper. I begin by briefly examining the place of the proper in *Being and Time*. Then I turn to a more lengthy examination of Heidegger's *Ereignis-Denken*. I have chosen to focus on his 1957 lecture, "The

Principle/Leap of Identity" (*SI*, 2002; *ID*, 2002) because in this work he theorizes the *Ereignis* as an event that opens up and exposes *Homo approprians* to such an extent that it disrupts its appropriative and identification capacities. In later chapters, I demonstrate how Agamben, Esposito, and Nancy exploit and exaggerate this formulation in their own theories of community. Finally, I end with an overview of essays written by Agamben and Nancy on Heidegger's theory of the proper.[1] What follows is not a comprehensive and authoritative account of Heidegger's theory of the *Ereignis*, but an extrapolation of different elements that are important for understanding how Agamben, Esposito, and Nancy conceive of community.

## I. The Proper

In "The Ends of Man," Derrida argues that for Heidegger, the "themes of the *house* and of the *proper* are regularly brought together," such that the "motif of the *proper* (*eigen*, *eigentlich*) and the several modes of *to propriate* (particularly *Ereignen* and *Ereignis*) . . . dominate the question of the truth of Being in *Zeit und Sein*" (1982, 129, fn. 25). In fact, if there were one theme that traverses his "so-called *Kehre*," it would be the "magnetic attraction" between "the question or the truth of Being" and "the thinking of the proper of man" (1982, 124). Whenever Heidegger raises the problem of ontological difference, he appeals to the proper in the specific senses of nearness and proximity, that is, his broader theme of presence.

Heideggerians have long engaged in a debate concerning how to translate *das Eigen*. After the publication of *Being and Time*, the field was divided on how to translate the *Eigentlichkeit/Uneigentlichkeit* dichotomy: "authenticity/inauthenticity" or "ownership/unownership."[2] Most preferred "authenticity" because it addresses the problem of representation. French existentialists also popularized this translation, but in his "Letter" Heidegger criticized them for reducing the problem of existence to the banal search for "meaning" and then conflating it with the search for an "origin" (1993). The second translation allowed thinkers such as Ricoeur to address the problem of ethical responsibility in terms of identity and property. To claim self-ownership, he argues in *Oneself as Another*, an ethical subject must conduct herself in a decisive manner by standing behind and owning up to her actions (1992). These translations are plausible, but they place limitations on Heidegger's broader critique. Derrida notes, "the value *proper* (propriety, propriate, appropriation, the entire family of *Eigentlichkeit*, *Eigen*, *Ereignis*) . . . is perhaps the most continuous and most difficult thread of Heidegger's thought" (2002, 48). Derrida presents a third alternative that is more general than the first two translations: "properness/improperness," which is repeated by Agamben, Esposito, and Nancy.

Much has been written on the passage from improperness (*Uneigentlichkeit*) to properness (*Eigentlichkeit*) in *Being and Time*. What is important is that Heidegger's notion of being-towards-death provides a fundamental challenge to *Homo approprians*. An appropriative subject is incapable of entering into the passageway that leads it from the improper to the proper. Thus, it will only be prepared if its appropriative disposition is disrupted and incapacitated. Whether the disruption is de-propriating, expropriating, alienating, or merely temporarily jarring is a widely debated issue among his interpreters. What matters is that if Dasein is to properly hear the call of Being, Dasein must let go, release, and abandon itself. Death represents one's ownmost (or proper) end, which can never be appropriated because it is inappropriable. Our task is to recognize that not everything in our lives is appropriable. If we can, it might just help us to reconceive of our way of being-in-the-world in a manner otherwise than *Homo approprians*.

Over the course of the following chapters I shall return to the problem of death and appropriation in Heidegger, because of its importance in the debate about community. Heidegger, as each of our three philosophers will repeatedly point out, never managed to translate this formulation into an *eigentlichkeit* notion of being-with. In *The Inoperative Community*, Nancy attempts to translate this individualizing notion of death into a model where the death of the other (not one's own death) opens up the possibility for entering into relations in a non-appropriative modality. He will later drop this reading, which was probably wise given the connotations of translating Heidegger's account of being-toward-death into a notion of community. The end result would be an authoritarian model of community that requires subjects to sacrifice themselves on behalf of the common good, a model of community not unlike that of the communitarian models found in Anglo-American political theory. Later Nancy will search for a middle ground where *Homo approprians* is disrupted, but not necessarily appropriated. There must be an alternative that is not appropriative. I will return to this point, but for now two more elements must be addressed in Heidegger's treatment of *eigentlichkeit* in *Being and Time.*

First, there is a close relationship between *eigentlichkeit* and *ethos.* In being-towards-death one is liberated from their world, untied from its constraints, and relaxed. Loosened, if you will. But, this loosening is not a negative form of freedom where the subject is absolutely liberated from all forms of responsibility. Being faced with the inevitability of that which one can never be freed from, one's own death, forces Dasein to become *resolute* or *decisive* (*entschlossen*). For Heidegger, this is not an automatic process, which would be contradictory; rather, Dasein has to make a decision between becoming resolute or taking the simpler path by conforming to the mundane, indecisive, and oblivious ethos of *das Man.*

Second, in *Being and Time* Heidegger did not develop his *eigentlichkeit* modality of being as an ethical doctrine. In the so-called "social" passage on "solicitude/caring-for," he distinguishes between "leaping-in-for" (*einspringen*) others and "leaping-ahead-of" (*vorausspringen*) others (*BT,* §26).[3] He characterizes the former as an *uneigentlich* modality. To stand-in-for others is to appropriate their autonomy. It is, in more existential language, to take away their capacity to stand out for themselves (ex-sistere). Such an action would be akin to an intervention where one steps into the other and substitutes oneself as the other. Heidegger was vehemently opposed to any model of intersubjectivity that is founded on an internal mediation between subjects. Instead, he argued that to leap-ahead-of another would be an *eigentlich* social act. If conducted with the utmost respect and care for the other's autonomy, including their capacity to make their own decisions, the act could occur in a nonappropriative fashion. One might, for example, provide a hand or advice, but only in response to a request and only to the extent that the provision provided does not overstep the request. An unsolicited provision or one in excess of the request would remain an *uneigentlich* form of solicitude.

* * *

At the "Ends of Man" conference dedicated to Derrida in Paris, co-organizer Philippe Lacoue-Labarthe posed a pointed question about the relationship between the philosophical and the political in Heidegger.

How, Lacoue-Labarthe asked, is it possible to extract the "thematic of the proper" from Heidegger's "vain aristocratism," association with the Nazis, "tragic heroism of self-sacrifice," and his unquestionable political leanings on the "right" (*RP*, 59–62)? Can Heidegger's "'economistic' ideology" of the proper be politicized without inheriting this baggage (*RP*, 60)? Of course, this was precisely the task he and his fellow director Nancy set out to accomplish at the *Centre de recherches philosophiques sur le politique* in the early 1980s.

Of the three main texts in the second wave of writings on community in the 1990s, *Being Singular Plural* represents the closest analogue to Heidegger's ontological philosophy. In this text, Nancy revisits his earlier efforts to rewrite Heidegger's existential analytic as a "coexistential analytic." Given his allegiance to Heideggerian philosophy, Nancy was widely criticized in France and abroad during the 1980s and early 1990s. Many were unsatisfied with his relatively cryptic statements about his own politics. Nancy Fraser even accused him of being complicit with the forces neoliberalism (1984).[4] As a deconstructive philosopher, he was critical of the "totalitarian" gesture practiced by traditional leftists. Platformism, vanguardism, and Maoism were too prescriptive for Nancy.[5] But as the philosopher who cowrote "Retreating the Political" and established the short-lived *Centre de recherches philosophiques sur le politique* with Lacoue-Labarthe, he had a difficult time shaking the image of being anything but an apolitical and obscure thinker. He responded in the late 1990s and early 2000s by writing a series of texts that were more explicitly political—or at least easier to situate on the political spectrum. *Being Singular Plural* is part of this series. During this stage, his musings on ontology were supported by more substantial political analyses and his references to the tradition of political economy became more extensive. He found his political voice and started to write commentaries on political affairs during this period. He also started to analyze the overlapping vectors of the proper: the model of the metaphysical subject (authenticity, ownness, identity, autonomy, etc.) and political economy (property). Despite his infusion of politics into this work, his theory remains the most committed to reformulating ontological philosophy as conceived by Heidegger.

In chapter 4, I argue that Agamben is likewise committed to revisiting Heidegger's theory of ontology, but he is less inhibited when translating this problematic into other terrains. Prior to writing *The*

*Coming Community*, he sought to rethink the proper in terms of the problem of first philosophy. In these texts, the proper was addressed through the philosophy of language, linguistics, semiotics, etc. In the *Coming Community*, Agamben often cites the improper modalities of different groups of people who represent a challenge to the properness of communication, morality, and ways of being. Impropriety represents an opening beyond the proper/improper. This strategy is carried forward into his *Homo Sacer* series. Here Agamben examines how modern biopolitical dispositifs reproduce the distinction between proper and improper lives. He strives to disrupt and render inoperative these dispositifs in order to arrive at an ontological ethos, way of being, or form-of-life that is inoperative and free to use things without resorting to proprietary categories. Across his works the proper/improper dichotomy occupies a prominent role.

Although a quick glance at the chapter titles and references of *Communitas* could lead one to conclude that of the three main texts this work is the most Heideggerian, the opposite is actually the case. Prior to writing this book, Esposito had clearly dedicated much less time to studying and writing on Heidegger than the other two philosophers. As the only philosopher whose formal training and professional post are in political philosophy, his publications clearly reflect his lifelong commitment to this field. Community for Esposito is the problem *par excellence* for modern political philosophy. Questions of ontology, especially ontological difference and plurality, remain in his work, but they are largely overshadowed by his commitment to political and ethical theory. He is also less invested in meddling with the protracted and cumbersome methodological issues that arise in Heidegger's ontological philosophy than are Agamben and Nancy. From the opening pages of *Communitas*, it is quite clear that Heidegger's ontological reading of the proper is directly translated into the discourse of political economy. We might even say that Esposito translates the ontological reading of the proper back to the dispositif from which it originated. For Esposito, the proper derives from private property. Ultimately, Esposito wrote his work after the other two and he inherited the entrenched Heideggerian reading of the proper established by the previous two texts. In *Communitas*, the proper is a problem for political economy, and in his subsequent writings it becomes a problem for biopolitics. Ontological questions are gradually supplanted by biopolitical questions in his work.

From early classical anarchist critiques of the property prejudice to contemporary critiques of human rights discourse and identity politics, the conflation of the proper and the idiom is starting to be challenged across multiple fronts. Many contemporary communists are searching for an opening to completely overhaul the communist exigency so that our notion of community is no longer expressed through this conflation. The literature on community is a key citation for this movement. The authors draw from a strain in Heidegger's *Ereignis-Denken* that provides an opening where the common can be considered beyond the semantics of the *proprium*. For this reason alone, it is paramount that we look more closely at his formulation. This does not mean, however, that Heidegger can be read as a communist. He was a romantic conservative who sought to preserve the proper and the idiom in a silent, apophantic form of communication. Translated into community, his solution would result in an ascetic clan of excommunicated brethren living an apolitical existence somewhere far beyond the distractions of the modern world. So rather than travel backward with him into the Black Forest, or worse, to his infamous rectorship address (1985) and his community of destiny (*BT*, §74), our three main philosophers part ways with him after he opens up this problem. They stop short, to speak in Nancean terms, before arriving at his conclusion.

## II. The *Ereignis*

In his lecture on "The Principle/Leap of Identity," Heidegger returns to the problems that the proper presents for ontology.[6] Instead of conceiving of a proper relationship between Dasein and its being, in this lecture he focuses on reconfiguring the relationship that occurs across the ontological difference between beings and Being. *Homo approprians* is incapable of entering into a proper relationship with Being and its own being because it seeks to take, appropriate, and master everything in its sight, including Being. Heidegger argues that humanity should not try to master Being; rather, humanity must belong to Being. He employs the *Ereignis* as a disruptive mechanism that prepares the subject for entering into this new relationship with Being by deconfiguring it. The superlative forces of the *Ereignis* render the appropriative capacities of *Homo approprians* inoperative such that it is exposed and forced to let itself go. In this modality of letting go, the subject of the *Ereignis* is placed in a passive, deferential, and submissive position.

Although Heidegger's model of the disruptive event simply reverses the terms of appropriation, and it ultimately replaces the proprietary framework with an authoritarian one, it is still necessary to examine how he seeks to disrupt the appropriative subject. His formulations have profoundly influenced subsequent attempts to disrupt the appropriative subject. In the following I will focus on how he reconfigures the event, the modality of the evental subject, and the ways that we conceive of relationships. This examination is paramount for understanding how Agamben, Esposito, and Nancy each reinterpret the event of existence as an event that disrupts the appropriative subject. I begin by providing further context for this lecture, and then I turn to his description of the event.

* * *

Heidegger maintains that with the proliferation of nuclear energy, the "atomic age" has brought us to a precipice of our own making. It forces us to make a "decision" (*Entscheidung*) about the "plan man projects," "whether he will become the servant [*Knecht*] of his plan or will remain its master [*Herr*]" (*ID*, 33–34; *SI*, 97–98). The problem we face, however, is not clear because we are living in a period of generalized indecisiveness. In our current conditions, everything is so obtuse that no one or nothing can be identified as the source of authority. That is, no one is capable of stepping away from, cutting through, separating, and disentangling the obfuscated world we have created. In short, no one is capable of making a decision. This is the quintessential formulation of crisis theory, which for Heidegger is a crisis of the first order because what is at stake here is more than a way of being, but being itself.

In this lecture, he unravels a dynamic tension located in the very heart of humanism: the intertwinement of in-/decisiveness and explosion/implosion. This tension is a result of the metaphysical horizon of modern humanism. On the scale of in-/decisiveness, we have cut ourselves off from our own work. Science has separated and carved up our material world so extensively that we now contain atoms—the *atomos* represents the ultimate limit of decisiveness because it cannot be cut. However, we have stumbled upon this technological feat in an indecisive and obtuse fashion. On the other end, we have been misled to the point where we are now imploding in and upon ourselves. After factoring in that we have arrived at a point where we only tentatively possess that which posits the very limitation of divisibility, which simultaneously contains the ultimate explosiveness of division, and that we have stumbled upon this position in an indecisive manner, we have to recognize that we are now faced with a core, fundamental crisis. It brings us upon the ends of the ends of humanism—the implosion of sheer immanence. For Heidegger, the atomic bomb serves as a metaphor for the pathos of metaphysical theory because it bears the imminent possibility of our collective annihilation. Its presence raises the stakes for traversing the metaphysical framework. His most popular statement on this theme is "The Question Concerning Technology" (1993).

The main solution proffered by the principle of identity for a crisis is the decisive mediator, which raises two immediate problems First, were one to cut into the core of the atomic bomb, the result would be mass death. Atomic energy contains the very division that defines us, and as mere definite beings we are incapable of permanently containing our definitiveness. The only rational decision is one that most nations, including Japan after the tsunami, are still incapable of making, which would be to cut away from atomic energy altogether. Second, we are left with an impossible choice between being subservient to and masters over atomic energy. This raises a fundamental question: why should we have to choose between being servants or masters of atomic bombs? Heidegger's question is actually more acute. When everything is reduced to "man," he argues, we become oblivious to the "claim/call [*Anspruch*] of Being" that addresses us through the "essence of technology" (*ID*, 34; *SI*, 98). Being is presenced in the limitations of atomic energy. It is there where we are faced with our finitude. The atomic bomb, in short, represents the limits of metaphysical power. It is Heidegger's Frankenstein.

Heidegger weaves a conservative notion of belonging (*Gehören*) into this romantic prose. Because we have not heard (*gehört*) the call of Being, we have not been obedient (*gehorsam*) to Being, and thus we do not belong to (*gehören zu*) Being. The *Ereignis* serves as a mechanism that disrupts the power of the humanist framework and prepares the subject for entering into a renewed relationship with Being. It compels us to "withdraw" (*zurücknahmen*) from the "authority" (*Herrschaft*) of the technological world. It is a mechanism that liberates and emancipates us from the "reign of the [humanist] frame" while delivering us toward Being (*ID*, 37; *SI*, 101). In the modality of the *Ereignis*, we are open to hearing, being attentive to, and obeying, the claim/call of Being.

One last point before I turn to the technical elements of this mechanism. The lecture reaches its romantic pinnacle in his call for a more personal form of servitude (*Dienstschaft*). In this lecture he plays with the two German words for servant, *Knecht* and *Dienst*, which are both translated as "service" in the English text. The former represents an impersonal service where one is either a "servant" (*Knecht*) or a "master" (*Herr*) of its "plan." In German, *Knecht* refers to farm laborers, even slavery (*Knechtschaft*). It also connotes a plan or purpose. The "word *Ereignis*," however, implores us to "serve" (*Dienst*) in a personal sense (*ID*, 36; *SI*, 101). "The Word" *Ereignis* is neither a nomination nor a noun, but the "leading word."[7] *Dienst* is rooted in the second-person, personal possessive pronoun *dein* (your). It is a kind of servitude that is germane to a manor or a household. Heidegger claims that we have but two options: either remain indecisive and submit to the destructive pathos of impersonal servitude or submit to a personal form of servitude, that is, humanism versus ontology. He implores us to submit to a conservative/conservational type of servitude.[8]

* * *

In this lecture Heidegger attempts to work though the problem of belonging-togetherness (*Zusammengehörigkeit*) in relationships. He is concerned with the ontological relation between being and Being, but his insights can be also be used to examine relationships on a more generic plane. Heidegger claims that metaphysics leads us to conceive of relationships in a manner where togetherness determines belonging, which ultimately destroys the relational element. He searches for openings to rethink the ontological relationship in a manner where belonging determines togetherness.

Heidegger strives to conceive of relationships that are direct and immediate, and thus without a mediating third. If there is to be a relationship of "two" elements, they must be "with" each other. This is not possible for the metaphysical principle of identity because it produces an identity between the two through an abstract mechanism: "a mediation

[*Vermittelung*], a connection [*Verbindung*], and a synthesis [*Synthesis*]: the unification into a unity [*die Einung in eine Einheit*]" (*ID*, 25; *SI*, 87). This leaves us incapable of "say[ing anything] about the nature of identity," "at least not directly/immediately [*unmittelbar*]" because the "principle already presupposes what identity means and where it belongs" (*ID*, 26; *SI*, 88). Identity is a product of a synthetic action that gathers elements together such that they appear to be the same.[9]

When togetherness determines belonging, belonging is passive, objectified, and appropriated. Why, Heidegger asks, is belonging understood as "to be assigned [*zugeordnet*] and placed [*eingeordnet*] into the order [*Ordnung*] of a 'together,' established in the unity of a manifold, framed together [*zusammengestellt*] in the unity of a system, mediated by the unifying centre [*einigende Mitte*] of an authoritative synthesis [*maßgebenden Synthesis*]" (*ID*, 29; *SI*, 90)? Isn't this an external action that gathers each part together and makes them the same? Moreover, this is a recipe for "ordering." A unifying third synthesizes the parts so that they are ordered, classified, and associated together. Finally, how is it possible to step outside or transcend this entanglement and become the one that can place each of the components together (*syntithenai*)? We find this formulation whenever metaphysics represents belonging as a "*nexus*" and "*connexio*," that is, a binding-together, which he calls a "necessary connection/knot/tie [*notwendige Verknüpfung*] of the one with the other" (ibid.). The end result is a nonrelation because there are no longer "two" elements, just the "one," that is, *unitas*.

This formulation of belonging-*together* speaks volumes to the endless accounts of how the masses are disempowered when they are collected, aggregated, gathered, grouped, hoarded, serialized, totalized, and so on, together in social and political thought. Many have attempted to find a way for the gathered-together to be re-unified such that they actually *belong*-together. Most appeal to a grand unifying third, either in a personal form, such as Hobbes's Leviathan or Weber's charismatic leader, in a group form, such as Luxembourg's spontaneous mass or Lenin's vanguard party; in an amorphous form, such as the *inter* that brings subjects together, such as Husserl's transcendental we or Merleau-Ponty's intercorporeality; or even in a theological form, such as Levinas's third party. Regardless of the ontological status of each of these thirds, they represent the pitfalls of universalism.

In an attempt to correct his simplistic dichotomy between the Us-object and the impossible We-subject in *Being and Nothingness*, for example, Sartre turn to the "group-in-fusion" in his *Critique of Dialectical Reason.* The group-in-fusion was supposed to syncopate the overpowering forces that gather together, or synthesize, and render the group a passive collective in such a way that it would remain open and resistant to these forces. The only way such a group could conceivably remain resistant, however, was in the face of a common and life-threatening enemy (the third). Not only were the members of the group-in-fusion lined up against a third, but they were also thirds themselves. Each active member acted as a mediating third. This ultimately led to the group being closed on an intermediate level. As their activity was heightened a net was woven through and around the group, creating a mediating nexus of sorts, which when their activity ceased would form the basis of their conversion into a serialized collective, ultimately taking the form of a hierarchical, ordered, and bureaucratic political party.

In more traditional accounts of community, community acts as a metaphorical house that shelters and protects people. The collectivizing forces that hold such a community together are centripetal. They are so powerfully charged that the community becomes an impenetrable fortress, which is closed to outsiders and repressive to insiders. Resistance to collective identity is often met with fierce opposition. The only escape from such a community is to defect and renounce it and/or to be excommunicated. There is a slight misunderstanding in how this narrative has been traditionally formulated, which Heidegger's account of togetherness helps to clarify. In the narrative of the traditional community, community is treated like a static entity. Centripetal forces, however, are actively employed through a whole series of operations that work by holding each of the components together. These operations must be constantly reinforced across a myriad of fronts, whether in the token gestures that are meant to remind someone that they belong to the group, such as when a teammate winks at her fellow teammate right after their coach had accosted her for a mistake she made to remind her that they're "in it together," or in the more violent ways that outsiders are excommunicated, such as when children of "illegals" are arrested in their classrooms and sent to deportation centers. When community is conceived as *com-unity*, the parts must be constantly gathered and regathered together. Whether this means bringing a part back into to the fold or ensuring that no one tries to circumvent the group, the community is constantly being contained. Without containment, no one is content.

Heidegger's solution to the problem of togetherness is the *Ereignis.* The *Ereignis* acts as a pathway that opens up a "peculiar/idiomatic together" (*eigene Zusammen*) (*ID*, 29; *SI*, 90). He employs a series of measures to ensure that the relationship between "man" and "Being" remains open. First, he characterizes the event by its "excess" (*Übermaß*) in order to traverse the dialectic of alienation and appropriation. When the world is conceived under the auspices of the lack, he argues, the lacking subject always seeks to reappropriate that which has supposedly taken away from it (*ID*, 31; *SI*, 94). Second, instead of appealing to "appropriation" (*Aneignung*), Heidegger uses the awkward formulation "over-propriation" (*Übereignen*) (*ID*, 31; *SI*, 94). Although this term is translated as *appropriation* in the English text, the closest English equivalents would be *transference*, *metastasis*, and, if we wanted to emphasize the theological undercurrent in this text, *transubstantiation.*[10] Third, he argues that over-propriation gives rise to a particular type of relationship that he describes as a constellation (*Konstellation*) rather than a nexus, interweaving, or interrelation (*Verflechtung*). Fourth, the openness is only made possible because the relationship occurs in a "spring/leap," which is the "abruptness of the unabridged turn *into* that belonging, which could foremost grant a towards-each-other of man and Being" (*ID*, 33; *SI*, 96). It is a "strange spring," that "leaps away or defects from" (*Sichabsetzen*) the metaphysical principle of identity. As such, the synthetic gesture is disrupted, but the "two" are still "sufficiently over-propriated" to ensure that they can enter into an immediate relationship with each other. Only after this is clearly understood is it possible to read the following two phrases: "Man and Being are *übereignet* to each other," which the English text translates as "appropriated," and "They belong to each other" (*ID*, 31–32; *SI*, 95). When relations are constituted through an appropriative act they are conflictive and discordant, not mutual and concordant as would be expected for relations where each belongs.

To disrupt the appropriative orientation of the metaphysical subject, Heidegger employs four terms that are etymologically related to *das Eigen* (*Ereignis*, *Übereignen*, *Vereignen*, and *Zueignen*).[11] *Vereignen* and *Zueignen* represent what happens on either side of over-propriation: within "the frame [*Ge-stell*] there prevails a strange *Vereignen* and

*Zueignen*." Over-propriation requires that each term be in concert with the other and that their activity be mutual (*ID*, 33; *SI*, 97). On the one side, "man is delivered over to the *vereignet* of Being," which the English text translates as "man is delivered over to the ownership of Being" (*ID*, 36; *SI*, 100). On the other side, "Being is *zugeeignet* to the essence of man," which the English text translates as "Being is appropriate to the essence of man" (ibid.).[12] In this translation, "man" is "owned" by Being and being is treated as the "essence" of "man." Even if we ignore that the verbs are in the past tense, the English translation formulates this double movement as a type of synthesis that intertwines Being and man, and thus annuls their ontological difference. Thus an alternative translation is required, including for "Event of Appropriation."

Heidegger's *Contributions to Philosophy*, written two decades prior to his lecture on identity, presents an alternative translation. François Raffoul, for example, provides an excellent analysis of these terms. He translates *Zueignung* as "owning-to," *Übereignung* as "owning-over-to," and *Ereignis* as "enowning" (2007, 91). "[O]wnhood," he argues, "is not a possessive appropriation but rather designates an 'own' that is in play at the very event of being" (2007, 90). He concludes that in the *Ereignis*, a proper selfhood emerges "in the *belonging-together of man and Being*. Man and Being are appropriated to each other and belong to each other. . . . *Ereignis* is the name of such co-belonging, trans-propriation" (2007, 93). Although I am considering a different lecture, this reading could be applied. In fact, it is very close to Agamben's reading of "Time and Being," which I examine in the next section.

In the lecture on identity, the proper (*das Eigen*) is present in all four dimensions of Heidegger's formula, that is, *er-/über-/ver-/zu-eignen*. In the three transitive verbs, the root becomes *eignen*. *Er-eig-nis* also derives from the same verb. The suffix *nis* ("ness") renders *Ereignis* as an abstract noun. It derives from the gerund *das Er-eignen* of the verb *ereignen*. The suffix *nis* connotes an active conditioning that is immeasurable. As such, we should not translate this term as I did above with "propering event," but as "propering eventness." Many commentators on his *Ereignis-Denken*, including Nancy, have recognized this aspect of the word. Heidegger's play is confusing because he mixes elements of *Mittelhochdeutsch*—the spoken and written dialectic from the eleventh to fourteenth centuries in his beloved southern Germany—with modern German. For example, *Eignen* is the modern German translation for the *Mittelhochdeutsch* term *eigen*. *Vereignen* and *zueignen* also derive from *Mittelhochdeutsch*.

*Vereignen* roughly means "to give up proper possession in order to face the strangeness." Its "boldness strengthens and intensifies the *proprium*, which sharply transfers over into strangeness."[13] One does not hand over or transfer one's ownership, as if it were in one's power to make a gift of it and to present it in the form of a deed, which would be a modern reading, but one relinquishes, releases, abandons or *lets go* of one's self-ownership, property in things, and everything else one has appropriated. The very structure of *vereignen* connotes relinquishment. The prefix *ver-* gives a sense of an intense loss or movement away from. One must completely give oneself up, over, and away to be wholly exposed and enter into a proper relationship *with* Being.

In this leap of faith into the unknown, *Homo approprians* is transformed into a submissive servant. This motif, of course, is present in the mytholegem of dispossession in the narrative of Jesus of Nazareth. Pious and ascetic movements in Christianity often elevate Jesus of Nazareth's form of life as an exemplary case where one's ethos is defined by the renouncement of worldly possessions and human laws. This message of complete and total abandonment also reverberates in many revolutionary movements. Change, revolutionary transformation, even Heidegger's *metastasis*, can only happen when we commit to relinquishing, abandoning, abdicating, and just letting go. Agamben, Nancy, and Esposito, like most continental philosophers, also draw from this motif. The latter two emphasize the opportunities for rethinking community that are present in the radical exposure. Agamben, however, tends to carry the logic of abandonment further. He also has a habit of making affirmative references to ascetic forms of life, especially those practiced by the Franciscans who renounce property in search for a nonappropriative way of using things. What Agamben often forgets to mention is that they renounce property to devote themselves to a more conservative and authoritarian notion of belonging. Heidegger was more concerned with an ontological economy than a political economy. To enter into the house of Being, which was probably located deep in the Black Forest, one must be a pious being.

Idiomatically speaking, *vereignen* is also significant in German. It supplements and disrupts the senses of togetherness present in its modern German cognate "*vereinigen*": to unite, to merge, to bring together, to connect, etc. The modern term derives from *verein* (unite, union, etc.). *Einigen* is an action that unites (*per unitatem*). It literally nullifies the possibility of entering into a proper relationship, a relationship with difference, because it forms a unity. *Vereignen*, as the older and more relational term, signals an abandonment of the modern toward-one (*ver-ein*) orientation, which must occur if we are to disrupt and leap beyond the principle of identity. He seeks to restore the original nonmediating and nonsynthetic sense of the term.

On the other side, *zueignen* is not appropriation (*Aneignen*), but a leap toward the proper (*zu-eignen*). It is a leap *toward* Being (probably in the form of being) that is made possible by disrupting the principle of identity (*ID*, 36; *SI*, 101). *Zu-* is an intensive prefix and one that signals a movement "toward." Like *vereignen*, it disrupts the fusional orientation that nullifies the two. It also carries a sense of openness that is not present in its modern supplement *aneignen*. In modern German, this verb is still used in the sense of "to dedicate." This *toward* orientation plays a pivotal role in Nancy's philosophy.

*Vereignen* and *zueignen* convey a loose yet idiosyncratic sense of "over-propriation." They open onto the constellation. "This suitability is valid" only, argues Heidegger, "when Man and Being are made proper to each other," which is "*simply experienced*, i.e., the inward turn in that which we name the *Ereignis*" (italics added, *ID*, 36; *SI*, 100).[14] There is a hint of mutuality here. Over-propriation is a crossing-over and a leap into strangeness. Thus, *Ereignis* could be translated as the "eventness that makes proper," which I will call "propering eventness" in shorthand. Only within and during propering eventness does "belonging have priority over the 'together'" and "the essence of identity is a property [*Eigentum*] of *Er-eignisses*" (*ID*, 38; *SI*, 103).

At this point in his lecture, the "title" qua "principle" of the law of identity ("*Der Satz der Identität*") has been translated into a "title" qua law of a "spring" away from "metaphysical authority" (*ID*, 39–40; *SI*, 104–5). His allegorical solution does not climb through and beyond the intertwinement of the world; it disrupts and traverses the work of the frame and springs beyond the gathering activity that bind us together. Each element in this exercise diagonally draws together the forgotten diachronic dimensions of language with its modern synchronic dimensions. He works through, disrupts, opens, and unfounds the ways we are gathered together in the contemporary use of language.

### III. Interpreting the *Ereignis*

In the following section, I focus on a few key exegetical essays that Agamben and Nancy have written on the *Ereignis*. Each argues that the *Ereignis* serves as a mechanism that disrupts the proprietary subject's appropriative capacities by exposing and opening them up. For Agamben, the *Ereignis* acts as a peculiar passageway that renders it possible to become a proper self (**se*). In his own work, he uses this motif of the auto-opening in his search for an ontological ethos, which he calls "whatever being" in *The Coming Community* and later "form-of-life." Nancy interprets the *Ereignis* as an onto-opening (*onto-ouverture*). If there is an "auto-opening" (*auto-ouverture*) in the event of existence, he claims, it is only in "the mode of the onto-" (*UPF*, 135; *BP*, 102). He carries this motif into his other writings where he searches for ways to conceive of being-with that occur in the modality of the "ex-." In the following, I begin by examining Agamben's more etymological account of the *Ereignis*, then I turn to Nancy's more existential reading.

* * *

Despite being published quite early in his oeuvre (1982 in *aut-aut*), Agamben's analysis of Heidegger's *Ereignis* in "*Se: Hegel's Absolute and Heidegger's *Ereignis*" foreshadows many of the problems that have come to define his philosophy. Agamben argues that from his earlier accounts of death and finitude to his later writings on the *Ereignis*, Heidegger constantly searched for ways to absolve the self. In the following section, I focus on how Agamben formulates the relationship between the self and the proper in the *Ereignis*.

Throughout this paper Agamben emphasizes the relationship between the **se* (self) and **leu* (to loosen, divide, free, separate) in the motif of absolution. He begins by examining the etymological connection between the **se* and absolute. "The Latin verb *solvo*, from which the adjective 'absolute' is derived," he claims, "lets itself [*si lascia*], in fact, be analysed as *se-luo* and indicates the work of loosening, freeing (*luo*) that leads (or leads back) something to its proper **se*" (modified *PI*, 169; *PE*, 116).[15] Given its "etymologically arbitrary" relation to "both the verb *eignen*, 'to appropriate [*appropriare*],' and the adjective *eigen*, 'proper' or 'own' [*prioprio*]," "*Ereignis* is not so far from the meaning of the **se*" and in fact it connotes a sense of "ab-*so*-lution [*as-so-luzione*]" (*PI*, 170; *PE*, 117). The absolution (*ab-*se-*leu*) that occurs in the *Ereignis*, then, is not a synthetic operation that gathers parts together; rather, it is a process that dissolves and exposes the subject in such a manner that it is forced to abandon itself.

Part of the problem of understanding the **se* is that it straddles two seemingly contradictory meanings in the semantics of Indo-European languages. On the one hand, the **se* indicates "what is proper," such as a habit, custom, or ethos that is "proper to a group." It is thus related to the "*idios*, 'proper' (*idioomai*, 'I appropriate,' and *idiōtēs*, 'private citizen')." On the other hand, the **se* "exists in an autonomous modality" (modified ibid.). It is that which "stands by itself" and "separated," such as in the "Greek *heauton* (*he* + *auton*)" or "the English 'self'" (ibid). Thus on the one side it refers to a "relation that unites" and the other "a relation that separates, the proper" (*PI*, 170; *PE*, 116–17). Heidegger's *Ereignis*, claims Agamben, cuts right through the middle of this confusion.

It is necessary to backtrack here for a moment. When discussing the principle of identity, I focused on the etymological relationship of *Gleichheit* (sameness/likeness) and *zusammen* (together) in German and English. I demonstrated how gathering together is a synthetic action that constitutes sameness. What I did not point out was that in this lecture, Heidegger also addressed the confusion of "sameness" with "identity." This arose, he argues, when ancient Greek was translated into Latin. That "which is identical [*Identische*], in Latin '*idem*,'" he points out, "is in Greek *τὸ αυτό*" or "the self/same" (*das Selbe*) (modified *ID*, 23; *SI*, 86). However, the proper cognate for *idem* in Greek would be *homo*, whereas *auto* would be better translated as *ipse*. Since this mistranslation stuck, we have been forced to deal with its many ramifications. "Self-sameness" (*auto-idem*) became the principle formula for conceiving of identity.

In his essay, for example, Agamben argues that Heidegger's *Ereignis* concerns the problem of the "*Selbst*, the '*same*' [*stesso*]," or the semantic connection between *eigen* and *Selbst* like that between *idios* and *he* (*PI*, 170; *PE*, 117). Agamben interprets the *Ereignis* in such a manner that it disrupts the traditional reduction of *auto* to *idem*, the self to sameness, which would open a pathway to becoming an ungrounded *ipseity* (selfhood). This reading is congruent with Heidegger's earlier writings on death and finitude. It is also clearly articulated in Raffoul's (2007) reading of Heidegger's *Contributions to Philosophy* and Ricoeur's monumental study of this problem, *Soi-même comme une autre* (1992). *Soi-même*, or *se stesso* in Italian, are translated into English as "oneself," however both could be translated literally as *self-same*. Even the Italian *se stesso* generates this confusion because *stesso* (same) is formed by combining *iste* (that) and *ipse* (self) as **st + istum*.

Both Hegel and Heidegger, claims Agamben, attempt to resolve this aporia by resorting to "dwelling in division" (*dimora nella scissione*) (*PI*, 172; *PE*, 118). This division is internal to the self, he argues, because it is the bearer of division. To make this point Agamben enlists Heraclitus's testimony "*ēthos anthrōpō daímōn*," which he translates as "For man, *ethos*, the dwelling in the 'self' that is what is most proper and habitual for him, is what lacerates and divides [*daímōn*], the principle and place of a fracture" (*PI*, 171; *PE*, 118). In order "to be-self" (*esser-sé*), a human must "divide itself" (*dividersi*). One could read this as a disruption of the traditional formulation of *Homo approprians*, where the subject is only made proper by appropriating that which is alienating, or by rendering the improper proper. This is how the problem of internal difference is usually solved as a pathway through which the self must pass and overcome before it can become a proper self. This is also a problem Agamben addresses in his book on community and in the *Homo Sacer* series.

At the end of this paper, Agamben expands on the posthumanist and posthistorical dimensions of Heidegger's *Ereignis* in ways that he will later integrate into his own philosophy. Translated into his more recent prose, this text poses the problem of an ontological ethos whose modality of being-thus (or form-of-life) occurs as a liberation from human destiny and from the practical ontology of having-to-be (*dovere-essere*). In this ethos one is nothing other than its modality of being. In the *Ereignis*, the self is abandoned "to what has neither property nor destiny," which he calls a "pure *as-sue-faction* [a habituation] and habit" (modified *PI*, 189; *PE*, 131). It is an *ethos* of abandonment. For Heidegger, it is impossible to think the proper because it only comes in the form of the *Ereignis*, which transmits an "untransmissible transmission."

If there is an end, it can only be one where the "ungroundedness of man—the hominization [*ominizzazione*]—is now proper" (modified *PI*, 193; *PE*, 134). Our task is to focus on this "*ethical* dwelling in **se*." This is a posthistorical, posthumanist notion of a human. The human is free to reposit her foundation in her "own action" (*proprio fare*). With a hint of what lies in store for his thinking, he even claims that sacrifice, and the identification of an excluded yet included "bare natural life" (*nuda* *vita naturale*), will not suffice because it attempts to create artificial grounds that cover over our ungroundedness. Although the *se is the "proper of man" (*proprio dell'uomo*), we should not treat it as either an unavowable sacred thing or as an arbitrary and violent nothing that is found in the "pathos of contemporary nihilism." Rather, as the ethos and proper of man, the **se* "is the social praxis itself that, in the end, becomes transparent to itself" (*PI*, 197; *PE*, 137). Later he will appeal to a notion of "free use" and even later "common use" in this ethos. Either way, for Agamben, the *Ereignis* performs the function of opening up and liberating the self, an auto-opening.

* * *

Instead of performing an etymological reading that focuses on the auto-opening and the freeing of the **se*, Nancy conducts an existential reading that examines the relationship between the onto-opening and the ex-. Like Agamben's, Nancy's reading is more than an interpretation because it is representative of what he does in his own philosophy. Across his writings on community and ontology, Nancy conceives of a notion of being-with that occurs in the existential modality of the ex-. He draws heavily from Heidegger's attempt to rethink the place of the proper in his *Ereignis-Denken* in this work. In the next chapter, I examine the trajectory of this project, but for now I will examine two essays where Nancy engages in a more systematic interpretation of the *Ereignis*, "A Finite Thinking" (*UPF*, *AFT*) and "The Surprise of the Event" (*ESP*, *BSP*), and his reading of *Being and Time* in "The Decision of Existence" (*UPF*, *BP*).

Like Agamben, Nancy translates *eigentlich* as "proper," not as "authenticity" (*UPF*, 132; *BP*, 100).[16] Authenticity, he claims, "implies, in an essential manner, the idea of pure origin or of provenance" (ibid.). Heidegger refused to use the German equivalent "*echt*, *Echtheit*." *Eigentlich*, however, "says nothing other than the 'proper,' that which properly appertains to" (ibid.). In a different paper, he points out that the decision of existence "does not take into account a floating 'authenticity,' in the air, but the very *proper* of the impropriety through which existence exists, each time and constantly" (*UPF*, 133; *BP*, 100).

Where the two differ is how they interpret the *Ereignis*. Nancy offers a more existential reading. Both advance that it is an event that opens up, exposes, and ultimately expropriates the subject, but for Nancy the subject of this event has been so extensively disconfigured that it is no longer possible to perform a reflexive action that turns back on and appropriates it self in order to enter into a proper ethos. For Nancy, the only possible thing left to appropriate is the *ex-*, the movement toward as a passageway, which he claims is the most proper of the existent. This is a reading that combines Heidegger's earlier formulation of the decision of the existence in *Being and Time* with his later formulation of the *Ereignis.*

Nancy's philosophy is grounded in the Heidegger-inspired notion that we dwell in division. His fundamental concept of *partage*, for example, carries a double sense of being "shared out" and "divided up." The negative modality of being shared out and divided up in the existential event must be reconceived in a communal manner where each shares with each other in a modality of coexistence. What is shared in and through coexistence is nothing that has been or could be appropriated and thus not something that could be redistributed. It is merely an ontological modality. Although Heidegger never managed to conceive of the *Ereignis* in a relational or pluralized manner, how he formulated it has fundamentally shaped Nancy's philosophy of coexistence.

Existence, Nancy argues, occurs with a notable "absence-of-foundation" (*L'absence-de-fondement*), his translation of Heidegger's "*Abgründlichkeit*" (*UPF*, 19; *AFT*, 9). That is, it occurs through a leap away from the essence of foundationalism (*ab-esse*). Contrary to the tradition, this does not signify a "lack of being" that must "be sustained [*soutenu*], justified, or originated insofar as it is and in that it is," but that "being refers to nothing, neither to substance, subject, nor even to 'being,' unless *to* a being-toward, to itself, to the world, which also makes the opening or the throwing, the being-thrown of *existence* [*l'être-jeté de l'existence*]" (modified, ibid.).[17] In Heidegger, this is merely a transmission to the "infinite," such as his "thought beyond the world," which Nancy claims is a "Christian sense of the world" (*SM*, 91; *SW*, 54).[18] For Nancy, "'being the existent'" does not "transmit" a "quality" or a "property"; only the self (**se*) is transmitted, "transmitting nothing other than the *toward* of the transmission *to* the existent, the being-to/towards of sense [*l'être-à du sens*], giving existence being insofar as [*en tant que*] sense, not the 'meaning of being' as [*comme*] the content of a signification, but the being-sense of being" (modified *UPF*, 20; *AFT*, 9).

This "transmission to/toward" is a passageway that does not give anything for which something would be expected back in return. Rather the *toward* puts the existent in "debt" (*dette*), "having *to* be (existence, self)" and thus "having to appropriate itself insofar as the inappropriable of the groundlessness that would have been its being" (ibid.). This is not an appropriation of Being, or of its sense, but an appropriation in the sense of *toward*-itself, such as the sense of *ad-propriare* that Heidegger used when distinguishing between *zueignen* and *aneignen*. For Nancy, being closest to one's most proper in the modality of the *toward* was present in Heidegger's notion of being-towards-death. Death is inappropriable, so the only that thing that can be appropriated would be the modality of the toward.

Nancy further examines the appropriation of the toward in "The Decision of Existence." Here he emphasizes the relationship between the modality of exposure and decisiveness. "Thought in its decision is not the thought that undertakes to found Being or found itself in Being. It is only the decision that ventures and affirms existence on its proper absence of foundation" (*UPF*, 111–12; *BP*, 84). The decision to affirm one's existence is itself a divisive (*de-caedere*) action that occurs within the divisiveness of the exposure. This poses a dilemma. On the one hand, the decision "is what most escapes existence" as "that to and in which existence is most properly 'thrown'" (*UPF*, 115; *BP*, 86). On the other hand, the decision "offers existence its closest [*plus proche*], its most proper or its most intimate advent: *Ereignis*" (*UPF*, 115; *BP*, 86). The existent is faced with a decision about that which is by definition undecidable, hence untenable, which is the very divisiveness of existence. How can division be grasped and retained, he asks, when we dwell in division? To do so would be to deny our proper being-toward.

The decision "is nothing but the exercise of the appropriation of the decision, which demonstrates that the decision of this appropriation always precedes it and does not appertain [*appartient*] to it" (*UPF*, 115; *BP*, 87). There are two sides to this argument. Structurally, the *Ereignis* disappropriates the ontic subject, which is evident in his translation of "the appropriating/disappropriating event" (*l'événement appropriant/désappropriant*) (*UPF*, 132; *BP*, 100). Unlike Descartes's cognitive *suspension*, this is merely a "suspension *insofar as* being," which Nancy rephrases as "*ego sum, ego existo*" (*UPF*, 134–35; *BP*, 102). An existent "*has* nothing" (ibid., 85/114) precisely because there is nothing to "hold" (ibid.). Being is neither "something," nor a "property." It is inappropriable because it has nothing to offer (ibid.). In "A Finite

Thinking," he makes a similar statement, "'There is' is not of the order of having . . . the verb 'to have,' here, slips from appropriation to Being through instantaneous diffraction, dislocation, and dissemination of the 'to have' of the 'to be'" (*UPF*, 24, fn. 1; *AFT* , 12, fn.14).

Contrary to Agamben, Nancy considers this passage as an "onto-opening" rather than an "auto-opening." The auto is appropriated/disappropriated in the strange "*se tenir*" of the "opening." The opening is where the existent "holds itself, holding and seizing *itself*, in this place or in this archi-original taking-place, *as difference opened up from its sameness of being*" (*UPF*, 135; *BP*, 102).[19] Decisiveness is "*the very consistency of its existence*" because the decisive existent "opens itself to its proper being" or "appropriates the inappropriable event of its advent to Being in its leap from a groundlessness of being" (*UPF*, 135–36; *BP*, 102–3). Existing, therefore, "has nothing more proper than this infinite appropriability of the inappropriable being-proper" (ibid.). This, claims Nancy, is the "truth of 'finitude.'" A "proper decision" is merely feigned because it exceeds thinking. It is neither "hostile" nor "indifferent," but a thought about its "proper limit" and "difference" (*UPF*, 145; *BP*, 108). Since an existent is faced with its most proper limitation, the decision is limited. The only thing an existent can appropriate is "its most proper being: existence itself insofar as opening" (*UPF*, 134; *BP*, 101). That is, its being toward, which again Nancy argues is represented in Heidegger's *Ereignis* as the *Zueignung*.

Does Nancy argue that Heidegger's *Ereignis* traverses the frame that "holds" (*tenir*) together the work of "taking" (*prendre*)? Not exactly. Like many others, he reads this movement as a mere reversal of taking by turning to the notion of "surprise" (over taken). Nancy states, "Tension, the extension of the leap—the spacing of time—the discord of Being as its truth, voilà the surprise" (*ESP*, 199; *BSP*, 173). The surprise does not "destabilize a subject that was there, but it takes [*prend*] someone there where he is not, or again it takes him, seizes him, paralyzes him *insofar as he is not there*," which is the "leaping at Being" as the "most proper mode of 'being there'" (ibid.). It is the surprise of "nothing"; that is, no (identifiable) thing. It has neither temporal nor spatial precedence. It is "the nothing of a leap into nothing," "which is the affirmation of the ek-sistent tension: its intensity, the intensity or surprising tone of existence" (*ESP*, 200; *BSP*, 173). The existent is so divided up and shared out that it is incapable of either "grasping" or "holding itself" (*se tenir*), which would be required for "self-appropriation" (*ESP*, 190; *BSP*, 164). This is a different reading than he conducted in his early essay on the decision.

One of the main issues in this entire problematic is how the proper is interpreted. When conducting his more existential reading of the decision of existence or of the broader event of existence in the *Ereignis*, Nancy tends to emphasize the relationship between the proper and presence. The proper in this reading is that which is most near and proximate. In "The Surprise of the Event," he argues that the *Ereignis* addresses issues raised by phenomenology and theology. It does not consider an objectifiable thing, an "event," but the "eventness of its event" (*l'événementailité de son événement*), which is "the non-phenomenal truth *of the phenomenal itself insofar as such*" (*ESP*, 187; *BSP*, 160–61). Eventness is not "present," but "presence of the present" (*ESP*, 193; *BSP*, 167). The *Ereignis* "exceeds the resources of a phenomenology, even though the phenomenological theme in general has, without a doubt, never been animated by anything else" (*ESP*, 195; *BSP*, 169). There is no "hidden presence" that must be dis-covered. Presence, he continues, is not even "un-presentable" because it is never "presentifiable." Rather, presence is simply the "difference that structures the present" that is "right at [*à même*] the present itself" (ibid.). Its modality can only be represented by "insofar as such" (*en tant que tel*), not "as such" (*comme tel*) (*ESP*, 195–96; *BSP*, 169).

Alongside other post-phenomenologists, Nancy distinguishes between the phenomenological method of "intentionality" (an immanent stretching toward) and "extensionality" (stretching away from). He calls for a "negative" "tension" that "tenses: tension and extension" (*se tend: tension et extension*) (*ESP*, 196; *BSP*, 170). This compliments Heidegger's call for a disruption of the intentional orientation that leads us to project toward something, which also prevents us from "letting go." Heidegger's focus on the pathway, rather than the thing intended, sidesteps this problem. Nancy's emphasis on ex-tension serves the same purpose. Tension, he argues, is "the only way something can appear as the 'passage' and the 'process'" (*ESP*, 196; *BSP*, 170). It is the "non-temporal, non-local ex-tension of the occurrence as such," such as Heidegger's "*Spanne*" that signals "the spacing through time that suddenly appears [*surgit*]" (ibid.). In the extensive occurrence, "there is a rupture and a leap" (ibid.). The leap leaps away from the standing order, ek-stasis, while leaping "right at Being." In his brand of existentialism, tension plays a prominent role and ek-sistence is a modality that is extensive (*ESP*, 199; *BSP*, 173). Thus, while Agamben emphasizes how the absolving characteristics of the *Ereignis* (loosen, divide, free, letting go, etc.) open up the *se*, Nancy's existentialist interpretation focuses on how the extensive characteristics give rise to an onto-opening.

* * *

In his less exegetical essays, such as "Compearance," Nancy translates *Ereignis* as a "disappropriating propriation." A communist revolution, he argues, must occur through an "ex-appropriative" movement. In "Our World," he claims that according to Derrida, "ex-appropriation" is "an essential lever in the Heideggerian project: to carry the 'proper' (which had already become indefinite and/or infinite in Kant, as that which is proper to man as a being 'of ends,' and in Marx as the produced, alienable and reappropriable property of the social/individual being) to the power of that which lies out of reach at the heart of existence itself, and which thus constitutes the *proper of the ex-* or the *ex- as proper*" (2003, 51). The *proprius*, however, is neither *commonius* nor *alienus*. It fosters a peculiar, special, private, and exclusive sense of belonging. This becomes apparent when the proper is conflated with the idiom. According to Derrida, an idiom "resists translation" because it is peculiar, different, private, and singular; as such, idioms cannot be compared (2005, 102). The "idiom, precisely [i.e., *praecedere*, pre + cut short], means *the proper*, what is proper to" (2005, 99). But, an "absolute idiolect or idiom would no longer be a language at all," Nancy argues, because "*it could no longer be translated so as to be the untranslatable that it is.* A pure idiolect would be idiotic, wholly deprived of relations and so of identity" (*ESP*, 178; *BSP*, 154). In ancient Greece, for example, the *idiōtēs* was a private, peculiar, excluded, citizenshipless, and thus apolitical economic entity. The idiot had neither the property nor the common identity that would provide a passage out of the private and into the public (*ESP*, 66; *BSP*, 45). For Nancy, however, the idiom is not an "absolute and vertiginous law of the *proper*," which means that "in appropriating its proper purity," the idiom "alienates itself *purely* and simply" (*ESP*, 178; *BSP*, 154). The "proper name" is only "the idiom of an idiolect" in myth (*ESP*, 182; *BSP*, 158). Nancy does not retain the properly proper (the absolute proper), an evident tautology, but that which is "proper to" the "ex-," which is certainly not a dwelling or an idiom in the sense of peculiarity (as in a private, nonevident, ethos/characteristic).

*Idios* is that which is both proper and peculiar to an individual. The *idios kosmos* is the private world, which is not to be confused with the *koinos kosmos*, or the shared world. The point here is not that the idiom should not be used for politics, a cliché that has been repeated for over two centuries, but that it cannot be used precisely because it is untranslatable, meaning that it excludes relations. Communists can make no use of the conflation of the proper with the idiom, which means that we must expose and traverse the dispositif of the proper.

Why retain the proper, even if it is only used in a diminutive state? Why not consider the "ex-" as a movement away from the proper, including appropriation, toward ex-propriation? We can do this by adding an improper translation to my already inappropriate translation of *Ereignis*. It could refer to an evental activity that cyclically returns to the proper that chips away at it. This is already happening, but we need to push this further. It would be wrong to read this as a call for a sacrifice of the proper (or Proper) because it is just a word, not a thing, substance, or hypostatic referent. Sacrifice, after all, is an idiopathogen of the proper.

Finally, we have to re-address the Marxian line promoted by Balibar and repeated by Elliot in "Community and Resistance in Heidegger, Nancy and Agamben" (2011). Why appeal to the radical passivity of the *Ereignis*, which prioritizes receptiveness over action, asks Elliot? Is it not the case that the "underlying approach to community shared by Nancy and Agamben" is precisely the "negative and privative logic" that promotes an "incommunicable source of all acts of communication and common existence" (2011, 267)? Besides overlooking the differences between each thinker, this question is formulated on a misnomer. It has been posed in terms of a defense of the model of revolutionary appropriation. Although the terrain is drastically different today, Elliot's question is really no different than the questions Marx and Engels asked of Stirner. Given the litany of crises we face today, one does have question whether *Homo approprians* is capable of solving our problems. What might a communism look like that is not grounded in the dispositif of the proper, which is at its basis a doctrine of private property, economic and political? How Agamben, Esposito, and Nancy formulate this problem in terms of an alternative notion of politics and/or ethics and in terms the fundamental issues of ontology, will be the focus of the following chapters.

# 3

# The Existential Community

> [I]t seems to us as indispensable today to recognise that what completes itself (and does not cease to complete itself) is the great "enlightened," progressivist discourse of secular or profane eschatology, and that is to say the discourse of the reappropriation of man in his humanity, the discourse of the actualisation of the genre of the human—in short, the discourse of revolution.
>
> —*RP*, 111

From his early formulations at *Centre de recherches philosophiques sur le politique*, to his first serious writing on community, to his recent writings on globalization and democracy, Nancy has been charged with being nothing more than an ornate and politically vacuous deconstructive essayist. Many English commentators have even denounced him for abandoning politics while favoring the ontological. While addressing these critiques, Martin Crowley has recently pointed out that Nancy does not prioritize the ontological and existential to the detriment of the ontic and political, but that these two regions are "co-originary" and "equiprimordial" (i.e., Heidegger's *gleichursprünglich*) (2014, 141).[1] In slightly different terms, Philip Armstrong has succinctly demonstrated that in his deconstruction of the tradition of political philosophy Nancy performs an "an-archic displacement of the political *arche*" (2009, xxi). Both defend Nancy against the charge of scribing an apolitical political philosophy.

Despite his predilections and his many hyperbolic claims to the contrary, Nancy's political philosophy is political. In fact, this philosophy circles around a paradox that he has been grappling with since the early

1980s. This is the paradox of *weak politics*, understood in the many senses of **weik* (bend, yield, soft). Nancy has sought to carefully articulate a delicate relationship between existence and politics. He deconstructs traditional political philosophy, the political and politics, in search of openings that will hold politics back from dominating existence. This does not mean that existence takes precedence over politics, in the sense of either preceding or taking over; rather, politics have to be reconceptualized, beginning with the political, so that politics can serve the purposes of holding open the space that is necessary for us to coexist in the existential sense of existence. In this sense, politics must be weakened and radically scaled back. In his more practical moments, he will admit that the only institutions capable of such a task in our society are our current political institutions. We might even say that this task is the political task, despite the contradiction, par excellence of politics for Nancy. The problem for him becomes one of rethinking the relationship between politics and existence, where politics do not overlap and appropriate existence. Politics cannot not be tasked with making existence happen. Existence must remain beyond the jurisdiction of politics. Although Nancy is critical of biopolitical philosophy, his formulation is quite similar to Agamben's critique of the way modern governmental machines attempt to control and regulate life. For Nancy, existence resides at the end of politics, but it is not the ends of politics.

A second point is that when reading Nancy, we cannot underestimate the significance of his reiterations of Sartre's dictum that "'Marxism is the unsurpassable horizon of our time.'" For both, communism can only be expressed through the ecstatic event of existence: the ex- can only occur as the cum- and the cum- can only be realized, not recognized, in the ex-. Nancy does not try to marry existential notions of the ecstatic event with the Marxist model of revolution, however, because he is working from a post-Marxist, deconstructive, and postphenomenological perspective. Instead he develops a model of "existential communism" where coexistence appears, or more properly stated compears, in a manner that is not congruent with traditional formulations of community. Unlike Sartre, then, Nancy does not seek to existentialize politics and make a politics out of existence; for him, especially in his more recent writings, the two should be held in slightly separate spheres.[2]

In this chapter, I trace the trajectory of Nancy's theory of community by focusing on a select group of texts where he most directly engages with political philosophy. I begin with his statements on the retreat of the political in the early 1980s and end on his recent reflections on democracy and globalization. Some of my omissions might strike the reader as inappropriate, but my intent here is not to provide an exhaustive account of his entire oeuvre. Instead, I have sought to trace a single thread in his political philosophy. I have selected particular texts that provide enough material to paint a picture of how Nancy has systematically deconstructed the dialectic of alienation and appropriation in search for an alternative way to conceive of community.

My reading emphasizes two fundament elements in his deconstruction of this dialectic: the proper and the problem of belonging-together. On the one hand, Nancy plays with the many senses of the proper in his works, including the proprietary notion advanced by political economy. But most of Nancy's work focuses on the symbolic economy, including the problems of sensibility and appearance. Nancy often counterpoises the appropriative logic that operates in the *authentic* notion of the proper with a notion of the proper as that which is most near and proximate. This is a relational sense of the proper that is inappropriable. He also challenges the logic of visibility, appearance, and meaning with a more tangential notion of sense and sensibility. On the other hand, he draws heavily, especially in the 1990s, from Heidegger's deconstruction of the problem of belonging-together. Throughout this chapter, I focus on how Nancy deconstructs the myriad ways that relationships are calibrated according to the model that gathers people together in a relationship, which he usually characterizes as the *partes extra partes* model of society. On this end, his critique is not too different from Sartre's earlier critique of "Us-relations" or later critique of "seriality." Together, these two strains culminate in a single problematic: how to dis-contain relationships from the representative framework, possibly superstructure, that unifies people by producing a symbolic identity. The collective (re)appropriation of symbolic identity, he claims, is not an appropriate solution because alienation is not a reflection of a misappropriated authentic identity. It is, according to him, an expression of the senseless of the world and, in very general terms, of being-with or community.

## PART 1. THE 1980S

Although they were written quite early in his career, the texts that Nancy wrote during the 1980s on community and political philosophy are not merely formative texts. His essays for the *Centre de recherches philosophiques sur le politique* (*RP*, 1996) and *The Inoperative Community* (*CD*, 1986; *IO*, 1991), to cite but two, stand out as important contributions to political philosophy in the 1980s. He has recently noted that he was "astonished" when Blanchot responded to this first essay on the inoperative community in *The Unavowable Community.* Blanchot had responded, he claims, "to someone who was a young philosopher without authority" (*LCD*, 18–19).[3] He was, in so many words, honored and unequipped to fully respond at the time, but what was said here profoundly influenced his own philosophy of community that he articulated in the 1990s. In the following section, I briefly cover some of the main themes Nancy developed in the 1980s.

> The communitarian and/or communal premise, the *Gemeinschaft* against the *Gesellschaft*, all of it contains the terrible germs that we know so well and that today can be used again for the flags of diverse ethnic and ethno-religious identities. I completely understand these kinds of reservations and I share them, since with the definition of an "inoperative community" I wanted precisely to speak of a community that does not put into effect any community. This is why I have continued to let the lexicon that I had been using slide from "being-in-common," "being-together," and "separation," arriving at "being-with" or the pure and simple "with," as one will see in *Being Singular Plural.*[4]

### I. The Political

There is no landmark text that marks a decisive shift in Nancy's oeuvre; rather, his theoretical trajectory from his earlier to later writings on political philosophy circles around specific axioms that he continues to address. If one were to summarize his political philosophy in single phrase, one would have to say that Nancy is the preeminent contemporary philosopher to address the problem of open relationships.[5] This problem is clearly articulated in his co-written

"Opening Address" for the *Centre de recherches philosophiques sur le politique*. He continues to raise the many philosophical and political issues that were only briefly addressed in this short but prolific text. In fact, the very parameters for re-thinking the communist question that he and Lacoue-Labarthe established in this address are reasserted with full philosophical force and precision in his subsequent writings on the common and the political.

In their opening address, Nancy and Lacoue-Labarthe claim that their political allegiances and the politics they hope to see espoused at the centre remain committed to Sartre's dictum "Marxism is the unsurpassable horizon of our time." Not "really existing socialism," however, which they liken to totalitarianism, but a radical revision of Marxism.[6] Mainstream political philosophy is no longer equipped to meet this task. Even revolutionary philosophies continue to rely on the same humanist principles that have contributed to the contemporary implosion of politics. The political today, which was the early 1980s when they gave the address, "is completed to the point of excluding every other area of reference" (*RP*, 111). Typical metaphysical solutions, usually articulated through mythological notions of transcendence, are now impotent because metaphysics can no longer find a pathway leading beyond the political. Even trying to conceive of an elsewhere is now impossible because all manners of thinking have been absorbed by the political, such that the political is now everywhere and "everything is political." Practical solutions presented by mainstream political philosophy—"social transparency," "the utopia of the homogenisation of the 'social body,' the hope attached to management or to enlightened direction"—are now but mere fantasies concocted by humanist philosophers whose ideas belong to a previous era. Rephrased with a Heideggerian inflexion: today, belonging is determined by togetherness and relations do not exist in their proper sense because they are dissolved in a state of sheer sameness; put in Arendt's terms, private life and public life have been consumed by the social (*RP*, 129).

In their critique of totalitarianism, Nancy and Lacoue-Labarthe draw attention to the relation between *being-ecstatic* and *relationships*. They address this relation through Claude Lefort's reading of the "lacuna of the political" in Marx and Marxism. Mainstream political philosophy addresses this problem in two generic ways. On the one hand, the political can be conceived as a "transitory political form." This approach is found in many revolutionary philosophies of action, such as the theory of spontaneity or permanent revolution, but it is also found in populist movements oriented against the formal political structures of the state and professional politicians. Sartre's group-in-fusion represents one of the most detailed studies of this approach, yet in the end his theory could not solve the problem faced by all who advocate this approach: the problem of continuity. Because the political is elevated to an ecstatic status—an absolute, extensive, yet, complete event—where relationships exist precisely in the confrontation with formal political structures, to remain political, relations must maintain a permanent state of active transition. This is the confrontational model of politics, the politics of opposition and struggle. It only exists as an ecstatic or metastatic event. Solutions for this aporia are plentiful in the history of modern political philosophy. Some attempt to overcome this impasse by concocting an eschatological formulation steeped in mythology and negative theology. Some dilute the absoluteness of the event by concocting authoritarian, or vanguard, formulas to contain and control the event. Others appropriate the formal structures and then continue to mythologize the established order as a permanent order of revolution. In each approach, the eventness of the event, or the ecstasy of open political relations, remains but a fleeting and unobtainable possibility.

In the less revolutionary formulation, the political can be fused to the state. Proponents here search for a means to limit the state so that there are checks and balances against "the total immanetisation of the political in the social" (*RP*, 115). Classical republicanism, contemporary theories of active citizenship, and proponents of civil society all figure within this perspective. Here the trick becomes one of distinguishing between the formal and informal elements of politics. Lacoue-Labarthe and Nancy argue that this approach also falls flat because it derives from the model of the "proper subject" where the key distinction rests between civil society and the state or between sovereignty and domination. In fact, neither *in statu nascendi* nor *separatio* proves to be an adequate solution because both are conceived within the horizons of metaphysics. Behind each lurks the model of the "subject," "an archē-propriety always leading back behind the figures of absolute depropriation which were supposed to be constitutive of the proletariat just as much as they were of sovereignty" (*RP*, 117).

Their powerful critique of the metaphysics of the subject should not be read as an apolitical call for indifference or political apathy. Since the neoliberal era is dominated by "political economy," "class struggles or political struggles" continue to be important for rethinking the relation. "The so-called question of the relation," they contend in "The 'Retreat' of the Political," "remains, to our mind, *the* central question" (*RP*, 133). The task at hand is to radically revise the meaning of the struggle without subordinating it to the logic of political economy. The question of the relation, of the social bond, or in Nancy's later writings, of singular plurality, must be readdressed again. The retreat of the political provides the opportunity to rethink the political, not to abandon it.

## The Existential Community, Take One

"The Inoperative Community" represents Nancy's first concentrated reflection on the problem of community. Many of the insights and formulations he makes in this work are further developed in his subsequent writings. The text itself is more entrenched in the Heideggerian theory of existence, specifically in George Bataille's rethinking of death as that which is most proper and inalienable in a postoperative and communal manner. Nancy uses this perspective to readdress the Western Marxist tradition. Although there are many interesting dimensions to this text, including the delayed debate with Blanchot, I will set aside most of the details of this encounter because I merely want to extrapolate a few formulations that he returns to in his subsequent writings on community.[7]

Nancy begins by re-raising Sartre's mantra that communism stands as the "'unsurpassable horizon of our time'" (*CD*, 11; *IO*, 1). After the letdown of really existing communism, the Hungarian Revolution of '56, Mai 68, and many other events, this horizon, he claims, has "disappeared"; yet in the wake of this loss, there remains the kernel of the "communist exigency" (*CD*, 28; *IO*, 8–9). The task today, he states, repeating the logic of the retreat of the political, is to use this disappearance to rethink the exigency. Communism, he claims,"stands as the emblem of the desire to discover or rediscover a place of community at once beyond social divisions and beyond the subordination to technopolitical dominion, and thereby beyond such wasting away of liberty, of speech, or of simple happiness as comes about whenever these become subjugated to the exclusive order of privatization; and finally, more simply and even more decisively, a place from which to surmount the unraveling that occurs with the death of each one of us" (ibid.). Echoing Arendt's critique of the *animal laborans*, Nancy argues that the traditional model of communism leads to an essentialist notion of community. Community represents the actualization, or realization, of the productive essence of humanity. Community is the common and finished product of human labor. In an Aristotelian, or Agambenian, sense, the operative community represents the *entelechia* of human *dunamis*, which he will call the "unitary entelechy of common being" in *Being Singular Plural* (*ESP*, 81; *BSP*, 59). In "The Inoperative Community," he criticizes this model for being *productive* in a double sense. Community represents the "goal" of "beings producing in essence their own essence as their work" (*CD*, 14; *IO*, 2). Not only is this potentiality-actuality formulation ideologically suspect, it produces a totalitarian closure of community. It produces a mythological notion of human essence, where essence "is set to work" (*CD*, 14–15; *IO*, 3). It is precisely this productive myth that Nancy attempts to "interrupt."[8]

Nancy's interpretation of the general deployment of Marx's theory of community is not off base. The same logic can be found in most humanist and Hegelian readings. As I discussed in the first chapter, the proper community represents the realization of *Homo approprians*. One only has to read *The German Ideology* in conjunction with his essay "Estranged Labor," even *The Grundrisse*, to arrive at this conclusion. In capitalism, humans are alienated from their "species-being" (*Gattungswesen*), which is their capacity to produce. To overcome their alienation—from species-being, the product, the process of production, and others—the proletariat must collectively appropriate the mode (forces and means) of production and render them common to all. Only after this appropriation process has been properly communalized can species-being be realized in the *life of the species*. A communist community, collectively owned and produced by all, represents the realization of human essence. Although each provided a nuanced account of this formula, it was applied by figures as diverse as Antonio Gramsci, Karl Korsch, György Lukács, Rosa Luxembourg, Herbert Marcuse, Mihailo Marković, Antoine Pannekoek, and Jean-Paul Sartre, to name just a few. It is this tradition of Western Marxism that we must deconstruct, according to Nancy, but not, of course, in the direction of Louis Althusser.

In an important subsection of this essay, which we could call the

"Horizons Behind Us," Nancy briefly discusses how community has been broadly conceived in Western political philosophy (*CD*, 28–35; *IO*, 9–12). He argues that Rousseau established the paradigm of the lost community. Rousseau created the myth that modern society was built on the ashes of a lost community. Community became a romanticized model of relationships where communal "bonds were tightly, harmoniously, and unbreakably woven together" (*CD*, 30; *IO*, 9). This ideal, however, was the product of a retrospective projection that was actually based in the critique of modern society. Modern society, for Rousseau and many subsequent political philosophers, was merely a "simple association and a dividing up [or sharing out, *répartition*] of forces and needs." As such, community represented the image of a perfect "organic communion" where members communed together in the very essence of community. Rather than a collective whole whose internal relations are more divisive than common, community is constituted by a state of sharing: "of sharing, diffusion or the impregnation of an identity by a plurality wherein each member only identifies with himself through the supplementary mediation of his identification in the living body of the community" (ibid.). Two familiar incarnations of this image are family and love, which are often representative of the masculine model of fraternity or brotherhood.

For Nancy, these discourses reckon back to a notion of a communion, which can never be fulfilled and can only be understood through the narrative of the lost community. This perceived withdrawal or retreat does not reveal something that was lost; rather it reveals that "*community has not taken place*" (*CD*, 30; *IO*, 11). The loss is merely a product of a retroactive projection, such that what is projected is not appropriable. It is the projection itself, he contends, that we have to reconsider; community is not "what society has crushed or lost," but "is *what happens to us*—question, waiting, event, imperative—in the wake of society" (*CD*, 34; *IO*, 11). This reading, that community occurs in the wake of society, was also advocated by many classical sociologists, including Ferdinand Tönnies himself. Nancy differs in that he chooses not to romanticize and resurrect the mythological lost community. Nor does he appeal to what former generations of sociologists called the "micro-model" of community. Against this tradition, Nancy does not search for a secure place where each belongs to the common property. Although his community does occur in the everyday, even between neighbors, this has nothing to do with the romanticized notion of a local neighborhood, parish, or association found in the Toucqueville-inspired communitarian theories of community.[9] Nor would the formulations of "social capital"—a buzzword in mainstream sociology—stand the test of his re-evaluation of community.[10] For Nancy, the notion of place is spaced out, divided, and shared. It is neither secure nor contained. And each may be conceived as a neighbor—dwells near—but only insofar as each is exposed and compears beside others.

In the closing pages of this essay, Nancy provides a rough sketch of his alternative theory of community. Community must be conceived in terms of a sharing or division (*partage*) "between singular existents that are not subjects, and whose relation—the sharing/division itself—is neither a community, nor an appropriation of an object, nor a self-recognition, nor even a communication that is heard between subjects" (*CD*, 64; *IO*, 25).[11] Two aspects in his formulation are important for our purposes: appropriation and appearance. First, following Bataille's reading of Heidegger, Nancy appeals to the death of the other as an example of an inappropriable experience. Not only is one's own death inappropriable, but the death of the other also exposes and extensively places us out-of-position. This imposition is so powerful that it leaves us incapacitated, thus without being capable of appropriating anything. Put differently, in the ex- of existence, we leap into a void which does not have the ground that is necessary for us to firmly take a stance, ground ourselves, and thus to appropriate our relations, the other, or ourselves.

Second, Nancy conceives of the phenomenality of these relations in a postphenomenological manner. Compearance is key here. Besides the reference to being summoned to compear in front of the court of law, compearance is the plural phenomenon of singular existents *compearing* together. It is not a thing that can be appropriated and re-presented, but precisely the co-appearance of singularities in their common exposure. Singularities compear as existents in the ecstatic eventness of compearance. Compearance is really a verb or modality for Nancy. As such, compearance is the presencing of community. In the modality of compearance, each compears together divided and shared. This is how community can be conceived in a largely existential framework.

In his later works, he will drop the references to death, communication, and literary communism, but already we have the early makings of his deconstruction of the traditional model of community. Since each is exposed to each other in the modality of compearance, that simultaneously shares out and divides each existent; there is no "bond" or "communion" (*CD*, 74; *IO*, 29). Neither the *se nor the community is completed in this absolving event. It is merely an opening itself, an opening toward each other, or a dis-containing of each that places them in an uncontainable relation. Put more simply, community occurs in the dis-containment of the tradition, of the subjects, and precisely as this manifold dis-containment process.

## PART 2. THE 1990S

In the early 1990s Nancy began to systematically deconstruct the authentic model of the proper in postrepresentational terminology. During this stage he developed a distinctively "Nancean" postphenomenological notion of existential communism. I begin this section by focusing on two important texts, "The Compearance: From the Existence of 'Communism' to the Community of 'Existence'" (*LC*, 1991; *TC*, 1992) and *The Sense of the World* (*SM*, 1993; *SW*, 1997). In both, Nancy raises the issue of symbolic appropriation. In the essay, he returns to Sartre's "communist horizon" (*LC*, 60–61; *TC*, 376). The book represents a methodological account of Nancy's deconstruction of sensibility and appearance. Across these texts Nancy deconstructs the phenomenological notion of sense in order to arrive at a properly existential notion of the sense, which is a sense that is thoroughly embedded in the world yet is not treated as a phenomenon that appears, and thus cannot be appropriated and represented. In a manner, these texts represent his version of Derrida's *Specters of Marx* (1994), only in his treatment there remains nothing left of the specter or anything else that falls under the register of vision.[12] This work also sets the course for his magnum opus, *Being Singular Plural*, where he employs compearance as a post-phenomenological supplement for the model of symbolic appropriation.

### III. Communism and a Deconstructed Phenomenology

The first third of *The Sense of the World* is arguably the most methodological passage in Nancy's oeuvre. Rather than establish a new scientific method, he searches for a passageway (*methodos*) that opens up the possibility of touching upon, not conceptualizing, the sense *of* sense in a nonappropriative manner. He is primarily focused on the intellectualistic strains of phenomenology based in Husserl's work.

He meticulously seeks to divorce his methodology from this tradition in an effort to arrive at a heavily deconstructed, postphenomenological, and existential notion of the sense of sense.

Nancy argues that the so-called contemporary "crisis of sense" provides a unique opportunity to completely overhaul how we have made sense of sense and thus of the world. What is actually happening in the *mondialisation* of the world needs to be understood not as a crisis, but as an opening up of the world to a new "exigency of sense" (*LSW*, 20; *TSW*, 9). This exigency carries an important lesson for rethinking community in an inclusive manner. Microcommunitarians are incapable of heeding this exigency because they seek to "make sense" of the demand of sense by reducing it to their particularistic and authentic notion of the proper. They hold fast to a model of the "world" "as the signifier of a proper and present signified, the signifier of the proper and the present as such" (*LSW*, 12; *TSW*, 3). For them, sense is something that can be appropriated, possessed, and thus contained. But what is becoming "obvious," not "clear" though, is that this traditional interpretation misses the fact that today there is an "excess of sense over all appropriable sense" (*LSW*, 12; *TSW*, 2). Sense rests not beyond the world, in a transcendental other, but in the world. The world is sense. It is, recalling the last chapter, the being-toward of relationships. If we want to attune or adapt to the exigency of the *mondialisation* of world, the sense of the world, then we must do so in ontological terms and only if the register of sense is changed "from having to being" (*LSW*, 19; *TSW*, 9).

Nancy is critical of the traditional phenomenological method, specifically Husserl's. Phenomenology incessantly "turns back on itself to appropriate its own process," which results in a containment of "transcendence" (*LSW*, 35; *TSW*, 18). Unlike the phenomenological epoché, where the phenomenologist is expected to "arrive at the constitution of an originary signification"—the thing-in-itself—he claims that we have "*to hold the step of thought suspended over this sense that has already touched us*" (*LSW*, 24; *TSW*, 11). He calls this gesture a "suspended step/not suspended" (*pas suspendu*). This suspended, not suspended, step allows the "excess or the initial spacing" to come forward (*LSW*, 35; *TSW*, 18). This excess, he notes in a distinctively Heideggerian vein, is the "exceeding of the origin—and of sense—is not to be seized. It is to be received or to 'let-be' and to act, simultaneously."

Instead of seizing, containing, and thus appropriating sense, we must let it be and receive it as such—at least if the "as such" is not understood in the sense of a presentation, but in the sense of letting it touch us in a manner than cannot be reduced to a cognitive or intellectual register. What comes forth is *signifiance*. *Signifiance* is the "dissemination" of sense, which comes before signifying and appropriable sense. We touch sense, rather than signify and thus appropriate it. We experience this "touch of sense," he argues, in our exteriority—being-toward (*LSW*, 21–25; *TSW*, 10–11). This is a new pathway, which began with the "end of philosophy," that is, of metaphysics.

Not even Heidegger's critique of the problem of intelligibility, he contends, where the *aletheia* supplements the *adequatio*, is up to this task. It too remains entrenched in the discourse of revelation and thus suspect to problems of appearance—presentation, representation, and appropriation. Nancy seeks to evade this problem by thinking about the "*being* or *sense* of appearing," rather than the thing itself that appears (*LSW*, 33; *TSW*, 17). Raising the stakes of the Heideggerian distinction between "taking" and "letting," Nancy claims that even postphenomenological formulations cannot account for the "coming of sense." Even they have "infinitely presupposed" the coming of sense: "one does not let oneself be taken in, carried away, or put out by sorts" (*LSW*, 34; *TSW*, 17).[13] This coming of sense, he claims in a later passage on Derrida's notion of différance , cannot be substantialized, but rather is an action that requires a "letting-coming," "letting-overcome," and "letting-go" (*LSW*, 59; *TSW*, 36). Letting, recall, signifies not just a letting pass by without attempting to seize it, but also a loosening, widening, and opening—in short, an unobstructed passageway (*laxus*). For Nancy, this might be more akin to laissez-passer, than laissez faire. What is called for here is not a radically political passivity, but an ontological passivity. It is precisely this *Ereignis*-like construction of the ontological passageway that Nancy will later use to formulate the relationship between politics and existence in his model of weak politics.

In an important footnote, Nancy agues that his reading is different from both Heidegger's "pathos-laden mode" of the truth and Badiou's "cooler mode" (*LSW*, 33–34; *TSW*, fn. 19). Truth "occurs only on the level of punctuation, not on the level of enchainment." There are three possible readings here. First, truth is presented in "the form of constitutive self-evidence," but in this reading "sense is always appropriated by truth in advance." Second, one could turn to the model of the "inaugural *decision*," but this represents an "empty truth." Nancy elects to follow a third way, via Jean-Luc Marion, and calls for a "*coming* of sense and to sense," which is "without origin," "end," or "subject." This modality is akin to the overwhelming surprise that occurs in the eventness of the event, which he reads as the experience of liberation (see *The Experience of Freedom*).[14] All three readings were present in Heidegger, but for Nancy only the third way is capable of being open to the "towards" of the "dis-position (spacing, touching, contact, crossing)."

Nancy also moves his philosophy further in the direction of a plural notion of existentialism. For Nancy, "finitude is the truth of which the infinite is the sense" (*LSW*, 51; *TSW*, 29). Finitude is not "privation," but being-in-common. "Being-deprived," he contends, "has no consistency except insofar as it is reappropriated—deprivatized—in an infinite being" (*LSW*, 53; *TSW*, 30). "*Privation annuls itself*," whereas "*finitude affirms itself*." Existence "traverses the essence and transports it beyond itself," its "'proper' essence." In the ex- of existence, existence is always "before" and "in front of itself," a stretching toward or *extensiveness* (ex-*tenere*), such that it is moving toward "that which it *essentially* is not." To exist is to be "exposed to and by the *ex*." Heidegger's being-toward-death, he now claims, can be conceived as "being-*toward*-the-world," "being-toward in its plural singularity" (*LSW*, 56; *TSW*, 33). The sense of being, of sensing and knowing itself, in this notion of existence, he claims, is in a manner entirely different from the tradition of "sensitive or cognitive appropriation" (*LSW*, 58; *TSW*, 35).

In two subsections of this book ("Politics I" and "Politics II"), Nancy provides a detailed account his deconstruction of political philosophy in a manner that he later readdresses in *The Creation of the World or Globalization*, which should be read as part two of this work. In "Politics I," he claims that identity politics are ill-equipped to deal with the contemporary crisis of sense (*LSW*, 141; *TSW*, 90). We must, he repeats, find a way to address the opening of sense, of the in-common, without attempting to transform it into a figure that represents our togetherness. This solution, he contends, is a byproduct of "ecotechnics," which, in a section on Marx and labor, he defines as "the global structuration of the world as the rearticulated space of an essentially capitalist, globalist, and monopolist organization that is monopolizing the world" (*LSW*,

159–60; *TSW*, 101).[15] What is at stake in ecotechnics is the crisis of democracy, however, today all of our solutions are drawn from political theology. Either one turns to a negative political theology and appeals to the "unnamable, ungroundable instances of justice and law" (*LSW*, 144; *TSW*, 91) or to the secularized version, which appeals to a configuration. But, what matters is "becoming-worldly," not "becoming-secular," which is still a theological notion. Of course, this is a topic of primary importance for deconstructing Christianity (2008, 2013). Becoming-worldly exposes the problem of bare or naked coexistence, which for him is the ontological problem of being-with. This, once again, is quite a similar formulation to those writing about the relationship between the biopolitical governance of life and economic theology.

In "Politics II," he returns to the closure of the political and the problem of thinking about relations in an open manner. Nancy distinguishes between the politics of the subject and the politics of the citizen. Both, he claims, belong to the "scheme of self-sufficiency" (*LSW*, 172; *TSW*, 110). Regardless of whether the reference is to the cosmopolitan metropolis or to the mythological nation, the citizens or the people always demand an appropriation of sense. In their place, Nancy advocates for a "politics of nonselfsufficiency," which he calls the politics of the "(k)not" or "tie" (*lien*). He calls for, to borrow from Armstrong, a networked sense of politics.[16] This tie is "neither interiority nor exteriority." It is not a thing, as in the res publica, but the "placing-into-relation." A "heterogenous" and "disjunctive conjunction" that turns inside-out and outside-in (*LSW*, 174; *TSW*, 111). While playing with the motif of the weaver, a common theme among Heideggerians, Nancy is clear that what he is speaking about is neither a social *contract* (draw or pull together) nor a *dénouement* (literally an outcome, but etymologically an unbinding or untying). There is no single tie or totality of ties, merely an interlacing of ties, which is never complete or closed. In such a "politics of knots," or of networks, "compearing precedes all 'appearing'" (*LSW*, 176; *TSW*, 113). This is a new form of politics, which comes with two demands. First, drawing from Balibar, he calls for an "intransigent politics of 'equaliberty,'" meaning that equality and liberty are mutually dependent. Second, he calls for a heavily deconstructed and antipatriarchal notion of "fraternity."[17] Both point to an open model of politics that is communal, nonheirarchical, liberating, equitable, and in line with his thinking about existence and critique of symbolic appropriation.

"The Compearance" represents the political companion piece to *The Sense of the World.* In this essay, Nancy heavily deconstructs the communist exigency in order to arrive an existentialist notion of communism. He says as much in the subtitle of the essay, "from the existence of 'communism' to the community of 'existence'"(*LC*, 1991; *TC*, 1992). Nancy uses the impending collapse of existing communism, which the essay was written just prior to, to deconstruct the problem of community in Marx, the classical tradition of communism, and Marx as a proper name. Much of what he says in this essay is repeated elsewhere in his work, so I will keep my analysis brief here.

In an atypical gesture, Nancy makes a categorical distinction between "four successive stages" of thinking about community: "(1) community as an object of the general problematic of order and disorder, aiming toward a political *eupraxis* (this would be more or less Antiquity and the Middle-Ages); (2) community as the site the problematic of 'unsociable sociability' (according to Kant), and aiming towards a regulation, from Hobbes to Kant . . . ; (3) community as the subject of a history (and) of itself; (4) community as task and ontological responsibility of *being*-in-common" (*LC*, fn. 15; *TC*, Fn. 15).

During our current stage, the stakes have been raised for completely rethinking community beyond the model of collective (re)appropriation. Rather than seeking to appropriate sense, the question today becomes "how does community appropriate the sense that it is" (*LC*, 76; *TC*, 383). Sense should no longer be *of* existence, but is existence. He again employs *signifiance* to highlight this "quality of existence" that is inappropriable. The "stripping bare" of sense "exposes" us to our "common condition," which is the division/sharing of sense or our "common division/sharing." *Communism*, he claims, "is the archaic name for a thought that is entirely yet to come" (*LC*, 62; *TC*, 377). Communism concerns the problem of being-in-common, which is more an "ontological preposition," than it is a "political option" (*LC*, 65; *TC*, 378).

Drawing from his earlier writings with Lacoue-Laberthe, Nancy argues that the end of the political—that is, the political of capitalist political economy—has to be reconceived. For Nancy, the new political program, if one could call it that, is "the to-come of the ontology of being-in-common" (*LC*, *87*; *TC*, 388). For Marx and most communists, the end of the political is conceived as the "withering away of the state." In this model, the political has to be *realized* as politics, which could only happen if the polis were to become "coextensive with all of real life and community" (*LC*, 89; *TC*, 388). There are two ways that the realization of the political can be interpreted. Either the polis represents the "sum" "of all activities," which is, again, the *partes extra partes* model of gathering together, or it represents the "distinct" and "separated" (*séparé*), where the se-parated are pulled apart and placed "in-common," that is, they compear together. Nancy of course, advocates for the latter interpretation. He argues that today politics must be understood as an emptying, rather than a fulfilling, of the in-common.

There is a parallel logic operating here between Agamben, Esposito, and Nancy, specifically around the distinction between emptying out and fulfillment. In *State of Exception*, Agamben refers to the "kenomatic state" and the "pleromatic state." In *Communitas*, Esposito places great emphasis on the emptiness—a term whose English etymology signifies not-having—of *communitas*. All are critical of models of politics that are predicated on (re)appropriation and fulfillment. For Nancy, this is a fundamental problem faced by those who aim to rethink the in-common. The "propriety" of the in-common, he claims, is "in-appropriable," yet the demand that it must be appropriated stands. This posits a serious dilemma, which all of Nancy's political philosophy circles around without providing a full solution: the relationship between community and the proper. The tradition of political philosophy incessantly turns to appropriation as the activity that produces community. Community is the fulfillment of the proper. For Nancy, Heidegger's *Ereignis* provides an alternative route. Heidegger's notion of "disappropriating propriation" (*propriation désappropriante*), he claims, serves as the starting point, not the final template, toward "rethink[ing] the 'proper'" (*LC/TC*, fn. 26).

Rethinking the proper, that is, rethinking politics beyond all models of the "self-appropriating Common Subject," requires an entirely new notion of politics, which at this stage in his thinking means that we must rethink the *interesse* in interest-based politics. This is necessary if we are to adhere to the "stakes" of existence. *Interresse* is "the interest (that which matters) of the *interesse* (at once: "to be inter," "to be separated," "to differ," "among" "to participate")" (*LC*, 94; *TC*, 390). Inter-being is thus an "interval" or the "between" ("*entre*"). In a postphenomenological manner, he claims that with compearance, there is nothing more than "a flash, which does not make a 'figure'" (*LC*, 97; *TC*, 391). There is nothing to symbolically appropriate, contain, and thus lay down as the basis of community.

* * *

In English we treat "between" and "inter-" as synonymous, but their lineages are quite distinct. "Between" comes from the Old English term *betweonum*, which is formed from "bi-" ("by") and *tweonum* (the dative plural of *tweon* or "two each"). This is rooted in the Gothic term *tweih-nai* ("two each"). *Between* signals a relationship by two, that is close and proximate without being closed and exclusive. Inter-, however, furnishes an entirely different sense. No conventional or etymological dictionary can provide a definitive source for inter-. Many list it as synonymous with "among," "between," or "enter-." A few argue that inter- represents a combination of *in* and *ter*. This gives rise to two common interpretations. First, it could derive from in-ground, as in *in-terra*. In this sense, *inter-* acts as a prefix that "buries" or "places under the earth." This sense is evident in the *interrare* in modern Italian. *Terra*, in Latin, literally translates as "dry land," which is rooted in the ancient Greek term *teresesthai* ("to become or be dry"). Thus, in-ter- grounds or is foundational. Second, it could also derive from "interior," such as "in-through" or "in-to." This reading further substantiates the hypostatic rendition of inter- as a foundational and internal connection. Both senses are present in the phenomenological notion of "intersubjectivity." In the first sense, it acts as the basis upon which subjects engage with one another. In the second sense, it acts as the connective web through which subjects relate with one another. When combined, "intersubjectivity" becomes the very *subjectum* of relations between intersubjective subjects. It is the very material upon and through which subjects are mediated. This logic is also evident in the ways that social phenomenologists have sought to think about a "collective we."

The problem with this formulation, as Nancy constantly reminds us, is that it oscillates between projecting the subject into the collective or into the individual. Etymologically, however, it is plausible to conceive of a third sense of the "inter-" that sidesteps the problems presented by the first two readings. This reading is not substantiated in the dictionaries, but it can be found by examining how the "inter-" has been applied in modern theory. It could signify "*in-three." For example, in Latin *tres* is "three." When *tres* is turned into an ordinal number it becomes *tertius*. *Ter* is the stem of *tres* after the letters have been transposed (i.e., metathesis). *Tertius* is also made by adding the suffix *ius*, which requires a *t* when the stem ends in *r*, as in *ter* + *(t)ius*; if separated it could be read as *in-ter*. *Ter* is "thrice." Thus, "inter-" could translate as "in-three." I should add, the same can be said about the French *entre*, *en-tres* (*in* + Latin word for three *tres*). In French, the "s" may have been dropped due to this language's complicated rules for phonological transformation. Etymology aside, what matters is how "inter-," qua "*in-three," has been used. In the nineteenth and twentieth centuries, for instance, Western social and political theorists began to treat the "inter-" as if it operated as the space of the third. How this third is conceptualized is of utmost importance for contemporary political theory (see Esposito, *TP*, 2012).

## IV. The Existential Community, Take Two

"Of Being Singular Plural" represents Nancy's ultimate statement on community (*ESP*, 1996; *BSP*, 2000). It combines the politics he espoused in his essay on compearance and the postphenomenological method he developed in *Sense of the World*. The text itself consists of thirteen mini-essays. He covers a wide range of topics, but in the following I only focus on a few passages where Nancy deconstructs the dialectic of alienation and appropriation. I use Heidegger's theory of the *Ereignis* as a template for examining how Nancy arrives at a deconstructed notion of community. I begin with Nancy's deconstruction of the problem of *togetherness* as articulated in traditional political philosophy. Then I turn to his co-existential analytic, which I read as an updated version of Heidegger's notion of *belonging*-together. For Nancy belonging cannot determine togetherness; rather togetherness needs to be held back from intruding upon belonging—weak politics must figure out how to prevent politics from intruding into the space of the common. This is not to say that Nancy's worldly ontology of singular plurality concerns the onto-theological problem of ontological difference between being and Being. In Nancy's philosophy, Difference is translated into an ontological division and sharing that occurs between us, in the world and in common.

### i. The Horizons Behind Us

Nancy immediately situates the problem of relationships in the ecstatic disruption of the horizon of the whole: "It is the opening or distancing of the horizon itself, and in the opening: *us*. We happen as the opening itself, the dangerous fault line of the rupture" (*ESP*, 11; *BSP*, xii). The stakes for rethinking relations, he argues, have never been higher. The early 1990s were marked by the conflict, often violent, of identities. For Nancy, these conflicts highlight the fact that humanity has yet to arrive at a shared world. Picking up his work on signification in *Sense of the World*, he situates his deconstruction of the proper within the problem of the meaning (or sense). Thinking about the "with," he argues, must address the "closure of meaning": "What does the above-named proliferation require of us, this proliferation that seems to have no other meaning than the indeterminate multiplication of centripetal meanings, meanings closed in on themselves and supersaturated with significance—that is, meanings that are no longer meaningful because they have come to refer only to their own closure, to their horizon of appropriation, and have begun to spread nothing but destruction, hatred, and the denial of existence" (*ESP*, 12; *BSP*, xii)?

Reiterating a point he has continued to make since his early formulations with Lacoue-Labarthe, Nancy argues that the central starting point for political philosophy and Western philosophy in general is the ancient Greek city. Philosophy, he asserts, "begins with and in the 'civil' [*concitoyenne*] coexistence insofar as such," which means that "the 'city' is not primarily a form of political institution; it is first of all being-with *as such*" (*ESP*, 51; *BSP*, 31). Earlier in the text he points out that the city "bring[s] to light of being-in-common *as dis-position* (dispersal and disparity)" (*ESP*, 42; *BSP*, 23). Traditional political philosophy mishandles this formulation by conceiving of the origin as the "one-origin." As such, the "dis-position of origins" is transformed into a "politics of exclusivity" and the "demand for equality" becomes confused with a notion of "'generic identity'" (cited in *ESP*, 43–44; *BSP*, 23). If we are to reread the meaning of the city in Western philosophy and politics, he contends, we must focus on the quintessential ontological problem: the "bare exposition of singular origins."

Heidegger, he claims, represents a necessary starting point: "it is necessary to reconfigure fundamental ontology (as well as the existential analytic, the history of Being, and the thinking of *Ereignis* that goes along with it) with a thorough resolve that *starts from the plural singular of origins*, from *being-with*" (*ESP*, 45; *BSP*, 26). Rethinking fundamental ontology in a plural fashion is simultaneously a political and philosophical task. The political must be weakened to allow for an ontology of existence. In this work, his primary target is the gathering-together logic that is employed in the political model of symbolic representation. Since compearance "is not of the order of appearance, of manifestation, phenomena, revealing, or some other concept of becoming-visible," we have to deconstruct the tradition that leads us to conceive of our relations as a thing or things that appear (*ESP*, 90; *BSP*, 67). We must learn how to "dis-identify ourselves *from* every sort of 'we' that would be the subject of its own representation" (*ESP*, 94; *BSP*, 71). Instead of trying to recalibrate the metaphysical principle of identity, which reduces difference to sameness, in an onto-theological register, Nancy returns to the heritage of the Western tradition and the paradigm of the Athenian theater. With the contemporary withdrawal of the political, it no longer makes sense, he claims, to continue to apply the principle of identity and make a spectacle of our relations. This paradigm contains three references: "to philosophy as the shared exercise of the *logos*, to politics as the opening of the city, and to the theatre as the place of the symbolic-imaginary appropriation of collective existence" (*ESP*, 94; *BSP*, 71). The theater appears simultaneously as "the political (civil) presentation of the philosophical (the self knowledge of the logical animal)" and "the philosophical presentation of the political." In short, it appears as the presentation of our *togetherness*.

The problem with this metaphor is that in fusing the *logos* to the *mimesis*, the *mimesis* is effaced by the *logos*. We mistakenly presume that the *logos*, which he employs in a general sense, can be presented, even present itself, as if it belongs to the "logic of presence" (*ESP*, 95; *BSP*, 72). Compearance, he argues, challenges this logic. It is not-a-thing, thus it is not presentable. When compearance is treated as something that can appear, it is reduced to the distinction between authentic and inauthentic appearance, that is, the "'good' *mimesis*" or "'good' (re) presentation" and the "'bad' *mimesis*" or "'bad' (re)presentation." In our current political imagery, authentic (re)presentation is presented as a "lost thing," which is juxtaposed to the inauthentic "popular and generalized" presentation (*ESP*, 96; *BSP*, 73). In reality, both are inherently unrepresentable. The former is perpetually in "retreat" while the other is "vulgar."

> The retreat of the political and the religious, or of the theologico-political, has no other sense than the retreat of every space, form, or screen onto which a figure of community can be projected. At the right time, the question has to be posed as to whether being-together can do without a figure and, as a result, without an identification, if the whole of its "substance" consists only in its spacing. But this question cannot be articulated in a completely appropriate way until the full extent of the withdrawal of its figure and identity has been grasped (*ESP*, 67: *BSP*, 47).

Nancy is being modest here because now is the time to raise this question. From Benedict Anderson's *Imaginary Communities*, to contemporary critiques of imperialism, empire, or neocolonialism, to the no-borders movement—to name just a few instances—the symbolic representation of "national," "ethnic," or "cultural" communities has been increasingly questioned. In fact, in the recent wave of critical texts on community outside of the debate between Agamben, Nancy, and Esposito, this question has been at the center of the discussion.[18] Nancy provides an interesting perspective on this discourse. According to Nancy, it is precisely in this withdrawal of the figure of community that acts as the symbolic representation of its internal relations that the critique must begin. He calls this withdrawal the "conditions of critique."

The retreat of the symbolic representation of the whole, of being-together, forces us to reconsider the problem of intelligibility, of the traditional dichotomy between appearance and reality or authenticity and inauthenticity. Traditional critical theory has a specific way of addressing this problematic: "society exposed to itself" (*ESP*, 73; *BSP*, 52). Nancy cites the work of the Situationists as one of the last great attempts to salvage this dichotomy. "The society of the spectacle," he claims, "is that society which achieves alienation by an imaginary appropriation of real appropriation" (*ESP*, 70; *BSP*, 48). So-called real appropriation could "consist only in a free, self-creating imagination that is indissociably individual and collective," while imaginary appropriation represents a commodified and inauthentic "replacement for authentic imagination." It is no wonder, he notes, that they were so popular among the artists and, I might add, still are today. A situation is an event where the creators appropriate their relationships and circumstances while making them proper to themselves. It is a moment, even if fleeting, of authenticity—*authentes* (acting on one's own authority and thus autonomously). This reading of the proper resonates with Agamben's interpretation of the *se, which he reaffirms in his more positive appeal to the Situationists in *The Coming Community.*

The Situationists are significant for Nancy, in that their approach represents a "symptom" of the retreat of the political. He commends them for distinguishing between "symbolic appropriation" and "productive appropriation," which most Marxists confuse. With Marx there is an assumption that the productive appropriation will "self-surpass itself" and become symbolic appropriation, as if this self-surpassing, or overcoming, occurs when there is an "appropriation of being-in-common understood as symbolic Being" (symbol meaning—"an ontological instance of the 'in-common,'" that is, "bond of recognition") (*ESP*, 71; *BSP*, 50). For the Situationists, the only self-surpassing that occurs is the "symbolization of production itself." Coexistence only takes "the form of the technical or economic co-ordination of the various commodity networks." The human sciences have fallen prey to this representation of society. Their formulations are less a "self-symbolization" of society and more like a "representation" of society "in the guise of symbolism" (*ESP*, 71; *BSP*, 51). Nancy claims this sociopsychological gesture is still rampant in the human sciences. One can hardly think of anyone other than Émile Durkheim when reading these lines.

The problem with this line of thinking, claims Nancy, is that to criticize "mere appearance" one has to simultaneously designate "the proper" as "nonappearance" (*ESP*, 72; *BSP*, 51). One must appeal to an "inappropriable secret of an originary property hidden beneath appearances" (*ESP*, 72; *BSP*, 52). The jargon of authenticity, in other words, remains the "most trenchant and 'metaphysical' tradition in philosophy" (*ESP*, 52; *BSP*, 73). Most modern critiques of "social alienation" remain straddled between such dichotomies as the authentic and inauthentic, proper and improper, or simply appearance and reality (*ESP*, 74; *BSP*, 53). Each of these dichotomies presumes that outside the order of appearance there rests another order or reality, which is always the "order of the Other" (*ESP*, 73; *BSP*, 52). The solution this formulation presents is to have the *Ego*—"whether generic, communitarian, or individual"—appropriate the improper order and convert it into a proper order. Nancy suggests that the time has come to replace this tired "ontology of the Other and the Same" with an entirely different ontology that begins with "being-with-one-another." Following Heidegger's critique of the metaphysical principle of identity, Nancy advises that time has come to depart from the tired distinction between authentic reality and inauthentic representation, that is, the philosophy of the intelligible. The world of sensibility, he reiterates, is the only way that being-in-common is intelligible (*ESP*, 76; *BSP*, 55).

Following his patterned return to the retreat of the political and the sense of the world, he asks, what can we appropriate when there is nothing left to represent our symbolic unity? The withdrawal provides a new opportunity to rethink our being-together without presuppositions. He claims that our current period of transition could even be characterized as yet another "'Copernican revolution,'" in the sense that "'social Being'" is now "revolving" solely "around itself or turning in on itself" (*ESP*, 78–79; *BSP*, 57). We are, to draw from his later lexicon, becoming a properly *mondialised world*. References to a transcendental figure, whether anthropomorphic visions of a first mover, the Levianthan, or the proletariat, are waning. Social reality today, he argues, is being "stripped bare." So rather than sound another alarm of monumental proportions, such as Habermas's legitimation crisis, or call for a new decisive figure to take over and occupy the place of the empty symbol, he treats this predicament as an opportunity to rethink, to borrow a phrase from Esposito, the "terms of the political." The entire terrain, possibly the *inter-* itself, from top to bottom and side to side, needs to be rethought.

In a deconstructive gesture, Nancy urges us to re-examine the meaning of symbol. The "truth" of the symbol, he points out, "is in making a *symbol*, that is, in making a connection or a joining, and in giving a figure to this liaison by making an image" (*ESP*, 79; *BSP*, 58). In a footnote he reminds us that for the Greeks, the *sumbolon* was merely a piece of pottery that friends or a host and guest would break when they "departed" (from *de-partire*). Later, when they met again, the pieces would be brought back together. Etymologically, he notes, symbol means "'put with.'" This is not a representation of reality, but "the real is in the representation" (*ESP*, 79; *BSP*, 58). It also has nothing to do with authentic and inauthentic representations. Rather, it signals a "joining" and "distancing" right between the put-with.[19] "Therefore the 'symbolic' is not simply an aspect of being-social: on the one hand, it is this Being itself; on the other hand, the symbolic does not take place without (re) presentation, the (re)presentation of one another according to which they are with one another [*les-uns-avec-les-autres*]" (*ESP*, 80; *BSP*, 58). With this stripped down and exposed sense of the symbolic, the modernist paradigm of "society facing itself" in a grand symbolic reflection starts to unravel. Compearance is starting to emerge as the watered-down, or simple, symbol of relations. It also signals something different than the traditional understanding of togetherness (*ensemble*). The term Nancy is working with is *ensemble*. It has two senses: either being similar—in the same time and in-simultaneous—or gathering together. I shall deal with the latter first and then turn to the former.

Nancy is critical of the gathering sense of togetherness, which, he argues following Heidegger, is the predominant sense found in metaphysical thought. In metaphysics, "ensemble" is usually treated as a process that is "extrinsic" to the subjects, as either "a qualification extrinsic to subjects" or an addition of a "particular quality" (*ESP*, 80; *BSP*, 59). This reading gives rise to the "impasse of a metaphysics—and of its politics." Either "social compearance is only ever thought of as a transitory epiphenomenon," or society is used as a "step in a process" that will lead to a larger "hypostatic unity of togetherness" (the common or individual). Two examples could be Sartre's fleeting group-in-fusion and the crude Marxist schematic of society-socialism-communism. Either way, "being-social" is "instrumentalized." It has to relate to something other than itself because "the essence of the 'social' is not itself 'social'" (*ESP*, 81; *BSP*, 59). In this extrinsic formulation, the social itself is closed off and replaced by a "simple, extrinsic, and transitory 'association'" or a "transocial presumption, the unitary entelechy of common Being."

Put in much less taxing vernacular, this dichotomy was present in the classical sociological theories of community. Classical sociologists believed relationships in modern society were extrinsic to individuals. In a society or *Gesellschaft*, individuals were merely gathered together through external associative processes. As such, societal relations were primarily alienating, both in Marx's economic sense and in a more social sense. On the other hand, in a community or *Gemeinschaft*, relationships were more authentic because each belonged. Each was internal to the common and the common formed the essence and the foundation of their relations. Two classical examples are Ferdinand Tönnies and Max Weber.

Tönnies helped to establish this dichotomy in classical sociological thought. Besides his study of this distinction in or *Community and Society* (1957), he wrote an influential essay on the notion of the "individual" where he compares modern *Gesellschaften* to the social contract model (1971). The social contract represents a union of separate and independent parties, whose interactions form the basis of the broader social unity. It not only serves as the ideological justification for privatized social relationships, it is also based on a contradiction. Unity is not constituted by separate parts, but by an external *compartmentalization process*, which, in the first instance, divides, separates, and shares out its parts, while in the second instance, it brings them back together as divided parts. This would represent what Nancy calls the type of gathering that brings together "isolated and unrelated parts" in a simple "juxtaposition": "*partes extra partes*" (*ESP*, 81; *BSP*, 60). As such, no one is an individual, in the proper sense of the term (indivisible), but just a divided share of the broader *Gesellschaft*. The so-called liberal "individual," Tönnies argues, is in reality a mere configuration of various divisions. This process is evident in the construction of the word *Gesellschaft*, which derives from *Gesellen* (journeymen, companions, partners) and the verb *sich gesellen* ("to join oneself"). The *Gemeinschaft*, however, represents what Nancy calls the "*totum intra totum*" model of unification, "where the relation surpasses itself in being pure" (*ESP*, 81; *BSP*, 60).

Max Weber also employed this distinction between external associative relations and internal communal relations. In his introductory essay on methodology in *Economy and Society*, for example, Weber draws from Tönnies's critique of the compartmentalizing effects of *Gesellschaft* to distinguish between "associative relationships" (*vergesellschaftung*) and "communal relationships" (*vergemeinschaftung*) (1978, 40–41).[20] Like Tönnies, Weber argues that in associative relations, people are mechanistically joined together. Across most of his writings on politics, bureaucracy, even science, Weber draws from this distinction to criticize modern relations while searching for a model that is more communal. His charismatic leader represents the antidote to modern associative relations (2004). And in *The Division of Labor in Society*, Durkheim sought to reverse this reading by arguing that modern solidarity was more internal and "organic" compared to classical forms of solidarity that were more external and "mechanistic" (1984).

For Nancy, the incommensurable provides an alternative path that avoids the pitfalls of the *intra* and *extra* formulations of togetherness. He claims there is a "point of equilibrium between" them.[21] Each supposes that there is a "pure outside" and "pure inside," which he points out like Heidegger, would render it impossible to conceive of relationships let alone togetherness. Rather than repeat the "collectivist" model of togetherness, togetherness must be reformulated as "being-together." In an ontological register, together can only be an "adverb" of Being, which "modalizes the verb": "Being is together, and it is not a togetherness" (*ESP*, 82; *BSP*, 60). This rendition of being-together is not possible within capitalism because it strips being-with bare. Everything is commercialized and reduced to the common measures of the marketplace. Even contemporary "human rights" discourse is commercialized. Not unlike Heidegger in his critique of *das* Man, Nancy criticizes the reduction of everything to a "common and average measure" (*ESP*, 106; *BSP*, 82).

The metaphysical tradition, Nancy claims, has but two means to overcome the "domination of mediocrity," "two difference measures of the incommensurable": the Other and the "with" (*ESP*, 105; *BSP*, 79). Since his early debate with Blanchot, Nancy has argued that the Other cannot be used to conceive of relationships. In this text, he states that whenever the "with" is calibrated according to the Other, Being is covered over. This formulation leads straight back into the community-versus-society impasse: "community (subsumption under the Subject, pure Being without relations)" and "association (accommodation of subjects, relation without essentiality)"—are calibrated according to the Other (*ESP*, 100; *BSP*, 77). Even if applied on a smaller scale, between the self and alter ego, the solution turns on the Hegelian model of "radical alienation." This dialectic of the same and/in/of the other, "reveals the power of the negative which holds the self to the other, the dis-alienating and reappropriative power of alienation itself as the alienation of the same" (*ESP*, 101; *BSP*, 78). Whether intrasubjective or intersubjective, each of these formulations passes over the "with."

In place of the gathering sense of togetherness, Nancy turns to the simultaneous sense of "together." "Together" (*ensemble*) means to be "at the same time (and in the same place)." Subjects *share* this space-time, not extrinsically, but not really intrinsically either. In being-together, subjects share in it and are shared/divided out: "they must share it between themselves and be shared out amongst themselves," which is the real sense given by symbolization (*ESP*, 82; *BSP*, 60).[22] They are to a great extent *shared.* This is, fundamentally and absolutely, the modalization of Being. Being always compears as being-with. The "with" can no longer be conceived as a predicate of Being or anything else that can be made into a presentation and subsequently appropriated. It is sheer modality. And it is only "between-us": "'With' stays between us, and we stay between us: just us, but only in the interval between us" (*ESP*, 84; *BSP*, 62).

Those who continue to advocate for "appropriation in general," or call for "the subject of the general reappropriation," he points out, will probably not be satisfied with his deconstruction of the tradition (*ESP*, 85–86; *BSP*, 63–64). Marx, claims Nancy, had an ambivalent intuition about capitalism. Capital signified the "general alienation of the proper" and "it exposes the stripping bare of the *with* as a mark of Being, or as a mark of meaning" (*ESP*, 86; *BSP*, 64). Both Marx and Heidegger expressed this ambivalence when thinking about technology. Nancy's model is more post-Marxist. We must stop trying to appropriate the "with" and instead turn our attention to the exigency of being-with that is exposed by capital. "[W]hat is at stake is not a reappropriation of the *with* (of the essence of a common Being), but a *with* of reappropriation (where the proper does not return, or returns only *with*)" (*ESP*, 86–87 *BSP*, 64–65). In other words, we need to stop conceiving of our relationships as a symbolic unity of togetherness that can be appropriated. The sym-bol is nothing other that our relations. The proper, if we can still use this language, is neither inside nor outside, but is presenced between in the "with," the *cum-*.

### ii. Coexistential Analytic

Nancy's ontology cannot be conceived of as an "ontology of society," which in Heideggerian language would be a "regional ontology," but an "ontology itself as 'sociality' or 'sociation'" (*ESP*, 58; *BSP*, 38). Following Heidegger, he claims that we have to rethink the relationship to the other in a nonsynthetic manner. This is found in his notion of "between us." The between, he claims, should not be conceived as a bridge or a connective link. Rather, the "'between' is the stretching out and distance opened by the singular insofar as such, as its spacing of meaning" (*ESP*, 23; *BSP*, 5). It is an open spacing that separates singularities from each other. People, he argues, are absorbed neither into an undifferentiated mass, such as Heidegger's *das Man*, nor into an intersubjective web, as in phenomenology.

When discussing others, or the Other, Nancy is clear that his theory does not appeal to the dialectic of alienation and appropriation and the formulation of *alien-proper*, but of the *alter* or "one of the two" (*ESP*, 29–30; *BSP*, 11). Recalling Balibar's critique of the celebration of alienation found in theories antagonistic to appropriation, Nancy proposes an alternative path that traverses the dialectic of alienation and appropriation. Our plural origins, Nancy argues, cannot be subjected to the logic of alienation and appropriation, either in the "dialectical mode where the subject must retain in itself its own negation" or in the "mystical mode" "where the subject must rejoice in its alienation" (*ESP*, 31; *BSP*, 12). In both modalities, alienation is overcome through the action of "reappropriation." These modes, he continues, are found in transcendental theories of the "exalted and overexalted mode of propriety of what is proper." Nancy claims the original relationship of being-with, exposed in compearance, is neither negative nor positive, but of an entirely different register: "originally divided/shared" (*ESP*, 31; *BSP*, 13).[23] The origin is accessed in a step before or between "loss and appropriation" in the modality of *touching*. This occurs in the very "coming to presence" of coexistence. Or in the *ex-* of exposure that occurs between us.

Nancy also distinctively characterizes the plural existential event in a Heideggerian tone. "The world springs forth [*surgit*] everywhere and in each instance, simultaneously," he contends; it "springs forth *out of nothing* and 'is created'" (*ESP*, 107; *BSP*, 83). Each "being belongs to the (authentic) origin, each is originary (the springing forth of the springing forth itself), and each is original (incomparable, underivable)" (ibid.). At this point, there is little difference between this characterization and the eventness of the event in the principle/leap of identity, but Nancy adds an important caveat: "all of them share the same originarity and the same originality; this sharing [or division] *is itself* the origin."

The sharing that occurs in this event does not follow the tautology of participation and sharing found in the dialectic of alienation and appropriation: participating *in* the taking and taking part *of* the participative activity. Nothing is appropriated. There is no pure outside and no pure inside. "What is shared is nothing like a unique substance in which each being would participate," he contends; rather, "what is shared is also what shares" (*ESP*, 107; *BSP*, 83). He claims this is a "materialist" "ontology of being-with." The "matter" is itself "what is divided/shared of itself." It is the sharing/division of bodies exposed to each other as simultaneously singular and plural. The "with" is nothing but shared/divided incorporeality; the modality of the "with" is nothing other than touching (neither taking-giving, nor holding-letting go), just touching (*ESP*, 116; *BSP*, 92).

Fittingly, this essay ends on a section called "Coexistential Analytic." Nancy argues that the existential analytic is both unavoidable and incomplete (*ESP*, 117; *BSP*, 93). He had intended to rethink Heidegger's subordination of *Mitsein* to *Dasein*, the Other, and synthetic thought. "Being," he contends, "is directly and immediately mediated *by itself*" (*ESP*, 118; *BSP*, 94). Not in the sense of a "dialectic" or "instrument," that is, operative thinking, but "negativity without use" / "the nothing of the with." There is no third party that synthesizes or mediates. "The 'with' is the permutation without an Other," whereas "an Other is always the Mediator; its prototype is Christ" (*ESP*, 118; *BSP*, 94). Nancy calls for a "mediation without a mediator," which he claims is the "mi-lieu, the place of sharing/division and crossing through [*passage*]; that is to say, *place* [*lieu*] *tout court and absolutely*" (*ESP*, 119; *BSP*, 95). In this milieu, "crossing," "intersection," "dispersal," and "radiating," we arrive at the "deconstruction of Christianity." "In its coming," he contends, "the existent appropriates itself." Referencing Heidegger's *Ereignis*—which he translates as the "appropriating event"—Nancy defines this self-appropriation as "transport and trans-propriation" in the "dispersal of the there" (*ESP*, 119; *BSP*, 95). No "proper self" arises in this event, rather the "coming is in itself and by itself, as such, appropriative." The only "propriety" is the process of "differencing" itself.

If one were to locate a proper in Nancy, one can only say that for him the proper occurs in the "ex-" of coexistence. Although ipseity does occur in this transitory or transpropriating event, the self does not return to itself, "'into itself,'" absolved from alienation and properly appropriated, but is turned "*beside* itself" (*auprès de soi*). For Nancy, this term signifies the "dispersal of the dis-position" (*l'écartement de la dis-position*). It is both "proximity" and "distance," such that there is no fixed point that can be grasped onto to measure ipseity. The only common measure here, if we can call it that, would be the incommensurable. This is how Nancy speaks of dis-containment.

For Nancy, the existential analytic must always be plural. The "structure of the 'Self' is the structure of the 'with'" (*ESP*, 120; *BSP*, 96). "Each is beside-itself insofar as and because [each is] beside-others." Contrary to the metaphysical tradition of gathering together, "from the very beginning, then 'we' are with one another, not as points gathered together, or as a togetherness that is divided up." Being-with is neither a sharing in a "common substance" nor a gathering that produces commonality. Being-with is simply the dispersal, a scattering of sorts. To be-with is to be bodies dispersed and disposed in *proximity* to each other. They simply touch. Nothing can be taken or held. Everything is utterly dis-contained. Consistency becomes disposition. The verb "to be" should be understood as a transitive verb. This, he claims, is the lesson of Heidegger's *da-sein*, "being-the-there," "disposing [of] Being itself as distance/proximity; it is 'to make' or 'to let' [*laisser*] be the coming of all with all *as such*" (*ESP*, 120–21; *BSP* 96–97). All this happens in the presencing of the present, such that it can only be subjected to representation after the fact.

Nancy ends this difficult essay by arguing that his ontology of being singular plural is both an *ethos* and a *praxis*. It is an ethical ontology where "the 'ethical' exposes what the 'ontological' disposes" (*ESP*, 123; *BSP*, 99). Later we shall examine Esposito's ethical ontology. Nancy does not carry this relationship as far as Esposito does. For Esposito, as I demonstrate in chapter 4, the results are a slightly more prescriptive deontological ethics, where the de-ontological stands for an intensification of ontology and the *deon* represents the sense of duty. As a staunchly deconstructive philosopher, and much to the annoyance of most of his readers, Nancy refrains from prescriptions. His model of weak politics provides, at best, openings and orientations for ethics. His politics belongs to the tradition of democracy, albeit from a radically deconstructed position. Esposito's politics belong more to the tradition, albeit radically deconstructed, of republicanism. After all, one is French and the other Italian. Or to put things in their own words, when thinking about com-munity Nancy privileges the *with-* and Esposito privileges the *munus*.

## PART 3. THE 2000S

Nancy's major works on community were written in the 1990s. In the new millennium, he turned his attention to other issues, such as the body, the deconstruction of Christianity, and aesthetics. He has, however, written several essays, contributed to multiple collected editions, and presented his work across the world. Of his many publications, two stand out for our purposes: "Urbi et Orbi" (*CWG*, 2007) and "The Truth of Democracy" (*TD*, 2010). The former consists of a deconstruction of the globalization of the world, while the second clarifies his theory of democracy. Together they provide a great summation of his political philosophy.

### V. Globalization

In "Urbi et Orbi", Nancy returns to the problem of the sense of the world. The essay consists of a lengthy deconstruction of Marx's theory of globalization while searching for a notion of *a* world that is not reducible to the logic of appearance. He begins by pointing to the two ways we understand globalization—either in a technical and economic sense, "globalization," which he likens to a process that gathers us together and represents our relations as a totality, or in the French sense of *mondialisation* [world-forming], which signifies a process that cannot be fully translated and thus hypostatized (*CWG*, 27–29). Marx also struggled with these two senses of globalization, he claims. For Marx, "globalization makes world-forming [*mondialisation*] possible" (*CWG*, 36). The question for Marx, and subsequent Marxisms, was what do with this possibility. For Nancy, the key to this problem is the meaning attributed to *value.*

Marx sought to invert the capitalist sense of value that had virtually colonized the world. Commodification created an opportunity to subvert the meaning of the "value of creation." Drawing from Arendt, Derrida, and Henry, Nancy argues that the "communist revolution" signified "the liberation of value as the real value of our common production" (*CWG*, 37). In becoming human, the domination of the many is replaced by a "self-production of human beings" in two senses: "production of human quality" and "production of each by the others, all by each and each by all." "Absolute value" in Marx's humanist eschatology, is "humanity creating itself by producing," producing itself, objects, and thus, its world. Nancy here is repeating his earlier critique of the operative model of community. Self-production is the realization and achievement of the *animal laborans* (the *entelechia* of human *dunamis*).

In this essay, Nancy claims that a problem arises in the way Marx conceived of "proper freedom." Marx treated the world as "the space of the play of freedom and of its common/singular appropriation" (*CWG*, 38). This can only appear as the "bad infinite"—an endless series without the possibility of reconciling potentiality and actuality (*CWG*, 38). Nancy insists that there is a way out of this circle. Instead of turning to the traditional appearance-versus-reality approach, where commodity fetishism is interpreted as a generalized mis-representation of the phenomenon of value and thus challenged by a collective form of symbolic re-appropriation (à la Situationists), Nancy directs us to the "thing in itself" that is purported to be represented in the phenomenon: "the character of a value 'in itself,' which precisely is not a 'thing in itself' but the actuality of a *praxis* that has 'value' by itself absolutely and in the materiality or the complex corporeality of the transformation in which it expresses itself, gives itself, and creates itself" (*CWG*, 39, fn. 11).

How, he asks, is it possible to conceive of *mondialisation* as the opening of the "good infinite," where "the finite inscription of its infinity" withdraws, and thus is incommensurable and beyond valuation itself? The modern gaze continues to treat the incommensurable as something that alienates us, which thus must be "apprehended," seized, and appropriated (*CWG*, 40). Yet the modern project, from Marx to onto-theology, also consists in a self-deconstructing process. This possibility is actually present in the way "world" is conceived in metaphysics. In metaphysics *a* world, not the world, "is a space in which a certain tonality resonates" (*CWG*, 42). In a world, we share in the "inner resonances." As such, a world does not form an objective and thus external unity that can be hypostatized and appropriated. A world is not presented, but is, he claims, following Heidegger, "presence." Second, "world" signifies a "disposition," or a "place," that we "inhabit." A world makes it possible for "something to properly take place." "To take place," he notes, "is to properly arrive and happen." The proper here, in this sense of the "world," is a "subject."

These two senses of "world" are present in the Greek terms *ēthos* and *ethos*. Both point to the "motif of a stand," which he notes, "is at the root of all ethics." We should also note that this motif is found in most French interpretations of the existential moment of ex-istence qua *standing-out.* Nancy claims that there is an analogous reference in "the Latin terms *habitare* and *habitus*," which likewise derive from *habere.* To stand, in the sense of *habere*, means to "occupy a place"—that is, to take over, *ob-capere*, a place—"and from this to possess and to have" (*CWG*, 42). Here we have all the makings of the appropriative gesture. A world qua ethos is the "proper mode," "what holds to itself and in itself," "a having with a sense of being," and so on. In this proprietarian sense of a world, the existent "resembles a subject." In "the proper mode of its stance"—stance is the translation of *tenue*, which derives from *tenir*, to hold—the sense of the world "circulates between all those who stand in it [*s'y tiennent*]" and share. In this short passage, Nancy uses existentialism to express the model of the proper subject of humanism. To take a stand, to stand out, in a world, is a propering event. Yet because this activity is steeped in the logic of appropriation and containment, the world of existence is reduced to a contained world. As such, this model of worldliness cannot account for the ab-solution that is found in the notion of the *Ereignis.*

In the metaphysical sense of "world" there is an opening that can be used to traverse the logic of representation and symbolic appropriation because the world is without "substance" or "support." Sense is merely circulated and shared. Such a definition, he contends, should confound the logic of representation, hence of symbolic appropriation. "Already with Marx, there was an exit from representation." In Marx, there was a sense of excess, in the "surplus value" of value itself. This excess cannot be subjected to a "shared appropriation" or—recalling the tautology of participating and sharing—"appropriating sharing" (*CWG*, 46). To treat the surplus as the accumulation of profit, he contends, is to return to the "bad infinite." Instead, he advocates a turn to the "actual infinite," where "a finite existence accedes, as finite, to the infinite of a meaning or of a value that is its most proper meaning and value." Capital, he argues, cannot "absorb all significance in the commodity" (*CWG*, 47). In the valuation of the world, there remains "an absolute value of value" that cannot be evaluated or accounted for by "political economy" (*CWG*, 48).

Nancy proposes that within the "productivity that disseminates sense" and the "growing order of symbolic wealth" there rests an "internal displacement" that holds open the possibility of inverting the signs:

"the insignificant equivalence reversed into an egalitarian, singular, and common significance" (*CWG*, 48–49). He does not call for a project or a party with a program, but as always in his existential fashion, for "a boundless leap outside of the calculable and controllable reality." This would be a sense of value "which does not derive from ownership (of something or of oneself) but in abandonment." He claims this is a sense of "poverty." His reference here is probably to the etymological construction of *pauper* qua *paucus-parare* or producing little, which is yet another sense in his model of weak politics and his allegiance to inoperativeness. Abandonment and poverty, as I demonstrate in the next chapter, are also terms that Agamben employs in his efforts to disrupt *Homo approprians*.[24]

For Nancy, creation must be conceived as "a form or symbolization of the world," but one where the sense of the future cannot be represented and thus appropriated (*CWG*, 53). It also calls for a deconstructed, or "*absentheistic*," notion of creation ex nihilo. This is made possible by the two processes that began with modernity: world-becoming detheologizes and "displaces value" and "world-forming displaces the production of value" (*CWG*, 51). Marx, he reiterates from his work in the 1990s, mistakenly conceived of the "reversal of the relation of production" as "a conversion of the meaning of production (and the restitution of created value to its creator)" (*CWG*, 54). Nancy advocates that we take a step back, to focus on "the value of the reversal itself." The sense of the world, he continues, is in the praxis of transformation itself. In this largely ecstatic configuration of the praxis of sense, "there is nothing," neither models, nor anything to appropriate (power or property), but the "agitation" of "the insatiable and infinitely finite exercise that is the being in the act of meaning brought forth in the world" (*CWG*, 55).

## VI. Existential Democracy

The only appropriate way to conclude this chapter is to return to his theory of democracy. I began by raising the question about the relationship between the ontic and the ontological, or between politics and existence. Politics as conceived within the ontic realm, which today is enframed by ecotechnics, is tasked with appropriating the symbolic and rendering the collective a proper whole. Of course, Nancy has provided alternative analyses, but since the 1980s the core objective of his political philosophy has been to deconstruct the dialectic of alienation and appropriation in order to find a passageway that opens unto the ontological. In the 1990s it appeared as if politics and the ecstatic event of coexistence were fused together in his notion of compearance, as if they were not equiprimordial but identical. But this "everything is political" model of the existential event would be Sartre's, not Nancy's. Recently he has clarified his position in a manner that resonates with his early writings. The political must be kept separate from the common, ontics from ontology, but only separate in the sense that politics ought to be tasked—and here is his prescription—with the role of rendering the in-common possible. *Politics ought to let us be in-common.* He is not calling for a laissez-faire politics, such as in the American version of libertarianism, but for politics to *figure out* how to loosen up and hold open the space where we can be in-common—in short, dis-containing the in-common in such a manner that the in-common is also protected from being contained again. This political prescription, as weak as it is, is clearly articulated in *The Truth of Democracy* (*TD*, 2010).

The English publication of *The Truth of Democracy* contains three papers that span nearly three decades of his writing. In a short piece he wrote in 1990 called "The Senses of Democracy," Nancy distinguishes between the political and the common (*TD*, 37–41). Politics concerns power and regulation, it is the sphere of configuration, whereas the common is the sphere of existence and sense. The democratic model of the "subject of revolt," of the ecstatic people, he claims, comes closer to recognizing this distinction than formal models of democracy, yet it too fails.[25] A decade later, he wrote "a simple note" on the phrase "everything is political" (*TD*, 45–51). This phrase, he argues, is a byproduct of modern political economy. With globalization, the market and democracy have become virtually indistinguishable. Modern democratic thought has been subsumed by the ecotechnical model of political economy, and politics today is trapped within the logic of measurement and evaluation. Even alienation can be measured and quantified. If we are to ensure that the place of the in-common is not appropriated and converted into a symbolic figure of unity, it is necessary that we find a way to hold open the space of the incommensurable. The politics of equality, which reduces everyone to a common measure, is not fit for this task.

The title essay was originally published in 2008 "to commemorate the fortieth anniversary of May 1968" (*TD*, ix). Here Nancy argues that Mai 68 provides some insight into how we can rethink the meaning of political action. During Mai 68, political action was decoupled "from the commonly accepted framework for exercising or taking power," either "through electoral means or insurrection" (*TD*, 10). These actions helped to deconstruct the traditional model of the ecstatic "subject of democracy." Instead of becoming subjects in the foundational and proprietary senses, these actions "exposed" the principle "objectives" of politics while simultaneously "opening" and exposing the subjects themselves. They were, in other words, *partagé*.

The spirit of these actions also points to a possible passage that gave rise to a new sense of politics. During the events, there was a sense of sharing in the "incalculable," which, he claims, is a type of sharing that is "most resistant to appropriation by a culture of general calculation" (*TD*, 16). It was a marked "break with all predictive calculations," including "all expectations of return." Traditional politics places valuations on things and people. But what is shared in common, which is different from the sense of commonly shared, cannot be evaluated or subjected to calculations. What lies beyond politics, which he repeats across many works, are such things as "art or love, friendship or thought, knowledge or emotion" (*TD*, 17). These should not be shared, divided, or redistributed by the formal political machinery. Instead, Mai 68 demonstrated that the only thing shared is the "share of the sharing (out) of the incalculable" (*TD*, 17). A democratic politics, then, should only "make possible the existence of this share, while its task is to maintain an opening for it, to assure the conditions of access to it, [yet it cannot] take responsibility for its content" (*TD*, 17).

Thus, contrary to the highly formalized models of redistributive justice, and in a manner strikingly similar to Arendt's critique of the social, Nancy claims that this is not the task of politics. Politics is about control, power, unification, but the common "has to do with not letting itself be hypostatized in any figure or signification" (*TD*, 21). Politics, he now clarifies, has to be "*distinguished*" from the common, first by remaining distinct, and second by ensuring that the distinction remains. Only in the modern, warped sense of democracy are distinctions "levelled out" or "mediocratized" in a "general equivalence" (*TD*, 23). How can we, to put things squarely within Heidegger's *Ereignis-Denken*, conceive of the common, or belonging in Heidegger's lexicon, without it being predetermined by a synthetic action that gathers the parts together? Politics, for Nancy, must be conceptualized in relation to the spring/leap that traverses the metaphysical principle of identity. Togetherness, Heidegger argued in a quote I cited in the last chapter, leads to a notion of belonging where each is "assigned and placed into the order of a 'together,' established in the unity of a manifold, framed together in the unity of a system, mediated by the unifying center of an authoritative synthesis" (*SI*, 90; *ID*, 28). Togetherness is an external action that gathers each together and makes them the same. If politics are to affirm anything for Nancy, the only affirmation should be, despite the contradiction here, the "incommensurable value," which is a different way of saying *singularity*, yet singularity understood always in a singularly plural sense (*TD*, 25).

All of this raises a difficult question, one that Nancy has been asked since the 1980s: then what is the role of politics? For Nancy politics should only be tasked with preparing the space for the "nonequivalent affirmation." Democratic politics should merely provide the contour, but it must renounce "giving itself a figure; it allows for a proliferation of figures—figures affirmed, invented, imagined, and so on" (*TD*, 26).

Nancy is critical of any model of politics that attempts to affirm, even if merely through negation, the extreme figure that has been alienated by an ecotechnological system of politics. In "A Note on the Term: *Biopolitics*," Nancy implies that *bare life*, probably alluding to Agamben and Negri, represents a biopolitical supplement for the proletariat (*CWG*, 93–95). If politics are affirmative, such as in Esposito's notion of affirmative biopolitics, it seeks to reappropriate the alienating conditions that created them in the first place. Biopolitics, he contends, "cannot address the problem opened by democracy," which is also "a problem posed by ecotechnology that demands, or that produces, the absence of a separable figure and the absence of identifiable end" (*CWG*, 95). Biopolitics, he argues in "The Truth of Democracy," "relies on a confused hypertrophy of the sense or meaning of politics" (*TD*, 33). This is a problem I shall return to over the course of the next two chapters when I address the political solutions of Agamben and Esposito.

Nancy's political solution is left up in the air, so to speak. Democracy for him means "going beyond the political order" (*TD*, 29). The *value* of democracy is merely "shared existence insofar as it exposes itself to its absence of ultimate sense as its true—and infinite—sense of being" (*TD*,

31). In a manner, he contends, "democracy equals anarchy"—"Neither God nor masters." The "power of the people," he continues, "is first of all the power to foil the *archē* and then to take responsibility, all together and each individually, for the infinite opening that is thereby brought to light" (*TD*, 31). This call for "finite inscription of the infinite," nullifies general equivalence, which produces the "indefinite," "indifference," and "tolerance." He calls for "affirmative difference" and "confrontation." Across most of his essays he tends to cite Balibar's notion of "equaliberty" and Negri's critique of empire, while also appealing to a deconstructed notion of fraternity, as models of affirmation with which he aligns himself.

Combining his early analysis of the retreat of the political, his critique of the operative community, his Heideggerian critique of identification, and his theory of truth, all outlined in this chapter, Nancy clearly states that if there is a "truth of democracy," it is simply that democratic politics "withdraws from all assumptions" (*TD*, 32). Democracy, he claims, "is first of all a metaphysics and only afterwards a politics" (*TD*, 34). The state does have functions, he concludes, but it should not concern itself with "the ends of man, of common and singular existence" (*TD*, 34). So if there is a politics in Nancy's political philosophy, the best we can say is that his politics is weak. It is weak precisely because it is tasked with holding open the space that is necessary to exist in-common. This is an ontological formulation, not a biopolitical one as we shall find in the following chapters.

# 4

# The Community Without Content

> For me, the problem is to try to diagonalize [*diagonaliser*] the proper and the improper, to think, in logic as well as politics, of a language that is beyond the proper and the improper, this is what strikes me as the problem of belonging.[1]

In *Improper Life*, Campbell duly remarks that to "some degree, all of Agamben's work may be inscribed in what amounts to a theory of the improper" (2011, fn.7, 163). Agamben translates Heidegger's "Being and being" and "proper and improper" into a biopolitical lexicon of "*bíos* and *zoē*, *Muselmann*/witness, and subjectification and desubjectification," which he treats "as the principle criteria for marking modernity" (2011, 40). Following Esposito's reading in *Bíos* (2008), he argues that Agamben overemphasizes the negative, thanatopolitical dimensions of biopolitics to the detriment of the affirmative aspects. Campbell provides a thorough examination of the many permeations of the proper/improper dichotomy in both Agamben and Esposito (2011, 31–82). Campbell focuses on the biopolitical relationship between life and the proper, which leads him to Heidegger's writings on technology and Hölderin. This and the following chapter, however, focus on community and the proper, which are articulated more in an ontological than a biopolitical lexicon. In fact, Agamben and Esposito only seriously started to engage in biopolitics immediately after writing *The Coming Community* and *Communitas*. These texts are heavily influenced by Nancy's writings on the proper and community, while the main Heideggerian problem of the proper is largely conceived in terms of Heidegger's writings on *das Man* and *das Ereignis*.[2]

Whether Agamben diagonalizes the proper and the improper or scribes a theory of the improper is a serious question that cannot be overlooked when reading *The Coming Community*. Philosophically, Agamben calls for an appropriation of the improper, of rendering the improper proper and thus one's own. When translated into the ethical and political terrains, the affirmation of impropriety leads to a series of problems that he has continued to address in his *Homo Sacer* series. In the text on community, one is left with the sense that he radicalizes difference to such an extent that he is open to the charge of promoting what Balibar calls *abyssal alienation*. Whether his exemplary case is represented by the bare life of the *Muselman*, the argot of the Roma, or the highest poverty of the Franciscan friars, Agamben has consistently appealed to the abject as a potential solution to the proper—the improper is that which is excluded yet included within the semantic field of the proper. Not only are the proper and the improper coconstitutive, improperness is the very means through which we are in common.

In *The Coming Community* and his earlier works impropriety is primarily articulated through language and communication. During this stage, he relies heavily on the notions of inoperativeness and impotentiality. Later, he turns to inoperativeness and common use as keys to rendering the dispositif of the proper in modern ontology, ethics, and politics inoperative. From his earliest writings on the philosophy of language, to the first installments of the *Homo Sacer* series on political theology, to the later installments on economic theology, he has continued to appeal to the political prescription—despite his efforts to think beyond the practical paradigm—that the task-at-hand for a coming politics is to realize improperness as that which is our most proper, or as our proper impropriety. Whether this amounts to an appropriation of the improper or a letting go of the proper is an issue of paramount importance for this chapter. This task only becomes apparent through a careful exposition of the dialectic of the proper and the improper.

All political philosophers struggle to reconcile their philosophical aims with their practical prescriptions. Nancy's critics, as I demonstrated in the last chapter, often charge him with prioritizing the ontological over the ontic. And despite his disdain for such a distinction and for providing concrete prescriptions, he has periodically revisited and clarified his own positions. Esposito too, as I will show in the next chapter, has been forced to clarify the practical implications of his theory of *communitas* and the subsequent theory of affirmative biopolitics. For Agamben, however, the question of a political task is rife with problems. Agamben draws together a critique of political economy, Heidegger's and Arendt's critiques of productivity, and contemporary inoperative political formulations, in his systematic critique of the productive paradigm that animates how we conceive of both ontology and politics. These core references are brought to the fore in his book on community. In his subsequent writings, especially in those where he performs a "theological genealogy of the economy" (*WA*, 8; *CCD*, 15) he even links this paradigm to the collapse of the economic in the political in early Christian economic theology and the related practical prejudice in the modern ontology of the effect. It is this strain that has created so much tension, even more so than with Nancy and Esposito, in the reception of his work. Many remain skeptical about the alignment of his philosophical aims with his political problematic, which in truth is no different than that of anyone else working on political philosophy after Hegel—how to think the absolute even in the most practical manner. Agamben is keen to tip the scale between the practical and absolute, to disrupt the practical prejudice in order to open a new ontology beyond the trappings of praxis. His critics read him as a philosopher who is so invested in conceiving in the absolute absolutely, without qualifications, that he leaves us with a useless and impractical form of politics that is more mystical than political. He is often read as a philosopher who muses in messianic and eschatological texts, provides only cryptic prescriptions, and is in the end a negative theologian who mistakenly views the most abject dystopian aspects of our world as a passageway into utopia. Put in more Marxist terminology, Agamben is read as an idealist who is incapable of grappling with real material relationships. According to this reading, his impotent and inoperative prescriptions lead to a radically passive model of politics, even weaker than Nancy's weak politics. Many question whether he completely abandons politics and resistance to found an obscure, passive, and ascetic model of ethics that is completely impractical.[3]

The ultimate aim of this chapter is to examine how Agamben conceives of community in relation to the proper and thus the dialectic of alienation and appropriation. To address this problematic I have broken this chapter into three parts. The first section has been written as a philosophical and political primer that I use to examine his more esoteric statements in his book on community. I focus on three key issues: being-in-language, impotentiality, and inoperativeness. I draw from the philosophical essays published in *Potentialities* (*PI*, 2005; *PE*, 1999) and the political essays in *Means Without Ends* (*MSF*, 2013; *MWE*, 2000). Not only were most of these texts written during the same phase of his writing as *The Coming Community*, there is actually considerable overlap in all of these writings, and they are much less esoteric than the passages in his book on community.[4]

In part two, I turn to *The Coming Community*. This work is often overlooked in the English literature on Agamben, even in the literature on debate about community.[5] Usually, it serves as a supplementary reference to help the author articulate a problem found in a different book. Most view this text as a turning point in his oeuvre where he starts to leave behind the problems of first philosophy and enters into the more practical terrain of biopolitics. Some even read it as the philosophical groundwork for his biopolitical project (Salzani, 2010). I believe that it is not quite either. The book represents a clear and focused articulation of his most important problematic: the subordination of being by modern politics and ethics. Agamben searches for peripheral and dissenting voices in the philosophical tradition of the West, which he uses to highlight possible openings for rethinking the relationship between ontology, ethics, and politics. He wants to find ontological modalities, ways of being, and mannerisms, ultimately an ontological ethos, that stops well short of becoming a prescriptive ethical ontology. Politics too, recalling Nancy's weak politics, must not be extended into the ontological. At this stage, he strives to conceive of an ontological ethos of being-thus, whatever being, that is without prescriptions and inoperative. Although it was present in his early writings, it is brought to the fore in the *Homo Sacer* series. Biopolitics, economic theology, effective ontology, the ontology of having-to-be, even the anthropological machine, all have the effect of reducing a being to its *whatness*, which is an ontic, factical, reduction of beings to things. The ontological ethos, being-thus, that he describes in *The Coming Community* becomes in his later writings form-of-life. This is the focus of part three of this chapter.

## PART 1. EARLY PHILOSOPHICAL CONCERNS

### I. Language and Absolution

> In the end, for me, [in *The Coming Community*] I sought to outline a theory of the event in language, i.e., being said in language, linguistic name as an arche-evental space, as a space of a transcendental act, which conditions language in all types of events. This might be an impossible task and it was not very clear in my book. My idea was to conceive of language no longer as a grammar, no longer as a language with linguistic properties, but as event. My idea was that the proper language of the event is an event in language. Being in language is that event which is neither proper nor improper, neither belonging nor not-belonging.[6]

*The Coming Community* was written during the peak of the "linguistic turn." The postmodern thesis, the clash of identities, the collapse of the Soviet Union, cultural globalization, and many other events were being conceived within the realm of language. Although Agamben is critical of how imaginary communities, to borrow from Benedict Anderson, are constituted, he maintains that communication is the medium through which we have to rethink community. The *logos*, he repeats many times, is the common. The problem with traditional notions of community is that they treat language as something that can be appropriated and thus rendered proper to a people. One has to look no further than the various formulations of community offered by communitarians in the Anglo-American world or their European associate Jürgen Habermas to find such a formulation. But for Agamben, claims Durantaye, language "has no *proper* meaning and no *proper* content" because it is simply "a medium for communication" (2009, 181).[7] Although humanity shares language, language is also what shares and divides us. Thus, Agamben searches for a way to conceive of language not as something we can dominate, but as a means through which we are placed in common. In the following section, I briefly examine a few dimensions of his argument, which I will later use to examine his notion of the coming politics.

Heidegger's hermeneutical critique of *apophasis* is key to understanding Agamben's philosophy of language. In *Being and Time*, Heidegger sought rethink the problem of manifestation, of the thing in itself, beyond the predicative actions of asserting and pointing out. He argued that "assertion" represents a "deficient" mode of interpretation. "When an assertion is made," he claimed, "some fore-conception is already implied; but it remains for the most part inconspicuous because the language already hides in itself a developed way of conceiving" (*BT*, §33). Hermeneutics should not assert anything; rather, it must find a way to dis-close the thing sought, which can only occur by *explicating*, unraveling or laying out, that which it interprets. Other hermeneuticians have continued to model their work on this distinction. In "The Task of Hermeneutics," for example, Ricoeur argues that interpretation "is above all an explication, a *development* of understanding which [and he starts to quote *B&T* here] 'does not transform it into something else, but makes it become itself'" (1981, 57). In *Truth and Method*, Gadamer claims that to explicate is to "bring to the fore" the "conditions in which understanding takes place" (2004, 295).

Although Agamben is not a hermeneutician per se, he does use the explicative method in his work. He attempts to clear away the fore-meanings (Heidegger's "as-structure") in order to dis-close the fore-structure. To assert something is to pleromatically fill in a gap in order to present a completed thought, which is an appropriative gesture. Assertion, from *asserere*, joins, links, and binds the asserted thing to series. Whether he is examining the emptiness of the law in the interstitial spaces of community or language itself, Agamben always prioritizes the kenomatic solution over the pleromatic one. Referencing Plato's *Phaedo*, for example, he claims that the "thing itself is not a thing; it is the very sayability, the very openness at issue in language, which in language, we always presuppose and forget, perhaps because it is at bottom its own oblivion and abandonment. . . . [I]t is what we are always disclosing in speaking, what we are always saying and communicating, and that of which we nevertheless are always losing sight" (*PI*, 18; *PE*, 35). Language, he continues, "says presuppositions as presuppositions, and, in this way, reaches the unpresupposable and unpresupposed principle (*arkhē anypothetos*)," which "constitutes authentic human community and communication" (*PI*, 18; *PE*, 35). Communication is the thing itself, but it is not a thing *in*-itself. Language is not a thing and thus neither a being nor an existent. It is but a means through which we experience our commonality. If we are to communicate in a genuinely common manner, then we must begin by challenging the presuppositional gesture.

In "Philosophy and Linguistics," Agamben articulates the same problem in relation to French linguist Jean-Claude Milner's distinction between *factum grammaticae* and the *factum loquendi* (*PI*, 57–77; *PE*, 62–76). The latter represents the "presupposition" that "there is language," that is, that "language exists," and that because "human beings speak," language is the "universal linguistic essence" (*PI*, 72; *PE*, 73). The *factum loquendi* merely insinuates the "pure existence of language, independent of real properties" (*PI*, 63–64; *PE*, 67). The task for philosophy is to find an opening to conceive of the *factum loquendi* without reducing it to the *factum grammaticae* (linguistic properties that belong to particular languages, studied by linguists). But philosophy struggles to address this fact because of its assertive modality. "Thought that seeks to grasp the *factum loquendi*, language as pure existence without properties," notes Agamben, "is always about to become a kind of grammar" (*PI*, 72; *PE*, 73).

In "The Thing Itself" and "The Idea of Language," he addresses this problem in relation to community. Drawing heavily from Heidegger, he claims that since "humans are thrown into language" and we "are condemned to understand each other in language," the "task par excellence" for a philosophy to come is to address the "dwelling of the *logos* in the beginning" (or "the *arkhē*" in the Italian version) (*PI*, 32–34; *PE*, 44–46).[8] The two twentieth-century thinkers who were most attuned to this task of eliminating and absolving presuppositions were Benjamin, in his notion of "pure language," and Heidegger, in his notion of *Sage*.

To overcome the presuppositional orientation, Agamben employs the term "exposure." The task of philosophy, he claims, is to "expose the limits of language" (*PI*, 34; *PE*, 46), "to expose this presupposition, to become conscious of the meaning of the fact that human beings speak," that is, the *factum loquendi* (*PI*, 63; *PE*, 67), "to redefine the entire domain of categories and modality so as to consider no longer the presupposition of Being and potentiality, but their exposition" (*PI*, 76; *PE*, 76), and to expose the "nonpresupposed principle" such as in Paul Celan's aphorism that "'*La poésie ne s'impose plus, elle s'expose*'" ("'Poetry no longer imposes itself; it exposes itself'") (cited in *PI*, 167; *PE*, 115). His choice of terms in this opposition is strategic. *Ex-ponere* is to put forth, explain, expound, or exhibit. This term connects to the broader etymological network of terms deriving from *ponere* (to put, place) that he enlists in many of his writings. To presuppose is to place, put, or set something beneath and prior to (*per-sub-ponere*), in short, to produce a basis or foundation. In his writings on the state of exception, for example, he employs presupposition to signify how positive law operates (*SE*, 2005). Agamben enlists exposition to challenge the positivist orientation in our world. The world of positivism is a contained world where things are treated as if they appropriable. Exposition, however, exposes, unravels, and leaves things out in the open, without defense or shelter, as they truly are, as improper. In a different parlance, exposition (*esposizione*) is a type of disposition, an imposition that renders the subject impotent and passive, which frees, opens, and prepares the subject to enter into relations without presuppositions.

In the 1980s and 1990s, Agamben's notion of the "*experimentum linguae*" performs this expository role. It acts as process of absolution that frees the *factum loquendi* from presuppositional thought. In *Infancy and History*, he defines it as an experience where language is not "experienced as this or that signifying proposition, but as the pure fact that one speaks, that language exists" (1993, 5). *Experiment* is a derivative of *experience* (*experientia* is a form of knowledge acquired through trial and test). It is simultaneously a pure experience of language and the event of language itself. In "Notes on Politics," he claims this experiment concerns "the matter itself of thought," which is "the power of thought" (*MSF*, 92; *MWE*, 116). He draws two political consequences from this notion: politics is the "sphere of pure means" and the "free use of the common" (*MSF*, 93; *MWE*, 118). In our world, politics is subordinated to the ends of the economy, but politics has to be reconceptualized so that it can address the *factum loquendi*, which is without ends. The *experimentum linguae* sets us on this course. Politics concerns the fact of our "being-in-language itself as pure mediality, being-in-a-mean as an irreducible condition of human beings" (modified *MSF*, 92; *MWE*, 116). Politics must become the "the field of human action and of human thought" (*MSF*, 93; *MWE*, 117). To conceive of a coming politics, one must begin from "*the exhibition of a mediality: it is the act of making a means visible as such*" (*MSF*, 92–93; *MWE*, 116–117).

The *experimentum linguae* also provides an opportunity to rethink the meaning of the common. From the "unrestrainable will to falsification and consumption" to the totalitarian demand for the "exclusion of any impropriety," the common is defined in opposition to the improper (*MSF*, 93; *MWE*, 117). Our political terrain, whether in theory or practice, is delimited by the "dialectic of the proper and the improper." The *experimentum linguae* provides an opening that helps us rethink the common "as a point of indifference between the proper and the improper." The common, he continues, must be conceived "as something that can never be grasped in terms of either expropriation or appropriation but . . . only as *use*" (*MSF*, 93; *MWE*, 117). The question for the coming politics must be "'How does one use a *common*?'" Heidegger, more than anyone else, points us in this direction with his notion of the *Ereignis*, which is "neither appropriation nor expropriation, but as appropriation of an expropriation" (*MSF*, 93; *MWE*, 117).

If one were to conceive of a "true [*vera*] human community" (*PI*, 35; *PE*, 47) or an "authentic [*autentica*] human community" and "human communication" (*PI*, 18; *PE*, 35), he claims in the opening essays of *Potentialities*, one can only do so without *presuppositions*. This means that common presuppositions, such as "a nation, a language" or "a priori communication" or any other common identifier, must be left aside. What really brings humans together, defines our common nature, is the "vision of language itself and, therefore, the experience of language's limits, its *end*." The dual political function of the *experimentum linguae*, to open politics up so that they are conceived as the sphere of pure means and so that the common is free to use, are issues he addresses in his political passages in *The Coming Community*.

## II. Impotentiality and Inoperativeness

In the new 2001 postface to the Italian edition of *The Coming Community*, "*Tiqqun de la noche*," Agamben claims "the paradigm of the coming politics" is "inoperativeness and de-creation" (*inoperosità e decreazione*) (*CV*, 92). Like the "sabbatical vacation," the "decisive question" for this work is not "'what to do?' but 'how to do?' and *Being* is less important than the *thus*" (*CV*, 92).[9] In his philosophy there is an important relationship between his notions of inoperativeness and impotentiality. Agamben uses these twin terms to address a wide range of issues, from the problem of historical destiny, to Bataille's notion of "*la négativité sans emploi*" or *désoeuvrément*, to the biopoliticization of the Arendtian problem of the conflation of politics and economics, to its original paradigmatic formulation in Aristotle's theory of potentiality.[10]

Agamben often employs impotentiality and inoperativeness to address the problem of historical destiny. In teleological models of community, community represents the realization of humanity's communal essence. Many interpret Aristotle's aphorism that "man is by nature a *politikon zoon*" in this way. If we are by nature social or political animals, then it is our destiny to create the perfect polis. The blueprint for a proper community is found in our nature, in *Homo approprians*, we might say. As such, it is our duty to work together to realize our human nature. "Simply because history designates the expropriation itself of human nature through a series of epochs and historical destinies," he claims in "Notes on Politics," this does not mean "that the fulfillment and the appropriation of the historical telos" of humanism must give rise to a "definitive order" in the form of a "homogenous universal state" (*MSF*, 89; *MWE*, 111). If our "anarchic historicity" indicates anything at all, it demonstrates that the opposite is the case. We must "take possession" of our "own historical being," which is our "own [or proper] impropriety." The only lesson that can be gleaned from history is that we must find a way to address the "becoming-proper (nature) of the improper (language)" and simultaneously the "becoming-improper (language) of the proper (nature)" (*MSF*, 89; *MWE*, 112). Sovereign politics, he claims, foreshadowing his later *Homo Sacer* series, is not up to this task. If there remains a possible "social power," *potenza*, implying potentiality rather than force, it can only be found in its "proper impotence" (*propria impotenza*) (*MSF*, 90; *MWE*, 113). Impotence is a gesture that "declines any will to either posit or preserve right," and it disrupts the sovereign paradigm that operates in state-centered politics. A "new politics" must find a way to conceive of a "*political* community" that "is ordered exclusively for the full enjoyment of worldly life" (*MSF*, 90; *MWE*, 114). In place of bare life, which is a product of sovereignty, he elevates "happy life" as the new principle of politics, which in his most recent writings on economic theology becomes "form-of-life" (see Mills, 2005).

This general problem represents a sort of third wave of the classical Marxist and anarchist approach to human agency. Many Western Marxists, including Luckács, criticized the orthodox Marxists for reducing Marxism to a schematic template of historical progression that eliminates human agency and contingencies. In the 1960s and 1970s, the New Left started to take up questions of free will, autonomy, vanguardism, and historical destiny in relation to identity politics. In

Italy and France, these issues were redirected toward the problem of economism, workerism, or productivity. Besides Bataille and Kojève, Agamben's notion of *inoperosità* is heavily influenced by the *Operaismo* movement, including the philosophies produced by this movement, just as Nancy's notion of *désœuvrement* is influenced by *Socialisme ou Barbarie* and the many political philosophers it produced. The "refuse to work!" slogan was not a call for generalized laziness or a state of inactivity, but a refusal to be subjected to the regime of capitalist production and regulation. A general strike, whether in real or social factories, would put a halt to the capitalist machine. The notion was intended to radicalize the meaning of "emancipation" to include all forms of exploitive labor writ large. Human activity will only be liberated and free after we are liberated from exploitive labor. Today, this strain is represented by the post-*operaismo* and postautonomous politics in Italy. Writers such as Hardt and Negri, Maurizio Lazzarato, and Paolo Virno have increasingly taken up the plight of the multitude represented by the precarious, immaterial laborers in post-Fordist societies. Each generation continues to draw from Marx and Engels's famous statement in *The German Ideology* that in a communist society "nobody has one exclusive sphere of activity but each can become accomplished in any branch he wishes, society regulates the general production and thus makes it possible for me to do one thing today and another tomorrow, to hunt in the morning, fish in the afternoon, rear cattle in the evening, criticize after dinner, just as I have a mind, without ever becoming hunter, fisherman, shepherd or critic" (1998, 87).

Agamben translates this general problematic into his theory of inoperativeness. His approach has also been a source of much consternation for his critics. Whether his formulation results in a negative or positive model of liberty–that is, whether he provides a template for conceiving of liberated activity socially, fostered by equitable conditions that create opportunities for everyone to experience liberation and provide checks on excessive individual freedom (both covered by social regulation in the quote above–is a problem I will leave open here. We must first establish the general contours of his theory of inoperativeness and impotentiality. I return to this problem below.

One of Agamben's clearest examinations of the relationship between work and politics in Aristotle is found in his essay "The Work of Man." Since the highest good for Aristotle, he argues, is "'the being-at-work [*energeia*] of the soul in accordance with excellence,'" how we interpret his notion of work is of critical importance not just for interpreting his philosophy but for our world, which has largely inherited his problematic (*PI*, 373; *WM*, 2).[11] Following Arendt, he argues that in our contemporary world we confuse the economic sense of work with the political sense of work. Aristotle distinguished between concrete economic activities performed in vocations (being a flute player, "the work of man") and the abstract notion of an "*argia*, of an essential inoperativeness [*inoperosità*] of man with respect to his concrete occupations and functions [*operazioni*]," which is the "work of man as man" (*PI*, 373; *WM*, 2).[12] The "end of history thesis" concerning the "fulfilled realization of human work" and hence of a possible posthistorical era of "*désoeuvrement*" or "*argos*," he claims, has its "logical-metaphysical foundation" in this formulation. This thesis can be interpreted in at least two ways depending on how one understands "man's *ergon*."

The most common interpretation of "work of man as man" is to attach the *ergon* to the *logos*. Western politics, he claims, has "been conceived as the collective assumption of a historical task (of a 'work') on the part of a people or a nation" (*PI*, 378; *WM*, 6). As such, the "political task" matches the "metaphysical task," which is "the realization of man as a rational living being." Since humanity is distinguished from other types of life on the grounds that in addition to sensitive and nutritive life we have practical-rational life, it becomes our duty to realize our "vital rational potentiality" (*PI* 377; *WM* 5). This can only be realized if the sphere of politics were to transform our state of merely "living" (*zēn*) into a state of "living well" (*eu zēn*). Politics represents the sphere where the "highest good"—individual excellence and distinction—can be realized. As such, politics is defined by "activity" (*operosità*) as opposed to "inactivity" (*inoperosità*). Marx's *Gattungswesen*, he claims, represents a "radicalization of this Aristotlean project." Further, because the *ergon* refers only to a particular "kind of life," it must exclude "the simple fact of living, of bare life" (*PI*, 378; *WM*, 5).

Agamben's emphasis on "life" in this passage helps him to draw a biopolitical conclusion. Gradually, he contends, this formulaic prescription of matching the metaphysical and the political tasks has been translated from labor to action, to life itself. With the end of WWI, the "paradigm of work" entered a period of crisis. Since nation-states could no longer identify with a "historical task" or the "work of man," he claims, their work turned to "the care of nutritive and sensitive life" (*PI*, 379; *WM*, 6). This resulted in the conflation of the economic with the political, which either "depoliticized" societies or turned "biological life" into the "supreme political task," that is, politicized life (*MSF*, 108–9; *MWE*, 140). Once "the home becomes the political paradigm," he warns, "then the proper, the most intimate facticity of existence risks turning into a fatal trap," which is the situation we are faced with today (modified *MSF*, 109; *MWE*, 140).

Contrary to the paradigm of work, he asks, what if "man" is "essentially *argos*," "without work, idle" or inoperative (*senz'opera, inoperoso*) (modified, *MSF*, 109; *MWE*, 141)? A human without a proper *ergon* could be conceived as a "pure potentiality" (*PI*, 373; *WM*, 2). This elevation of inactivity, of the *argos*, he maintains against the materialist and anti-intellectualist strains of modern politics, does not necessarily refer to a state of complete inactivity or laziness, but to the *skholē* that is necessary to provide the pause from work that allows us to reflect and think. He often turns to Averroes and Dante to provide evidence for this alternative perspective. Averroism, he claims, "links the political vocation of man to the potentiality of the intellect" (*MSF*, 109; *MWE*, 141). Dante elaborates on this interpretation by claiming that the "'highest potentiality in man . . . is to be a creature who apprehends by means of the possible intellect'" (cited in *PI*, 381; *WM*, 8). For Dante, politics must "correspond to the inactivity of man," "from a working that exposes and contains in itself the possibility of its own not existing, of its own inactivity" (*PI*, 384; *WM*, 10).

Even if it is not possible to conceive of an absolute form of "inaction," he proclaims, we must conceive of the figure of the multitude as "a working that, in every act, realizes its proper *shabbat* and in every work is able to expose its proper inoperativeness and its proper potentiality" (modified, *PI*, 384; *WM*, 10). Beyond the biopolitical reduction of politics to the *oikonomia*, the coming politics must find a way to address "this *argia*, this essential inoperativeness and potentiality," which must be addressed without reducing it to a "historical task" (*MSF*, 109; *MWE*, 142). Politics must "correspond to the essential inoperativeness of man" (modified, *MSF*, 109; *MWE*, 141). Politics should become "nothing other than the exposition of man's absence of work as well as his creative indifference to any task"; only then will politics "remain integrally assigned to happiness" (modified, *MSF*, 109; *MWE*, 142).

Agamben addresses this problematic in more specific terms in various passages of *The Coming Community* and in his essays "On Potentiality" and "Bartleby, or On Contingency."[13] In "On Potentiality" he distinguishes between "generic potentiality" and "existing potentiality" (*PE*, 179). The former represents the traditional interpretation and the latter his distinctive reading. For both, the main issue is *how* the "passage from potentiality to act comes about" (*CV*, *33*; *CC*, 35).[14] Generic potentiality is the kind attributed to children, whereas existing potentiality is attributed to an adult who already "has knowledge or an ability" (*PE*, 179). Unlike the child, an adult already possesses his "potential" and thus does not have to "suffer an alteration." Because of his "*hexis*, a 'having,'" the adult is also empowered to "*not* bring his knowledge into actuality (*mē energein*) by *not* making work" (*PE*, 179). This is an inoperative form of potentiality—impotentiality from Aristotle's notion of *adynamia*—that disrupts the generic potentiality and its imperative that one do something. This inoperative potentiality is a "potential to not-do, potential to not pass into actuality" (*PE*, 180). It is not necessarily a lack that needs to be fulfilled; that is, it is neither pleromatic nor appropriable.

Agamben generally draws three implications from this theory of impotentiality: not-being (*non-essere*), not-doing (*non-fare*), and freedom (*libertà*). First, he claims that impotentiality means that "potentiality . . . maintains itself in relation to its own privation . . . its own non-Being [*proprio non-essere*]" (*PE*, 182). This side of his theory resonates with Heidegger's existential notion of being-towards-death as one's most proper possibility. "To be potential," continues Agamben, means "to be one's own lack, *to be in relation to one's own incapacity*." It symbolizes the "*possibility of privation*." Second, because we possess impotentiality we have the power to not do something. In other words, we have the power to perform "inoperative work" (*l'opera inoperosità*) (*PI*, 289). Third, impotentiality distinguishes humanity from other animals. "*Other living beings are capable only of their specific potentiality*" (*PE*, 182). Human "*greatness*," however, "*is measured by the abyss of the human impotentiality*." Human freedom is located precisely in this "abyss of potentiality" (*PE*, 182–83). "To be free is . . . *to be capable of one's own impotentiality*."

In *The Coming Community*, he claims that supreme power is "a power that is capable of both power and impotence" (*CV*, 34; *CC*, 36). "If every power is equally the power to be and the power to not-be," he argues, "the passage to action can only come about by transporting (Aristotle says 'saving') in the act its own [*proprio*] power to not-be" (*CV*, 34; *CC*, 35). Proper agents, in other words, are only capable of acting when they transfer their incapacity. For example, Glen Gould's "mastery conserves and exercises in the act not his potential to play," which is the ironic position of "positive potentiality over the act, but rather his potential to not-play." The "not" in this formulation provides an opening for turning back on itself, for creating a pause or "passivity" of sorts that opens up the possibility of thinking about a "pure potentiality." This is not a simple opposition, but an exercise that is "contain[ed]" by a "third term: the *rather*," which in the Italian *piuttosto* connotes both a sense of a promptness or a swiftness that comes to pass in an *easy manner* and of a decisiveness that must be taken when faced with a tough decision. The rather, he continues, is the "power to not not-be" (*CV*, 87; *CC*, 104). To be "capable of the *rather*"—"can not not-be"—renders potentiality "necessarily contingent" and "contingently necessary" (*CV*, 87; *CC*, 105). This inoperative potentiality qua impotentiality must be, despite the apparent contradiction, realized in the coming community.

## PART 2. THE COMING COMMUNITY

The fragmentary nature of the chapters of this book, his obtuse prose, and the potpourri of references make it difficult to read and impossible to systematize. I have no intention of doing so here.[15] Instead, I examine how Agamben attempts to rethink the relationship between ontology, ethics, and politics. In modern ontological formulations, he argues, being is subordinated and ultimately deontologized by political and sometime ethical formulations. *The Coming Community* consists in a series of exercises aimed at creating tiny schisms that open up new passageways between ontology and ethics or politics where new ontological modalities, mannerisms, or means can be found. He thus shares a common aim with Nancy and Esposito, yet of the three, he is the most concerned with maintaining a stark separation between ontology, ethics, and politics. Agamben's ontological formulations are also far less ethical than Esposito's deontological formulation and far less relational than those found in Nancy's ontology of being-with. Agamben searches for an ontological ethos qua a way or modality of being, but he refuses to convert it into an ethical ontology. This is a position he later reaffirms in the *Homo Sacer* series. Politics, at least at this point in his writing, plays the role of creating abject and depoliticized subjectivities that could potentially create new openings for thinking about an ethos of being-thus that is without prescriptions and inoperative. Finally, and perhaps most surprisingly given the title of this book, it is hard to find a genuinely relational dimension in his ontological ethos of being-thus. At most, he describes the conditions that render ontological relations possible. In this section, I begin by examining the relationship between ethics and ontology, and I end by examining the relationship between politics and ontology in *The Coming Community.*

## III. Depoliticization

In a statement he will later repent, Agamben remarks that "there are no longer social classes, but just a single planetary petite bourgeoisie" (*CV*, 51; *CC*, 63).[16] The cultural revolution orchestrated by the petite bourgeoisie has inadvertently paved the way for thinking about a new ontological ethos. The petite bourgeoisie represents the core contradictions of our time, not just because of its false identification with its insignificant portions of the means of production à la Marx, or because it has failed to take over the reigns of the democratic state à la Weber, or because it has become the new managerial class of the service economy à la postindustrial thesis, but also because of its peculiar relationship to the proper à la consumer-society thesis. Who else could thrive in the midst of our commodified, consumptive, and commercialized society? "They know," he declares, "only the improper and the inauthentic," and they "even refuse the idea of a discourse that could be proper to them" (*CV*, 51; *CC*, 63). The petite bourgeoisie is, in other words, a class without "any recognizable identity." Agamben even extols the cosmopolitan ethos of this class on the grounds that it remains indifferent to cultural-linguistic differences. Nothing holds "any meaning for" a petite bourgeois, she has lost "any capacity for expression and communication" (*CV*, 51–52; *CC*, 63–64). For her, differences and diversity are "exposed in a phantasmagorical vacuousness." In other words, what is proper to a petite bourgeois is improper, not only in the sense of not-being hers, but also in the sense of complete indifference. Under her reign, the "senselessness" of the world is exposed. Even when faced with her "ultimate expropriation," "bare life" (*la nuda vita*) but also the "pure incommunicable," she still attempts to "cover over the secret" (*CV*, 52; *CC*, 64).

During this phase, Agamben regularly returned to the topics of consumerism, commodity fetishism, and the media—in short, the society of the spectacle. Rather than focus on the spectacular aspects of these phenomena—which Nancy used to critique the Situationists' model of symbolic appropriation on the grounds that it reduces the proper to the logic of presentation, appearance, and hence of authenticity—Agamben argues that the spectacle manifests nothing more than the fact of "language, the very communicativity or linguistic being of humans" (*CV*, 64; *CC*, 80). Since the *logos*, he claims in reference to Heraclitus, is "the Common," we have to recognize that with the "complete triumph of the spectacle" that "human sociality itself" is expropriated and alienated. The spectacle represents the "extreme form of this expropriation of the Common"—our "linguistic and communicative nature" (*CV*, 64; *CC*, 80). In addition to the "expropriation of productive activity," he exhorts us to take into account the "alienation of language itself."

In addition to the society of the spectacle, Agamben often references the more generalized phenomenon of the crisis of sense. Meaninglessness, he claims in a similar manner to Nancy, provides new opportunities, but for Agamben the point is to experience the event of language. For the first time, humans are "alone with language" and "abandoned without any final foundation" (*PI*, 33; *PE*, 45). This presents a tremendous opportunity, a "Copernican revolution" because "we are the first human beings who have become completely conscious of our language" (*PI*, 33; *PE*, 45). Rather than turn to the traditional solutions—rethinking the universal in a metalanguage or turning to the negative theological practice of the "unsayable"—Agamben claims that we need to rethink the limits of language in "finitude" and "polysemy." One of his most common examples is the relationship between foreign and native speakers. He cites Gaunilo's critique of Anselm's ontological argument as an early formulation of this idea. Contrary to Anselm, Gaunilo pointed out that those who held little if any comprehension of the meaning and significance of a particular language, such as an "idiot or barbarian," would not understand and thus confirm the ontological argument. Embellishing this point, he argues that they merely understand the "pure event of language before or beyond particular meaning" (*PI*, 27; *PE*, 41–42). When a completely foreign language is spoken, the outsider makes a decision to let go of the possibility of finding any meaning or signification in the words. Their attention is redirected to the "'voice alone.'" This experience, for Agamben, "opens thinking to an originary logical dimension that, indicating the pure taking place of language without any determinate event of meaning, shows that there is still a possibility of thought beyond meaningful prepositions" (*PI*, 42; *PE*, 42). Thus, outsiders—whose language, culture, or nationality is improper—are possible candidates for experiencing the *factum loquendi.*

In "Languages and Peoples," Agamben argues that modern political discourse is defined by the correspondence between two facts: the *factum loquendi* that "human beings speak and understand each other" and the *factum pluralitatis* that "human beings form a community" (*MSF*, 56; *MWE*, 66). Given the "fallen condition of language" or the "Babelic confusion of tongues," which he describes in relation to Benjamin's problematic in *Potentialities* (*PI*, 42; *PE*, 52), the political task is to find a way to readdress this relationship without reducing language to grammar (*factum grammaticae*). Modern states close off this relationship by fusing language, people, and state together in a single unity. But languages, he contends, are nothing but "the jargons that hide the pure experience of language just as peoples are the more or less successful masks of the *factum pluralitatis*" (*MSF*, 59; *MWE*, 70). If these two factums are to "come to light," if only "for an instant," then the language-people-state nexus must be disrupted. Stateless people, such as the "Gypsies" [*Zingari*], represent a potential disruption of this nexus. "Gypsies are to a people what *argot* is to language" (*MSF*, 56; *MWE*, 66).[17] Outsiders provide a critical perspective on how modern states synthesize people and languages. Like the Roma people, "all people are gangs and *coquilles*, all languages are jargons and *argot*" (*MSF*, 56; *MWE*, 67).

In *The Coming Community* he makes the same point in his discussion of Tiananmen Square. What makes the "coming politics" novel, he claims, is that they will occur in the "*struggle between the State and the non-State (humanity)*" (*CV*, 67; *CC*, 85). They cannot, however, happen in "a simple affirmation [*rivendicazione*] of the social opposition to the state" (*CV*, 68; *CC*, 86). To re-vindicate an opposition to the state would require that the opposition movement "form a *societas.*" But whatever singularities do not "possess/put in order [*dispongono*] any identity to vindicate." That is, they are not invested in positing themselves in a recognizable position because at best they exist in the manner of exposition, as being-thus. They merely "form a community without affirming an identity" (*CV*, 68; *CC*, 86). As such, whatever singularities represent a threat to modern states. "A being radically devoid of any representable identity, would be *absolutely* irrelevant to the State" (italics mine, *CV*, 68; *CC*, 86). His example here is, of course, the *homo sacer.* "Whatever singularity, which wants to appropriate belonging itself, its own being-in-language, and thus rejects all identity and every condition of belonging, is the principle enemy of the state" (*CV*, 69; *CC*, 87). The state cannot tolerate when they "peacefully demonstrate their being in common." Just like what occurred in Tiananmen Square, whenever they do manifest themselves, "sooner or later, the tanks will appear" (*CV*, 69; *CC*, 87). That is, the power to not-be (pure potentiality) will be appropriated or at the very least repressed.[18] Later this rejection of identity and his antistatism will be reasserted in his notions of form-of-life and destituent power, which I consider in the final part of this chapter.

In place of the appropriative models of resistance, Agamben calls for "messianic shift," which appeals to the logic of letting go. There is no privileged place today where one can "counteract capitalism." The Situationists mistakenly located their utopia "in the taking-place of what it wants to overthrow" (*MSF*, 64; *MWE*, 78–79). Instead, he argues that we need to find a point of indifference, such as is found in Nietzsche's "*experimentum crusis.*" This experiment provides a small "messianic shift" that "*integrally*" changes the world, yet simultaneously "leaving it," "at the same time," "*almost* intact" (*MSF*, 65; *MWE*, 79). In *The Coming Community* he calls this messianic shift a "tiny displacement" (*piccolo spostamento*) of the world. This displacement brackets off the *factum grammaticae*, our traditional orientation in the world, and thus the positivity of the world as such. In the experiment we are exposed to a non-place or not-place (utopia) that makes it possible for us to experience the *factum loquendi.*

Agamben often refers to the cabalist's parable of the "Shekinah" as an example of the tiny displacement. In this tale, four rabbis seek a solution for contemplating the presence of God. Agamben compares the actions of Rabbi Aher to the workings of the spectacle. Both separate knowledge from its reality, appearance from being, and thus sever the living connection to knowledge. The spectacle does this by isolating and rendering language autonomous. "Whereas under the old regime the estrangement of the communicative essence of humans took the form of a proposition that served as the common foundation, in the society of the spectacle it is this very communicativity, this generic essence itself (i.e. language), that is separated in an autonomous sphere" (*CV*, 65; *CC*, 82).[19] What unites us, in other words, separates us. In Agamben's rendition of the cultural globalization thesis, journalists and "mediacrats" are the archetypical agents who produce our communicative alienation. Exaggerating his point, he claims that above economics and technology, "the uprooting of all people from their vital dwelling in language" represents the crucial element that creates "single common destiny" for our now globalized species (*CV*, 66; *CC*, 83). He even claims that the sphere of language has been elevated to such heights that it is now an "essential factor in the production cycle" (*MSF*, 91; *MWE*, 115). In the globalized spectacle, our common linguistic alienation creates an unprecedented opportunity for us to "experience" our linguistic being for the "first time." We can experience "language *itself*," "the very fact that one speaks" (*CV*, 66; *CC*, 83). "Contemporary politics," he claims, "is this devastating *experimentum linguae* that all over the planet unhinges and empties traditions and beliefs, ideologies and religions, identities and communities." If this disarticulating process is carried to completion, by "bringing language itself to language," then we can possibly enter "into the paradise of language and leave unharmed" (*CV*, 66; *CC*, 83). The "first citizens of a community" are those who are without presuppositions or a State. In "'*Pardes*,'" Agamben contends that the *experimentum linguae* "opens onto an ethics" (*PI*, 370–71; *PE*, 218–19). Whoever can conceivably carry out this experiment "to the end and finds, in this sense, her matter (suffering, impassioned), can dwell—without remaining imprisoned—in the paradoxes of self-reference, can not not-write" (modified, *PI*, 371; *PE*, 219).

## IV. Ontological Ethos

Agamben argues the destructive ethos of the planetary petite bourgeoisie provides new opportunities. Since our identities are "already improper and senseless," and since there has never been a so-called "proper identity" (*identità propria*), they provide an opening for thinking about our "impropriety as such." If anything is to be made proper, it can only be our "being-thus," which is nothing more than a "singularity without identity, a common and absolutely exposed singularity" (*CV*, 53; *CC*, 65). If humanity could heed to their ethos, yet by redirecting it to the truth that we are nothing more than "*the* thus," then maybe we could "for the first time enter into a community without presuppositions and without subjects, into a communication without the incommunicable" (*CV*, 53; *CC*, 65). This might just put an end to the endless chatter of the world we currently inhabit and open us to the possibility of experiencing "the perfect exteriority that only communicates itself." This is a first-order task for our time. In the end, he admits in a highly instrumental rendition of social transformation, the petite bourgeoisie is ill equipped to complete the task of creating a "new planetary humanity"; they have merely set the stage for another class to take over this task.

Depoliticization creates a tiny schism that allows us to rethink the passageway between ontology and ethics, but the task we must now address is how the new ontological ethos of being-thus works. Being-thus is an ethos, not a moral conduct or part of an ethical doctrine. Agamben is critical of morality and ethics. He argues that morality is presuppositional because it converts the good and the bad, or the authentic and inauthentic, into predicates (*CV*, 15; *CC*, 13). Morality consists in separating the proper from the improper. To affirm the proper, the improper must be placed somewhere else, and rigid barriers must be erected around the proper to protect it from becoming contaminated by impropriety. Ethics, on the other hand, can only begin—he never says it actually happens—by recognizing the codependency of the proper and the improper. Drawing on the theory of negative apophantic assertions, he cites the ancient adage that "Truth cannot be shown except by showing the false" ("*veritas patefacit se ipsame et falsum*" (*CV*, 15; *CC*, 13). *Patefacer* (*pate-facere*) means to thrown open or to disclose. It is, he claims, "linked to *spatium*." Truth, he continues, can only be revealed when space is given "to non-truth—that is, as a taking-place [*aver-luogo*] of the false, as an exposure to its proper, most intimate impropriety" (modified, *CV*, 15; *CC*, 13). Ethics is more readily available, thus, for those who are excluded or merely share "tiny fragments" of "properness"; these people are open to "the possibility of an appropriation of impropriety as such" (*CV*, 16; *CC*, 13).

Agamben is not a systematic philosopher and the book is not written as an ethical treatise. Since he is critical of presuppositional thought, he is careful to not to appeal to any positive prescriptive models of ethics. And since he is opposed to operativeness, he is critical of various consequentialist models of ethics. One could argue that inoperativeness and communicating without presuppositions are two virtues that give rise to the good life and happiness, but if we were to be fair we would have to conclude that this is also one step too far. He does not make a virtue out of his preferred modality of being-thus, because this would be a moral code that instructs one how to conduct oneself and dictates what one must do. In *The Coming Community*, as with his more recent texts, he is interested in "'how to do,'" not "'what to do.'" Ethics can only commence from the fact that there is nothing to "enact or realize" whether this be a destiny, essence, or history (*CV*, 39; *CC*, 43). If there were an essence or anything else that has destined humanity to a particular pathway, then "there would only be tasks to be done [or realized, *compiti da realizzare*]" (*CV*, 39; *CC*, 43).

His clearest account of the modality of being-thus is found in the appendix "The Irreparable."[20] Here being-thus is read as a disruption of presuppositions and operativeness. Things are, he claims, "just as they are, in this or that mode, consigned without remedy to their way of being" (*CV*, 73; *CC*, 90). There really is nothing to be placed back in order, reproduced, rearranged, or otherwise brought forth, because there is no *telos* that orders the world. The world is "irreparably profane." Earlier in this book he argued that the irreparable is an eschatological reference to a world of postjudgment, where "things are consigned without remedy to their being-thus, that they are precisely only their thus" (*CV*, 38; *CC*, 39). In this nonreworkable and postjudgment world, everything is "absolutely exposed, absolutely abandoned." Being-thus, therefore, represents an ecstatic state where one is nothing other than his or her "mode of being" (*CV*, 77; *CC*, 93). It is neither a realization of one's potentiality nor a presupposed modality. Being-thus is "not otherwise," which he claims, is the "only correct way to understand negative theology" (*CV*, 78; *CC*, 93). "*Not otherwise*," he continues, "negates each predicate as a property (on the plane of essence), but takes them up again as im-propriety [*im-proprietà*] (on the plane of existence)" (modified, *CV*, 78; *CC*, 94).

Being-thus is a modality of existence. It is a "manner" (*maniera*), which contrary to traditional etymologies does not refer to the hand (*manus*) or dwelling place (*manere*), but to *manere* (to flow), such as in *emanate* (to flow out, rise forth) (*CV*, 27–28; *CC*, 27–28). It is a "*manner of rising forth*," (*maniera sorgiva*), which is not a modality one enters into but, again drawing from the Heidegger, "a being that is *its* mode of being" (*CV*, 28; *CC*, 29). This spring/leap, the *ex-manare*, is, he claims in an ontological tone, the "original mannerism of being." Only in this manner can we "find a common passage between ontology and ethics" (*CV*,28; *CC*, 28). Contrary to morality, a being that is rising forth cannot "*presuppose* itself" because it is *exposed* to its "qualifications" when it "*is* its *thus* without remainder" (*CV*, 28; *CC*, 28).

In the literature on community, each theorist appeals to this existential motif of exposure. For Nancy and Esposito, exposure divides up and shares out subjects (*partage* or *condivisione*). Exposure radically disrupts previously immunized subjects, to use Esposito's phrasing, and places them into a relation with each other qua singular plurals. Exposure is, to put things in very simplified terms, the very mannerism of our dwelling in division or of our being-in-common. For Agamben, exposure merely prepares subjects for the possibility of being in a relationship. More precisely, exposure creates the possibility of entering into communication with others. It is an existential modality that opens to the "unpresupposed principle" (*arché anypothetos*). Being "as such" (*tale quale*) exposes subjects to "the pure relationship with language itself" (*CV*, 80; *CC*, 96–97). This was expressed, he claims, in Heidegger's hermeneutic circle, the problem of apophantic assertions, and the as-structure of the world. Meaning and denotation, however, "do not count for all of linguistic signification," because there is a "third term," which he calls in reference to Plato's theory of ideas, the "thing itself" (*CV*, 82,; *CC*, 100). This thing itself is "never itself, but only the existent," which is "completely without refuge" because "it is in the midst of being, and being is entirely abandoned in the existence" (*CV*, 82; *CC*, 100). It gives itself over to the power of being. In the appendix he refers to this process as a "redemption" where one abandons oneself to the "irreparable loss of the lost," which occurs in the profanation of the world (*CV*, 85; *CC*, 102). In this abandonment one must "let the thus be" (*sia il così*). Or in his other lexicon, it is about being capable of the "rather," "the power to not not-be" (*CV*, 87; *CC*, 105). If we are capable of "[s]eeing something simply in its being-thus," we are, he claims, capable of love (*CV*, 88; *CC*, 105).

Exposure plays an import role in disrupting *Homo approprians*. For Nancy, exposure gives rise to the possibility of being-with. For Esposito, *communitas* itself is an expository force that disrupts the immunitary dispositif. It would be wrong, however, to conclude that Agamben leaves us with a privative notion of exposure as a pure mode of being alienated. Agamben actually shares a common reference with Esposito. Both appeal to an ontological notion of debt to overcome the privative notion of debt found in the contemporary articulation of the "economy of compensation" (*l'economia del risarcimento*). Both appeal to an alternative notion of debt by infusing this concept with an ontological and ethical inflection. Esposito's *munus*, for example, combines these dimensions in a deontological formulation that creates a communal sense of duties and obligations. Agamben, however, is not as eager to carry the ontological into the realm of duty. At most, his theory points to the ontological exigency of debt.

In *The Coming Community*, there are two main references to debt. First, debt is an ontological problem par excellence for Agamben. He draws from Heidegger's distinction between ontological and ontic readings of guilt in the passages on the "bad conscience" (*schelchtes Gewissen*) to make this clear (*BT*, §57–60). Ontic guilt, for Heidegger, belongs to the model of compensation. To be guilty in this sense means that one *has* a debt, either because one owes something in return or because one has committed an act for which one is responsible. It refers to a "lack" or a "privation" that requires a measureable form of compensation. This is a type of debt, in other words, that can be appropriated and rendered whole again. Ontological guilt, on the other hand, is a guilt for which there is no solution, especially no compensation, because it concerns the fact that one *is*. "*Being-guilty*," Heidegger claims, "*does not first result from an indebtedness, but that, on the contrary, indebtedness becomes possible only 'on the basis' of a primordial Being-guilty*" (ibid., §58). This is his famous throwness thesis, of the impossibility of being responsible for our origin—a responsibility, O'Byrne justly points out, that belongs to the forgotten mother (2010). The "not" cannot be conceived as a "lack" or "privation" from which one can be compensated or fulfilled (*BT*, §58). All that can be accomplished, claims Heidegger in a futural tone, is to hear the "appeal correctly," to understand "oneself in one's ownmost potentiality-for-Being—that is, to projecting oneself upon one's *ownmost* authentic [or proper] potentiality for becoming guilty"—to accept "Being-the-basis of a nullity" (*BT*, §58). "Existing authentically," notes Raffoul in *The Origins of Responsibility*, "can only mean taking over or making oneself responsible for this 'not,' "one's finitude" (2010, 265).

This sense of ontological debt also operates in Agamben's notion of the existential ethos: "Since the being most proper to humankind is being one's own possibility or potentiality, then and only for this reason (that is, insofar as humankind's most proper being—being potential—is in a certain sense lacking, insofar as it can not-be, it is therefore devoid of foundation and humankind is not always already in possession of it), humans have and feel a debt. Humans, in their potentiality to be and to not-be, are, in other words, always already in debt; they always already have a bad conscience without having to commit any blameworthy act" (*CV*, 39–40; *CC* 43–44).

The second reference in Agamben's notion of debt (*debito*) is etymological, which is a reference he shares with Esposito. The Latin term *debere* breaks down as *de-habere* or *de-having*. It is here that Agamben hints at, but much less forcefully than in Esposito's deontological prose, the relationship between ethics and ontology by reversing the order of *being* and *having*. This is a form of debt that is beyond the order of appropriation, because when one is in debt one is exposed and expropriated. This is a debt for which there is no compensation or remuneration because it is a type of debt that is, in Nancy's terms, incommensurable. One is rendered improper precisely because debt places one in a position that is "humankind's most proper being." This ontological exigency serves two important purposes in his effort to rethink the passage from ontology to ethics.

First, he plays with the connection between *ethos* and *habit*. The "only ethical experience," he contends, "is the experience of being (one's proper) potentiality, of existing (one's proper) possibility—exposing, that is, in every form of one's proper amorphousness and in each act one's proper inactuality" (modified, *CV*, 40; *CC*, 44).[21] Recalling chapter 2, Agamben returns the relationship between **seēthos* and *habit*. In his essay on the *Ereignis*, he claimed that the **se*, as the ethos and proper of man, "is the social praxis itself that, in the end, becomes transparent to itself" (*PI*, 197; *PE*, 137), which refers to nothing more than "the dwelling in the 'self,' which is what is most proper and habitual for him" (*PI*, 171; *PE*, 118). In his book on community he reintroduces this formula of the liberated self in relation to the event of existence. Existence he now claims is a "*habitus*, an *ethos*" where one is simultaneously "generated [*generati*] from one's own [*propria*] manner of being" and opened up to the possibility of the "free *use of the self*" (modified, *CV*, 28; *CC*, 28–29).

This liberating experience creates the possibility for the self to generate itself anew.[22] *Generare* is to bring forth, a process of procreation, to create a new *genus*. The sheer force of the event liberates the self from the operative logic of the world. It is thus free to use itself however it sees fit because it exists in the liberated time of the brief sabbatical. This freed time is neither useless nor inactive, but a time where the activity of the *argos* doesn't make sense to the commonplace activity of the *ergon*. One is free to be creative, in the multiple senses implicated in this passage, which is why he claims in an almost prescriptive fashion that "the only happiness possible for humans" is to be "generated from one's proper manner" (*CC*, 28; *CC*, 29). As an existent one can appropriate their impropriety and treat it as if it is their proper being. Yet this being "does not belong to it" because "it is," he claims, in reference to the problem of ontological difference, "perfectly common" (*CV*, 29; *CC*, 29). Impropriety, he claims in a manner that is more contrarian than diagonal, "is our second, happier, nature" (*CV*, 29; *CC*, 29). In this formulation, there is a reference to human freedom and free will, which are both present in his intellectualist reading of impotentiality qua *argos*. He is quick to point out that his formulation traverses the slip into "nihilism" and "decisionism," such as in the typical formulation that consigns humanity to nothingness, where one is left to "freely [*arbitrio*] decide whether to be or not to be" (*CV*, 39; *CC*, 43). Rather, he draws upon the ontological exigency "that humans are and have to be," which does not refer to an "essence" but to "*the simple fact of one's own* [*proprio*] *existence as possibility or potentiality*" (*CV*, 39; *CC*, 43).

Second, this ethos opens up to a possible ethics. To be a proper host or neighbor, claims Agamben in a prescriptive manner, one must not compensate "for what the other lacks" (*CV*, 24; *CC*, 24). Ethical relations are only possible in the space of "ease" (*agio*), which is "the space adjacent (*ad-jacens*, *adjacentia*)," which is "the empty place where each can move freely" (*CV*, 24–25; *CC*, 25). It is the space of love. In this sense, ease "names perfectly" Hölderin's "'free use of the proper.'" Evil, on the other hand, is found "in the decision to remain in deficit of existence," which is, of course, a modality where one seeks to "appropriate the power to not-be" and convert it into "a substance and a foundation" or to view potentiality "as a fault that must always be repressed" (*CV*, 40; *CC*, 44).

## V. Whatever

Two of Agamben's most prominent critics in Italy are Negri and Esposito. In *Bíos*, Esposito argues that Agamben's reading of biopolitics is too negative. He has also noted in "Dialogue on the Philosophy to Come" that although Agamben's "politics of 'pure means' . . . is a suggestive formula," it remains "very indeterminate" (2010, 84). Negri has been less restrained. He has likened Agamben's notion of "bare life" to a "'utopian escape'" (cited in Salzani, 2012, 228). In *Empire*, he and Hardt criticize the Bartlebian model of the refusal on the grounds that it merely indicates the "beginning of a liberatory politics." An "empty" and "solitary" refusal, they contend, "leads only to a kind of social suicide." What is really called for is a constitution of "a new mode of life and above all a new community" (2000, 204). Put in more traditional Marxist terms, the politics of refusal merely represents an initial phase of revolutionary action. At best, it represents the development of a private economic consciousness, not class-consciousness and certainly not a revolutionary consciousness that will give rise to revolutionary reappropriation. One might go even further and question the conditions of liberation in Agamben's formula. How can the so-called "lumpen proletariats" of our time, those that are completely abandoned, hold any transferable political currency, especially when they are forbidden from using traditional political means for their cause? But this would be a step too far.

In the last part of this chapter I turn to Agamben's more recent efforts to address these concerns, but for now it is necessary to end my examination of this book by turning to what is arguably the most contentious concept: "whatever" (*qualunque*). The first sentence of this work reads, "The coming being is whatever being" (*L'essere che viene è l'essere qualunque*) (*CV*, 9; *CC*, 1). Agamben uses this term to disrupt presuppositional language, the dualism of universality and particularity, and the operative logic that is employed in the generic potentiality that requires actualization. "Whatever" even provides a passageway beyond the duality of the common (genus or nature) and the proper. "*Common and proper, genus and individual*," he pronounces, "*are only the two slopes dropping down from either side of the watershed of the whatever*" (*CV*, 21; *CC*, 20).

To the English ear, it is hard to read this term without thinking about young adolescents whose very ethos is defined by their lack of concern or indifference to the world, "Whatever, I don't care" or "it doesn't matter to me." The implication is that they are willing to let things pass through them without latching onto them. Their orientation to the world, much to the consternation of older generations, is noncategorical. They are, in other words, without presuppositions or judgments. Agamben is critical of this commonplace notion of the whatever, which we find when put in terms such as "'it is not important which, indifferently'" ("'*non importa quale, indifferentemente*'") (modified, *CV*, 9; *CC*, 1). If we trace the term back to its origin in Latin, he notes, "*quodlibet*" actually denoted "being such that it is always important" ("*l'essere tale che comunque importa*") (modified, *CV*, 9; *CC*, 1).[23] The key term in this sentence is "important" (*importare*), which is translated as "matter" in the English text. An etymological dictionary helps to explain the significance of this term for Agamben. The *portus* was not just passageway, door, or entrance (*poros*) where any and all things from the outside were brought in (imported), because it was also a place of asylum (**per-*) where someone or something was granted safe passage (portal). It is an inviolable place that provides refuge from the right of seizure and judgment. Thus, the *portus* is not an indifferent and porous passageway without the capacity to let things pass; rather, the *portus* must be an empowered protectorate, which is capable both of letting in and protecting that which has been let in. This sense is present in the specific way he uses this term, but at this stage of his project the "how" is largely missing.

"Whatever being" is important because it matters just as it is, or in his terms, "as such" (*come tale*) and without predicates. In his later works, "whatever being" is translated into form-of-life, which is a life that is its *how* versus its *what*. "Whatever being" is an existential way of being-thus that exists in a brief sabbatical from the law, operative logic, and presuppositional identification, where one can be (*essere*), as he claims in *Opus Dei*, how one is without having-to-be (*dovere-essere*) anything else. In *The Coming Community*, even the essays collected in *Potentialities* and *Means Without End*, however, Agamben's resistance to making political prescriptions or even to describing potentially empowering modalities—such as in his more recently developed term "destituent power"—leave one wondering how "whatever being" can even be realized in anything but a fleeting and peripheral manner. Moreover, given that his exemplary alternative forms of life are found living in the most abject conditions, either imposed by external or internal mechanisms (Roma people or ascetics), and that the key texts he draws from are eschatological and messianic, many wonder if his work should be taken seriously. The two additional senses he emphasizes in "whatever," which I will now examine, have not helped his case.

In addition to its reference to the "will" (*libet*), he notes, *quodlibet* "has an original relation to desire" (*CV*, 9; *CC*, 1). Love is the quintessential experience of whateverness: "The lover wants the loved one *with all of its predicates*, its being such as it is" (*CV*, 10; *CC*, 2). To love someone, in other words, is to love them without presuppositions and thus prejudices. Etymological dictionaries show that the term means "what you will, what you please." It is a combination of *quod* (what), which is the neuter of *qui* (what), and *libere* (to please). If one approaches the other in the manner of the "whatever," then one is more open to the other's alterity. This is a manner of relating to the other where one is a position of ease, because one is relaxed and loose, and thus nonjudgmental. He is referring to a liberated and freed sense of love and desire, but unfortunately, to be at ease is also be in an extremely passive, languished position. One not only lacks vitality (slack and weak)—*homo sacer* and the *passion* of Christ—but they are also without spirit and wit—the *Muselmann* (*RA*) and Gaunilo's "idiot" (*PI*, *PE*).

He also plays with the humorous sense of *quodlibet*. The term was coined during the Renaissance. Composers would combine popular tunes or melodies into a song for comical effects. The end result would be a mélange or potpourri that, while familiar, would be starkly different from the originals. Because the references were familiar and popular, the listeners would be drawn in, but soon the unfamiliar mixing would amuse and capture them. The humorous qualities of the *quodlibet* were also used to great effect later in music and poetry, when authors would take to mixing several quotes. Benjamin stands here as a primary reference. Agamben's style of prose in this text refers precisely to the *quodlibet*. Making the familiar unfamiliar or strange was also a tactic the Situationists employed, drawing heavily from Dadaism and Surrealism, and one used often by existentialists and cultural Marxists such as Brecht. "Tricksters or fakes, assistants or 'toons,'" Agamben claims in an unforgettable line, "they are the exemplars of the coming community" (*CV*, 14; *CC*, 10–11). That is, when the proper is rendered improper and the improper proper, we can no longer distinguish between the normal and the abnormal.

Agamben is not the only author in this series of books on community, which includes many different works beyond the three main philosophers, to conceive of community through the alterity of the other. Besides Blanchot's better-known work, American philosopher Alphonso Lingis turned to the problem of alterity to conceive of community beyond ethnicity and nation (1994). His community of "those who have nothing in common," however, reads more like a travel journal written by a naïve Westerner tantalized by all the "foreign" traditions and people he meets in his search for interactions without common linguistic frameworks, symbols, manners, morals—that is, a community without presuppositions. While not quite at the level of poverty porn or slum tourism, his tone, personal narrative, and inability to acknowledge his own privileged position make this text read more like yet another exotic account of the Orient. What really matters in his text is what happens to the self when exposed to the Other. This is, in short, not a reciprocal relationship.

Agamben's approach is different. He searches for radically new modes of being exemplified by those that are included, but only by being excluded, that is, differential inclusion. This is a vastly different political position than the one found in Lingis's simple cosmopolitan ethos of cultural difference. Yet one still has to ask if Agamben remains too married, especially at this point in his project, to the jargon of authenticity. This is a relevant question for the works I have covered this far. Recalling Campbell's *Improper Life*, it must also be asked of the early installments of the *Homo Sacer* series that focus on the biopolitical distinction between *bíos* and *zoē*. When all of these texts are considered together, it would be hard to make the case that his ideal community represents anything other than a celebration of, recalling Balibar, abysmal alienation.

A community based on alienated identities is a community built on the unstable grounds of insecurity, notes Bauman in his contribution to this debate *Community: Seeking Safety in an Insecure World*. In such "multicommunitarian" models of community, "cultural differences are used as building materials in the frenzied construction of defensive walls and missile launching pads," and culture itself "becomes a synonym for a besieged fortress" (2001, 141). Without social justice, in other words, there is no community. "Tricksters or fakes, assistants or 'toons'" may be a source of entertainment, of an inoperative and incomprehensible form of humorous being, but "sooner or later," as

Agamben admits, "the tanks will appear" (*CV*, 69; *CC*, 87). Serious circumstances require serious solutions; otherwise laughter quickly turns into ridicule and violence. There must be an empowered protectorate that even if it is not taking, seizing, judging, and appropriating, can, at the very minimum, enforce the letting in and the letting be in such a way that it can occur inviolably. For Nancy, this was the role of weak politics. Agamben's reluctance to prescribe an ethics or politics to support his ontological ethos, at least at this stage, leaves his theory supported by nothing other than exigencies. Only in the past decade has Agamben started to seriously address this problem in his texts on economic theology. In these texts we also find the dispositif of the proper coming to the fore, whereas earlier it was understated and often muted by his focus on authenticity.

## PART 3. THE *HOMO SACER* SERIES

There are really two strains in this series. The first three books, *Homo Sacer*, *The State of Exception*, and *Remnants of Auschwitz*, focus on the question of sovereignty. The problem of the proper/improper, as Campbell has shown, remains an important issue in these texts; however, it is only in his subsequent writings where he really starts to examine how the dispositif of the proper dominates the ontological. Starting with his genealogical study of government, *The Kingdom and the Glory*, Agamben has turned his attention to the paradigm of economic theology. Agamben strives to expose and render inoperative this paradigm to conceive of an inoperative and modal ontology where form-of-life is free to exist without presuppositions; that is, a liberated ontological ethos.

It is beyond the purview of this chapter to enter into the minute details of his wide-ranging studies of economic theology. It is also beyond my expertise to enter into scholarly issues regarding how comprehensive, representative, and even accurate are many of the theological sources he employs in this research. Instead, I extrapolate a handful of themes that are relevant for the purposes of this chapter. In the following, I trace this problematic across several texts in this series.[24] I have also integrated three texts, although not officially part of the series, that are helpful for understanding the general problematic in his recent work because he is more forthcoming in them.[25]

## VI. Economic Theology and Political Economy

Starting with *The Kingdom and the Glory*, Agamben has sought to lay bare the theological foundations of the governmental paradigm of modern political economy. Aside from his messianic and Benjaminian prescriptions, this project can be read as an attempt to combine Foucault's paradigm of governmentality with Heidegger's critique of modern ontology. He does this by tracing the genealogies of governmentality and modern ontology back to their fundamental formulation in the Christian "Trinitarian *oikonomia*." To salvage the monotheistic doctrine of a single, divine being, the early Church Fathers developed the doctrine of the divine economy in the Trinity. They distinguished between the divine substance of God in all three persons (*parousia*) on the ontological level, and the tripling of God's *oikonomia* on the level of praxis or the government of the world. This ultimately led to a split in the classical ontological doctrine between "God and his action, between ontology and praxis" (*RG*, 69; *KG*, 53), which has given rise to two separate and incommensurable paradigms that have come to define the history of the West.

In *Opus Dei*, he returns to these paradigms and uses them to establish new parameters for rethinking ethics. In this text he also reasserts the Heideggerian roots of his claim. He argues that Western ontology is dominated by an operative and practical paradigm that subordinates being to praxis. In classical ontology, "being and substance are considered independently of the effects that they can produce" (*ODI*, 55; *ODE*, 41), a "being is what it is." In the practical ontology of the West, however, being is measured according to its praxis, "being is what it does, is its operativity itself" (*ODI*, 58; *ODE*, 44). In terms of Heidegger, he argues that "one cannot understand the metaphysics of technology" if it is only understood "in the form of production" because "[i]t is just as much and above all governance and *oikonomia*," which is "a form of management of human beings and of thing" (*ODI*, 76; *ODE*, 61).

In *The Kingdom and the Glory*, he argues, contra Foucault, that the paradigm of governmentality, which distinguishes between God's sovereignty and government of the world, must be traced well beyond the secular movements in the sixteenth century back to the idea of providence (*RG*, 127; *KG*, 111). Theologians and philosophers turned to providence to reconcile the splitting of classical ontology in the

Trinity. The "providential machine" was articulated across "two separate realities: being and praxis, transcendent and immanent good, theology and *oikonomia*" (*RG*, 157; *KG*, 140). Political theology comes to represent "the transcendence of sovereign power on the single God" (*RG*, 13; *KG*, 1). It belongs to the "political-statal" paradigm (*RG*, 82; *KG*, 66). Contrary to Schmitt, Agamben argues that Christian theology is an "economic-managerial" paradigm (*RG*, 82; *KG*, 66). Economic theology "replaces this transcendence with the idea of an *oiknonmia*, conceived of an immanent ordering—domestic and not political in a strict sense—of both divine and human life" (*RG*, 13; *KG*, 1). In the providential machine, the "two levels are strictly entwined, so that the first founds, legitimates, and makes possible the second," but "the second concretely puts into practice" or executes the orders and decisions of the first (*RG*, 158; *KG*, 141). The sovereign paradigm is the subject of political philosophy, while the second economic-governmental, or impolitical, paradigm is one of biopolitics.[26]

Modern biopolitics represents the "complete triumph of economy and government over every other aspect of social life" (*RG*, 13; *KG*, 1).[27] It is genuinely an administrative and governmental paradigm that is impolitical or postpolitical, which has gradually usurped the paradigm of sovereignty. To make matters worse, the governmental machine is supported by the modern effective, operative, or practical ontological paradigm—he uses many different descriptors—that completely separates being from acting, doing, operating, performing, and so on. Today praxis occurs in complete anarchy without any foundations in being. It would thus be a mistake to continue to turn to the theological-political paradigm for solutions because the "*central mystery*" of biopolitics is "*government*," "*the governmental machine*" (*RG*,303; *KG*, 276–77). Today, this economic paradigm has completely replaced "classical ontology."

In a recently published essay, "Stasis," he summarizes this problematic through an examination of *stasis* (civil war).[28] For the ancient Greeks *stasis* marked the "zone of indifference between the impolitical space of the family and the political space of the city" (*ST*, 24). *Stasis* operates in an "analogical manner" to the state of exception—"*zōē*, natural life, is included in the juridical-political order through its exclusion"—because in "the *stasis* the *oikos* is politicized and included in the *polis*" (*ST*, 30). Politics (*la politica*), he claims, represents a battlefield or field of forces (*campo di forze*) between the *oikos* and the *polis*, where "the political is economized" or "depoliticized," and the economic (or impolitical) is politicized. According to the ancient Greeks, politics were tasked with maintaining a "precarious equilibrium" between the division of the *oikos* and the *polis*. Periodically, a *stasis* was necessary to re-establish the equilibrium between them, such that the political could be repoliticized and the economic depoliticized. With the gradual ascension of the economic-theological paradigm, however, today our impolitical or biopolitical era is defined by a perpetual state of civil war. When governments are concerned with managing life and the economy, all forms of civil conflict, whether intra- or inter-national, are present in the "figure of terror" (*ST*, 32). Thus, despite the goal of modern theories of the political, starting with Hobbes, who sought to reverse the classical Greek "necessity of civil war," contemporary politics affirm this necessity, only now it is beyond our capacity to regulate and manage. The global political economy only exacerbates this problem.

Agamben continues to focus on the problem of language and absolution in his writings on economic theology. He now employs an "archaeological method," which he uses to expose and render inoperative presuppositional thought by performing an "archaeological *epoché* that suspends, at least provisionally, the attribution of predicates" (*SLI*, 24; *SLE*, 17). This method is grounded in the core problem of his current philosophy: the economic-theological *dispositivo* (translated as "apparatus" in English, but it could also be translated as "dispositif"). Across many writings, he addresses various ramifications that have arisen from the Church Fathers' unfortunate decision to translate *oikonomia* as *dispositio*. It also enables him to continue to make a play on the distinction between exposition and disposition, both from *ponere* (to put, place), such as is found in the operation of positive law (*CCD*, 19–20; *WA*, 12). Recalling the introduction to this book, Agamben defines a dispositif as "anything that has in some way the capacity to capture, orient, determine, intercept, model, control, or secure the gestures, behaviors, opinions, or discourses of living beings" (modified, *CCD*, 21–22; *WA*, 14). Today, he argues, beings are divided into two groups: "living beings (substances)" and "dispositifs" (modified *CCD*, 21; *WA*, 13). Our struggle today rests in "the relentless fight" between living beings and dispositifs. Dispositifs, he contends, cannot be captured from within. Their instruments are beyond correction and subversion. Rather, they must be exposed and rendered inoperative. Only then can we liberate all that has been captured and appropriated by dispositifs and open up the possibility for a free, new, or common use as well as a form-of-life that exists in a modal or relational ontology.

In *The Open* Agamben weaves his project through the Heideggerian problem of the closure of being caused by humanism and the core modalities of taking and letting. The "anthropological machine," he argues, "articulates nature and man in order to produce the human through the suspension and capture of the inhuman" (*LO*, 85; *TO*, 83), which today distinguishes between the real and fully human and the animalized human or bare life (*LO*, 43; *TO*, 38). Against the captivation (*Benommenheit*), absorption (*eigenommen*), and behavior (*Benehmen*) of the impoverished animal that lacks a world (*LO*, 55; *TO*, 52), or the everyday occupation of the human who remains captivated by and in things and seeks to appropriate them for herself (*LO*, 67; *TO*, 64), Heidegger searched for a modality that would expose and open the human to its animality. But Heidegger's fixation on the proper (*Eigen*) left us with two possibilities in this exposure. Either humanity can continue to try to appropriate and master its animality, or humanity can abandon itself to its animality and thus make it proper to itself (*LO*, 82; *TO*, 80). Put differently, either the technological human makes the improper proper or the romanticized "man, the shepherd of being" abandons its proper self to its impropriety. Neither solution (*solvere*, **se-luo*) is satisfactory. If "letting be" (*lasciar essere*) is the "supreme category of Heidegger's ontology," this formulation must be corrected. He turns to two familiar sources to find an alternative solution. First, Agamben employs Benjamin's concept of the "dialectic at a standstill" to render the machine inoperative, "stopped" "at a standstill," which opens up the "interval" or the "play between two terms" (*LO*, 83–86; *TO*, 81–84). Second, from the Gnostics, he argues that the passageway requires a "zone of nonknowledge," of "ignorance," which does not just "let something be," but "lets it be outside of being" as the "unsaveable" (*LO*, 93; *TO*, 91). To genuinely abandon the human-animal dialectic, in other words, we must let the animal and the human be, being-thus we might say, absolutely and unconditionally. This modality of "existing" (*esistente*) is "beyond the [ontological] difference between being and beings" (*essere ed ente*) (*LO*, 94; *TO*, 92). The result is neither a "new creation" nor a "more effective," "more authentic" human. Our task, he claims, is "to show the central emptiness, the hiatus that—within man—separates man and animal, and to risk ourselves in this emptiness: the suspension of the suspension, Shabbat of both animal and man" (ibid.).

## VII. Language and Ethics

In *The Sacrament of Language*, Agamben returns to the relationship between the *factum loquendi* (the fact of speaking beings) and ethics. Through an archaeological investigation of the institution of the oath, which "suspends" the "predicates" often attributed to "religion and law," he searches for a nonpredicated ethos in the event of language. Agamben is critical of the religious and legal characterizations of the oath on the grounds that each draws from the cognitive model of truth as an *adequatio* between words and things, facts, or actions. Both view the oath as an assertion (*asserzione*), which, in the same manner as the apophantic and predicative modality of the dispositif, gathers words and things together by joining, arranging, or attaching them to in a series or sequence (*asserere*). Truth is thus rendered "independent of the subject and is measured with logical and objective parameters" (*SLI*, 78; *SLE*, 57). But the split between word and thing creates a space where it is possible to transgress the relationship, to perjure or to lie. Religion and law thus arose as the protectorates of this division who secure the truth by punishing all inadequate transgressions. "Religion and law," he contends, "do not pre-exist the performative experience of language that is in question of the oath, but rather they were invented to guarantee the truth and trustworthiness of the *logos* through a series of apparatuses [*dispositivi*], among which the technicization of the oath into a specific 'sacrament'—the 'sacrament of power'—occupies a central place" (*SLI*, 80; *SLE*, 59). The curse represents nothing less than the punishment of perjury that befalls one who advocates and maintains an inadequate relationship between words and things, facts or actions (*SLI*, 49–50; *SLE*, 36). Prior the political-legal curse attributed to the *sacer* (bare life), however, the oath represented an "original *sacratio*," the "*sacrament of language*" "of the living human being through the word to the word" (*SLI*, 90; *SLE* 66). The oath is "a sacramental bond or obligation [*vincolo*] that links the human being to language" (*SLI*, 98; *SLE*, 72). It is the very "signifying power of language," to name and thus unify words and things, which is the "positive force of language" or the *logos* (*SLI*, 44–51; *SLE*, 32–37). This sacrament must also be exposed. Contrary to the "cognitive paradigm" of *Homo sapiens*, he argues, we must disrupt the relationship between law and the curse to "make possible another use of speech and the law" (*SLI*, 90–93; *SLE*, 66–68). The human word, in short, should not be consecrated but profaned.

Contrary to the sacramental function of the oath, its real function, he argues following Foucault, is "veridiction" (*veridizione*). Language and intelligence "above all pose problems of an ethical and political order," of the *Homo iustus* (the just human) and of its "*ethos*" (*SLI*, 93; *SLE*, 68). A veridication is not an objective truth linking the word and thing, but a truth that depends on the worldview of a subject. Its "sole criterion of its performative efficacy" is in its "relationship to the subject who pronounces it" (*SLI*, 78; *SLE*, 57). In an oath, one must "performatively affirm the trust and trustworthiness" of one's speech (*SLI*, 89; *SLE*, 65). The oath, he contends, demands that the "speaking animal [put] its nature at stake in language and to bind together in an ethical and political connection words, things and actions" (*SLI*, 95; *SLE*, 69). In such an act, "the subject constitutes itself and puts itself in play as such by linking itself performatively to the truth of its proper [*propria*] affirmation" (modified, *SLI*, 78; *SLE*, 57). The speaking being's problem therefore is not the "inadequation" (*inadequazione*) between names and things, but the "efficacy [*efficacia*] and truthfulness of his word" and thus of the speaking subject who is "capable of asserting and promising" his word through "his actions" (*SLI*, 92–93; *SLE*, 68). In subsequent texts, as I show below, he returns to the problem of the efficacy of actions in his critique of modern deontological ethics.

Agamben, once again, finds solace in the thesis of the Situationists. The society of the spectacle has broken the ethical connection that "unites words, things, and human actions" (*SLI*, 96; *SLE*, 70–71). In the "age of the eclipse [*eclissi*] of the oath"—*ekleipsis* (a leaving, abandonment, forsaking, or to leave/let out, *ek-leipein*)—new openings emerge for rethinking the relationship between the speaking being and its language. On the one side rests the accursed bare life that is reduced to its simple biological reality; on the other, recalling the petite bourgeoisie, stand the impolitical beings who are subjected to so many dispositifs that they speak nothing but "vain" (empty, void, worthless) words for which they can no longer claim any form of responsibility. Although the paradigm of language as a tool has been rendered inoperative in our world, this has also helped to isolate and disclose what is actually decisive in language: "in the place it leaves for the speaker." Recalling the event of language, he claims that language "prepares within itself a hollowed-out form that the speaker must always assume in order to speak," which establishes an "ethical relation between the speaker and his language" (*SLI*, 97; *SLE*, 71). In speaking, the human is presented with the opportunity to "*take the word, assume it and make it his own*" (*SLI*, 97; *SLE*, 71). This is an "*ethos*" where the subject is implicated "in his word," in the "concrete act of discourse," "the human being must put himself at stake." This implication, however, only occurs in the modality of explication, an exposition without presupposition, and, of course, an exposure that disrupts the dispositif. As with the modality of being-thus, putting oneself at stake is to abandon oneself. But, the question remains, how is this *ethos* an ethics proper, because this modality does nothing more than prepare the subject for the possibility of entering into ethical relationships, which he still has not prescribed? He says little concerning the relationship between individuals in this modality. At best it concerns the relationship between a subject and its word.

## VIII. Priests and Monks

Agamben comes closer to addressing the connection between an ontological ethos and ethics, as well as how this formulation relates to the dispositif of the proper, in *Opus Dei: An Archaeology of Duty* and *The Highest Poverty: Monastic Rules and Form-of-Life*. In these texts Agamben returns to the "ethical connection" (*nesso etico*), which he now articulates in terms of "the subject and his action" (*ODI*, 38; *ODE*, 25) instead of between the "speaker and his language" (*SLI*, 97; *SLE*, 71). He argues that if we are to find a genuinely ontological ethos or way of being, then it is necessary to sever the connection between ethics and actions in order to focus on the relationship between ethos and habitus. In these texts, he uses the figures of the priest and the monk to demonstrate the difference between these two configurations. The priest is a mere instrument of the operative and effective ontology that dominates Western economic theology, while the monk presents an alternative ethos qua form of life that is almost ontological, beyond the law, inoperative, and ineffectual. The impoverished lifestyle of the monk provides glimpses of how the ontological ethos can be conceived beyond the dialectic of alienation and appropriation itself. In this section, I begin with an examination of the priest and end with the monk.[29]

*Opus Dei* represents a systematic critique of deontological ethics. Agamben argues that this system of ethics in the West gained traction in the early formulations of economic theology, which created a schism between the subject and its actions. He traces this problematic through the "paradigm of office or duty" (*paradigma che l'ufficio*). In this paradigm, "being and praxis, what a human does and what a human is, enter into a zone of indistinction, in which being dissolves into its practical effects . . . it is what it has to be and has to be what it is" (*è ciò che deve (essere) e deve (essere) ciò che è*) (*ODI*, 9; *ODE*, *xii*). This paradigm "has changed, from top to bottom the rules of first philosophy as much as those of ethics" (*ODI*, 9; *ODE*, *xiii*). In it, being (*essere*) is subordinated to having-to-be (*dovere-essere*). It is a paradigm, he argues, that is driven by "operativeness" and "effectiveness"; "[o]nly what is effective and as such governable and efficacious, is real."

In early Church liturgy, the effective reality of the sacrament had to be protected from subjective qualities of the person performing the office (*ex opera operato*). By elevating the *opus operatum* (validity and effectiveness of actions) of the priest at the expense of his *opus operans* (moral and physical qualities of the agent), the priest was transformed into an animate instrument that merely performs a function. This formulation, which "conceive[s] of human actions as an *officium*" (*ODI*, 106; *ODE*, 91), disrupted the ethical connection between the subject and his action, such that "what is determinative is no longer the right intention [or moral character] of the agent but only the function that his action carries out as *opus Dei*" (*ODI*, 38; *ODE*, 25). In *The Highest Poverty*, he argues that this legal dispositif converts the "life of the priest" into an *officium*, whose being is defined not by his actions, but by his office alone, by what he does, not by what he is.

To sever the connection between ethics and action, Agamben appeals to his longstanding interpretation of Aristotle's theory of impotentiality. In *Opus Dei* he uses this theory to rethink the connection between habit and action. For Aristotle, he argues, habits "render possible, regulate, and operate the passage from" potential to action (*ODI*, 108; *ODE*, 93). "Habit is . . . the mode in which a being . . . 'has' a potential to know and act," and as such it is "the point where being crosses over into having"

(*ODI*, 109; *ODE*, 93–94). But, once again, one only has a potential in relation to its "privation" (*adynamia*, impotentiality). Contrary to the liturgical model, Aristotle's model requires the potentiality to "not exercise," to "not us[e]" one's potentiality, to ensure that one does not lose oneself in one's actions (*ODI*, 110; *ODE*, 94). *Habit is inoperative.* Unfortunately, Aristotle did not stop here. He enlisted virtues to govern the inoperative, privative, and impotential aspects of habits. Virtue is a type of habit that "renders it capable of passing into action and of acting in the best way" (*ODI*, 111; *ODE*, 96). It is here that Aristotle combines being and action (the ontological and the practical). One's "moral character" in this model is defined by the training needed to transform a virtuous act into a customary one.

The *officium-effectus* model of liturgical action duplicated and strengthened the operative ontology of Aristotle's potential-act model. By the time of Aquinas, the aporetic relationship between habit and inoperativeness was all but forgotten, because habit was firmly based in the will. Will served as the "passage from potency to efficacy" (*ODI*, 147; *ODE*, 128). From this point forward, the relationship between virtue and duty could be articulated. In a subtle manner, Agamben uses this analysis to emphasize how this liturgical formulation of debt conceives of de-having in a negative fashion (*debere*, *de-habere*). Religion, for Aquinas, consisted in "rendering to God the honor that is owed [*dovuto*]," a debt (*ODI*, 118; *ODE*, 102). He formulated, "for the first time" a pre-Kantian "duty of virtue" (*ODI*, 118–19; *ODE*, 102–3). But in the ontology of command, the "sole object" of virtue is "*debitum*." Here one's being "coincides totally with a having to be, virtue and *officium* coincide without remainder." *Dovere-essere* thus is intricately linked to the operative ontology. "In the idea of a being that is totally dissolved into a debt, into a having to be, law and religion necessarily coincide" (*ODI*, 122; *ODE*, 106).

Modern deontological ethics represents the pinnacle of the having-to-be, of the ontology of command and operativity. In addition to his re-centering of the subject, Kant's "'Copernican revolution'" firmly entrenched the ontology of command by secularizing the "liturgical tradition of *officium* and operativity" (*ODI*, 140; *ODE*, 122). Whether it be the subjective respect for the law or the objective constraint of the law, Kant's deontological subject only carries out its actions in relation to the law. "The problem of the coming philosophy," he claims in the last line of the text, "is that of thinking an ontology beyond operativity [putting-to-work] and command [having-to-be]," while ethics and politics must be "entirely liberated from the concepts of duty and will" (*ODI*, 147; *ODE*, 129).

In *The Highest Poverty* Agamben counters the priestly office with the monastic form of life. This work could be read as one his most prescriptive texts to date, especially in the *Homo Sacer* series.[30] He argues that "the most demanding legacy of monasticism" is its alternative way of conceiving of "human action": in place of "sphere of action" and "practice," monasticism shifts its emphasis to the sphere of "form of life and life" (modified, *AP*, 80; *HP*, 61). He turns to the early Fransciscans as an exemplary case where the central experience of monasticism is life, rather than doctrine and law (*AP*, 9; *HP*, xiii). Their legacy, he contends, leaves us with the "undeferrable task": "how to think a form-of-life, a human life entirely removed from the grasp of the law and a use of bodies and of the world that would never be substantiated into an appropriation. . . . [t]o think life as that which is never given as property, but only as common use" (*AP*, 9–10; *HP*, *xiii*). In the remainder of this section I focus on the two dimensions of this imperative. First, I examine the relationship between form-of-life and law. Second, I turn to his efforts to rethink use beyond the dispositif of the proper, at least in its political-economic inflection. Both lines are grounded in his theory of *habitus*.

What is interesting about this text is that Agamben comes close to articulating the possibility of community. In fact, in his largely positive evaluation of asceticism, which carves out an alternative relationship between form and life beyond the law and a theory of use beyond property, he underlines the communal dimension of this particular ethos. Of the various types of monastic orders, Agamben focuses on the cenobites, who despite the "monastic ideal, born as an individual and solitary flight from the world"—that is, *monos-terion* and *eremites*—gave rise "to a model of total communitarian life" (*AP*, 19; *HP*, 9). Cenoby derives from *koinobion*, which is above all else a life lived in common (*koinos bios*) (*AP*, 16; *HP*, 6). Contrary to the privative model, their common life is defined, in the Book of Acts, as a life without "'private ownership of any possessions'" because "'everything they owned was held in common'" (*AP*, 20–21; *HP*, 10).

One of the decisive features of cenobitic monasticism is the notion of "communal habitation." Contrary to the ancient Greek notion of habit, recalling Aristotle's theory of habits that links habit to the "way of acting or being" (*modo di essere o di agire*) and became "synonymous with virtues," the cenobites view habit as a "way of life" (*modo di vita*) (*AP*, 24; *HP*, 13). How they dress is intricately linked to how they are supposed to conduct themselves (*atteggiarsi*). This link between dress and conduct has an expository dimension to it. It puts forth, reveals, and exposes (he employs the Italian term "*esporre*" and the Latin "*exponere*") the "interior way of being," such that the attention paid to the "care of the body" (*la cura del corpo*) is turned toward the *morum formula* "'example of a way of life'" (*AP*, 25; *HP*, 14). "To inhabit together" (*abitare insieme*), he claims, monks had "to share" (*condividere*) a *habitus*, which was more than a "place or style of dress." The cenobites, in short, "attempt to make habit and form-of-life coincide in an absolute and total *habitus*"[31] (*AP*, 27; *HP*, 16).

Agamben praises the Franciscan "cenobitic project" for shifting the "ethical problem from the relation between norm and action to that of form of life" (*AP*, 92; *HP*, 72). In their habitus, life and form become so intertwined that their form of life can no longer be read as a "rule" or a "code of norms and precepts" (*AP*, 125; *HP*, 99); rather the dichotomy between life and rule "enter into a zone of indifference" (*AP*, 92; *HP*, 71). There is a concordance between form and life, where "*living* according to that form, that is of a life that, in its sequence, makes itself the very form," which is an entirely different relation than "applying a form (or norm) to life" (*AP*, 124; *HP*, 99). Thus, the form is not determinative of the relationship as it would be in an *assertion*, which applies a general rule and is measured according to the *adequatio*. In its most perfect expression, it is an exemplary *form-of-life* (*forma-di-vita*).[32] For the Franciscans, form of life is neither a "normative system" nor a "corpus of a doctrine"; rather it is an "exemplary" "conduct" or a "way of life," as in the form-of-life exemplified by Christ (*AP*, 129–30; *HP*, 103–4). The Franciscan form of life distinguished their ethos from the political and juridical model of the liturgical *officium*. Unlike the animate instrument that the liturgical priest represents, whose being is reduced to what he does, whose end is reached in his work (*artes in effectu*), and thus whose actions are measured by their effectiveness (*opus operatum*), the ideal monk is a being whose being is what it is, whose actions are simply ends in themselves (*artes actuosae*), and thus his actions are judged by the moral and physical qualities he possesses (*opus operans*). That said, Agamben is also at pains to demonstrate that this form of life is not configured in a contrarian manner. It is not configured in opposition to the model of the *officium*, such as in an anticlerical model, because it is a form of life that is "radically extraneous [*estraneità*] to law and liturgy" (*AP*, 148; *HP*, 121). To oppose (*opponere*, *ob* + *ponere*) the Church, in other words, would be to enter into its terrain and thus its terms. This would take the form of an antagonistic movement that would seek both to vindicate itself and to establish a new and "true Church." As such, oppositional power merely challenges the dispositif by establishing a new one, which, in the end, challenges nothing because it is a constituent form of power. The Franciscans, on the other hand, represent a destituent form of power. If their form of life is to remain pure, it must be formulated as completely indifferent—in the sense of the "whatever" or *qualunque*—to the liturgical *officium*.

The Franciscans sought to "*realize a human life and practice absolutely outside the determination of the law*" (*AP*, 109; *HP*, 110). This is evident in their notion of "common use" [*uso commune*]. They sought to conceive of the "use of goods without having any right to them (neither of property nor of use)" (*AP*, 136; *HP*, 110). However, it is on this front where the purity of the Franciscan doctrine ran into problems. In the heat of the conflict with the liturgy, property was considered to originate through either conquest or positive law. Both relied on a division between natural and human law. So the Franciscans sought to renounce human law and property rights (*abdicatio iuris*) by promoting a notion of the natural law where people were free to use things without staking ownership over them. William of Ockham, for example, argued that in the extreme case of necessity, people have a natural right to use things despite not having a positive right to own them. For Agamben, this represents an "absolutization of the state of exception," where the "exception becomes for them a form of life" (*AP*, 141–42; *HP*, 115). At the same time, their renunciations were contaminated by the law. Not only were they concocted as counterclaims to Church doctrines, they drew heavily from juridical language.

Instead, they should have concentrated on the relationship between use and habitus. Since habitus was conceived as a nonoppositional form of life, use itself "could have been configured as a *tertium* [third] with respect to law and life, potential and act," and thus it could have been used to define "the monks' vital practice itself, their form-of-life" (*AP*, 172; *HP*, 140–41). Instead of conceiving of use as "the pure and simple renunciation of the law," use could be conceived as "that which establishes this renunciation as a form and as a mode of life [*modo di vita*]" (*AP*, 173; *HP*, 142). In a destituent manner, he claims that this renunciative "form of life" does not establish a "new doctrine," as in constituting a new power, because it is expressed in "eschatological terms": "the final *modus*" (*AP*, 175; *HP*, 143)."The 'highest poverty,' with its use of things, is the form-of-life that begins when all the West's forms of life have reached their historical consummation" (ibid.).

The Franciscan doctrine of use, claims Agamben, is a model where "life could be affirmed unreservedly as that existence which is situated outside of the law" (*AP*, 177; *HP*, 144). If life is to be affirmed at all, it must occur outside of the law and thus beyond the biopolitical apparatuses. Our task is to conceive of a form-of-life that exists "outside the law" and of how to use things without appropriating them. Use must be entirely reconceived so that it is no longer defined, even if negatively, in relation to ownership. Use must be "translated into an ethos and a form of life" (*AP*, 178; *HP*, 144). These, finally, must be conceived in an inoperative manner.

## IX. Destituent Power

In the introduction I stated that the task-at-hand for a coming politics is to realize the improperness as that which is most proper, our proper impropriety. From his early writings on the philosophy of language, where he sought to think through the *experimentum linguae* that challenges presuppositional thought in order to reconceptualize politics as a sphere of pure means, the common as free to use, and impotentiality as the power to not-be, to the open ethos of being-thus, the free use of the self, and the whateverness of the coming community, up to his formulations on the operative and effective ontology of modern economic theology, his entire body of work has been formulated as a unconditional critique of practical ontology. Many of his solutions appear to be merely speculative or intellectualist, especially in the various affirmative examples he uses to describe an inoperative modality (*skholē*, *Shabbat*, asceticism, contemplative life). We might say, following Pierre Bourdieu, that his ideal disposition is an idealistic one that is only rendered possible through a "scholastic enclosure" (2000). After each publication in the *Homo Sacer* series, Negri has repeatedly pointed out that Agamben's "radicalized nihilism" is utterly impractical (2012). Not everyone can be an ascetic or have the luxurious lifestyle of an aristocrat. Who will do the work necessary to provide for such a "messianic banquet" if the dialectic between "man" and "animal" in the "anthropological machine" is left at a "standstill"?

At times, it appears as if Agamben's heavy-handed critique of political prescriptions leaves him with no room to maneuver. But it is precisely at this point where we have to backtrack, because the formulation of a "task-at-hand" points to an aporia in his work. Agamben is categorically opposed to any imperative that derives from the economic theology. To assign or assert a task to the coming politics is to translate his lifelong search for an unprescriptive *ethos*, now articulated in a form-of-life and his inoperative notion of common use, to the ontology of command of having-to-be and the operative ontology of putting-to-work. In one sense, this is a similar position to Nancy's critique of productive, operative, or more recently eco-technological, political prescriptions, as both are critical of the question "what is to be done?" However, Agamben carries this critique into the realm of ethics, especially in relation to deontological ethics. If there were a proper task-at-hand, it would be an assigned duty or tax (*tasca*). If there is a work, job, or task that must be accomplished (*se c'è un'opera deve essere compiuta*) that is at-hand, the only real thing to do would be to let it go, to dis-contain, because being should never be predicated. So in an answer to the question of what to do, Agamben can really only say nothing at all. Nothing should be done.

Agamben's call for a radical ethos represents a nuanced account of the liberating power of the revolt itself. His recent use of the "destituent power" (*potenza desituente*) helps to clarify this position. In the lecture "What Is Destituent Power?" Agamben uses this notion to provide a gloss of his work over the last three decades. He claims that destituent power articulates the "two fundamental concepts of [his] politics" inoperativeness and use. Destituent power, for example, opens up the possibility of thinking of the "essential inoperativity of man," not "as the cessation of all activity, but as an activity that consists in making human works and productions inoperative, opening them to a new possible use" (*DP*, 69). This is a new radical thought that fundamentally challenges the primacy of "production" and "labor" that is found on the Left. It is not a "suspension of labor," but a "temporary suspension of productive activity," such as in the feast or the Shabbat. Neither are defined by what is *not* done, but by how the "what is done" is "undone, is rendered inoperative, liberated and suspended from its 'economy'" (*DP*, 69). Revolutions and insurrections, he claims, belong to the model of power as constituting-constituted, which "destroys and always creates new forms" (*DP*, 71). His theory is more in line with the "anarchist tradition and twentieth-century thought" (*DP*, 72). His two main examples of a destituent power come from Pauline and Bejaminian messianism. Pauline messianism, for example, is a "form-of-life" that "unrelentingly deposes the social conditions . . . without negating them, but simply using them" (*DP*, 71–72).

It "will not be possible," he argues, "to think another dimension of life if we have not first managed to deactivate the dispositif of the exception of bare life" (*DP*, 66). Agamben claims that it is not possible to directly access the *dispositif of the exception*, the inclusive exclusion of bare life (*DP*, 72). If politics are to be inoperative and destituent, a philosopher can only (or should only) strive to exhibit and expose the form through which the arche of power operates. Such work was carried out in his *Homo Sacer* series. Bare life is a life that has been captured, excluded, and included as a *what*. To seize, even to oppose and de-constitute, this arche, he argues, would give rise to a reconstitution of the arche. Thus, the sole political task available for Agamben is to exhibit, to lay bare, and expose the dispositif of the exception. Such a task can open up new possibilities for a truly modal ontology. This would be a modal ontology, an ontological ethos, where "*my form-of-life relates not to what I am, but to how I am what I am*" (*DP*, 73). Form-of-life, he claims, is "a life that can never be separated from its form, a life in which it is never possible to isolate something like a bare life," which is "a life for which, in its way of living, what is at stake is living itself" (ibid.). The "habitual use," recalling the monk and Aristotle, "deactivates operativity in form-of-life." The stake for this life is precisely its "mode of living," the ethos of being-thus in *The Coming Community*, where "the single ways, acts, and processes of living are never simply *facts*, but always and above all *possibilities* of life, always above all potentiality" (ibid.). In the end, his modal ontology of de-having is a philosophy of exposure and de-positioning.

Whether this results in a diagonalization of the proper is another question. The disruption of the exception neutralizes the reduction of the political to the economic and the economic to the political that we find in the dispositif of the proper. Destituent power seeks not to appropriate that which has been deemed expropriated. It creates openings for rethinking politics and ethics. The form-of-life that occurs in the modality of destituent power is not "authentic" (*DP*, 74). He refuses to dictate what is to be done, and when he comes close to doing so he usually cuts himself off by inserting a messianic phrase, such as his call for a "politics to come," or referring to the inoperative modality of "contemplative life" of *theoria* (*DP*, 74). He also refuses to take the final step in his ontological philosophy by converting it into an ethical and/or political ontology. At most, his modal ontology renders it possible to think about the relationship between politics and ontology or ethics and ontology. Whether his ontology of the how enables us to rethink politics in anything other than an ecstatic or evental state remains a problem for his philosophy. If there is a communal dimension here, common use and habitus foster a communal ethos that is not only without content but occurs precisely in the ethos of dis-containment. One does wonder if there is anything more than a lifestyle politics here. These questions are hopefully answered in the conclusion to the *Homo Sacer* series *The Use of Bodies*.

# 5

# The Deontological Community

> [T]he common is not characterized by the proper but by the improper, or even more drastically, by the other; by a voiding, be it partial or whole, of property into its negative; by removing what is properly one's own [*depropriazione*] that invests and decenters the proprietary subject, forcing him to take leave of himself, to alter himself. In the community, subjects do not find a principle of identification or sterile [*asettico*] enclosure within which they can establish a transparent communication or even a content to be communicated.
>
> —*CI*, xiv; *CE*, 7[1]

Across many texts, Esposito claims that his theory of community differs from traditional accounts found in three representative branches of social and political theory: the organic model of *Gemeinschaft* in early-twentieth-century German sociology, the Habermasian model of the communicative-ethical community, and the Anglo-American communitarian model ("neocommunitarian") (*CI/CE*, *CIB*, *LT*, *TOP*). Despite their differences, he contends, each conceives "of community in a substantialistic, subjective sense" (*CIB*, 83). Each is conceptually derived from the "figure of the proper"—membership is exclusively staked on each owner's claim over their commonality—because belonging (*appartenere*) is conceived in a proprietary sense.

Like our previous two philosophers, Esposito draws from the Heideggerian critique of the dispositif of the proper. Whereas Agamben emphasizes the communicative and authentic declensions of this dispositif and Nancy the symbolic, Esposito squarely places it within the tradition of political economy. This declension is emphasized by the other two, but for Esposito it is first and foremost understood in proprietary terms. Esposito adds a new dimension to this debate by re-engaging this general problematic within the modern Western tradition of political philosophy. From his most ontological work, *Communitas*, to his subsequent biopolitical writings, up to his latest installments on the person, Esposito's primary aim is to work within, through, and across this tradition while simultaneously turning it inside out. He is, in other words, committed to *traversing* this tradition. Esposito confronts the myriad ways that the common has been misplaced in the tradition of Western political philosophy. This tradition is entrenched in the discursive regime of political economy, which mistakenly treats the common as something that is proper, that has particular properties, and yet simultaneously represents the proper of the collective. But the common is neither proper nor improper. The proper is at its core a privative notion and thus anticommon.

In addition to his focus on the proprietary declension of the proper, Esposito's theory of *communitas* stands out for at least two additional reasons. First, Esposito does not shy away from relating ethics and ontology by sidestepping the issue with a notion of an ontological ethos. Second, he provides a slightly more practical solution than Agamben and Nancy. In place of political economy, Esposito formulates a type of ethical economy, which in *Communitas* is articulated more in ontological terms, but in his subsequent writings it becomes more biopolitical. His ethical economy re-addresses the core communist problem of redistribution, only for Esposito that which is distributed is not pieces of property (personal or otherwise). In the ethical economy of the *munus*, the proprietary disposition of *Homo approprians* is radically expropriated. The *munus* also obliges each member to contribute to the community, not in terms of things given, but in terms of performing duties. The former model relied on a political economy of sharing, whereas for Esposito, sharing/division (*condivisione*) is articulated in an ethical ontology. This modality of sharing/division disrupts the giving-taking modalities of *Homo approprians*. And although his *communitas* is also conceptualized through a dis-containment process that forces this subject to let go of the hold it has over our world, the *munus* provides a more solid nexus through which a community can occur.

Esposito is a prolific political, or in his terms "impolitical," philosopher who continues to produce several texts per year. In the 1970s and 1980s he engaged in extensive studies on major thinkers in the Western and Italian traditions of political philosophy. With the publication of *Categories of the Impolitical* in 1988, his trajectory started to change. In the 1990s he continued to develop several political concepts that are now central to his philosophy, which brought him notoriety in Italy, then across Europe, Latin America, and more recently, in the English-speaking world. The scope of this chapter is limited to his biopolitical trilogy *Communitas: The Origin and Destiny of Community* (*CI/CE*), *Immunitas: The Protection and Negation of Life* (*IMI*, *IME*), and *Bíos: Biopolitics and Philosophy* (*BBF*, *BBP*); his subsequent writings in *Terms of the Political* (*TOP*), *Third Person* (*TP*), *Persons and Things* (*PT*); and a handful of selected essays. So the bulk of this chapter focuses on a highly productive period in his writing that was philosophically grounded in his monumental book on community, which spans a little over a decade.

The primary focus of this chapter is his notion of *communitas*. The philosophical groundwork for this project was established in *Communitas* (*CI*, *CE*), which I examine in part I. This work synthesizes the communitarian critique of the social contract tradition, Heideggerian existentialism, and the communist question. It is also his main contribution to the continental debate about community. Politically, he develops a radical model of republicanism where communal duties and obligations are prioritized over private rights, interests, and property. Existentially, his community unfolds in an ontology where *being* takes precedence over *having*. Rather than replace the contractual model altogether, Esposito conceives of a heterodox model of contractual exchange that I call a "deontological contract." In part II, I examine how he develops his theory of *communitas* in his subsequent writings. I begin by examining his distinction between *communitas* and *immunitas*, then I turn to his critique of communitarian philosophy, and I finish by considering his notions of affirmative freedom and obligations in his recent writings.[2]

## PART 1. *COMMUNITAS*

> Modern individuals truly become that, the perfectly individual, the "absolute" individual, bordered in such a way that they are isolated and protected, but only if they are freed in advance from the "debt" that binds them one to the other; if they are released from, exonerated, or relieved of that contact, which threatens their identity, exposing them to possible conflict with their neighbor, exposing them to the contagion of the relation with others. (*CI*, xxi; *CE*, 13)

*Communitas* stands out in Esposito's oeuvre. The text belongs to the continental debate about community. The questions he asks, the philosophical background, and the general problematic are similar to Nancy's main texts and Agamben's *The Coming Community.* All place much emphasis on Heidegger, and like Nancy, Esposito also dedicates much space to Bataille. Bataille and Heidegger, Esposito remarks in the appendix, are "necessary" references in the recent debate "in France and Italy" that provides "a new philosophical reflection about community" that is missing in mainstream, especially communitarian, philosophy (*CI*, 160; *CE* 148). Other than fleeting references at both ends of this book, however, Nancy is rarely referred to and Agamben only in passing in the introduction and again in the endnote referring to the debate in France and Italy.[3]

Despite the sporadic references to Nancy, this work is closely aligned with his project. During this stage, Esposito claims in a recent interview, Nancy "had a certain influence over my work," especially with "respect to the notion of community" (Saidel and Velasco Arias, 2012, 52).[4] *Communitas* was published two years after Nancy's *Being Singular Plural.* The first endnote of *Communitas* praises Nancy's *The Inoperative Community,* which Esposito claims in an allegorical fashion is "a text to which I owe an unpayable debt, as is the case for every *munus* given us in the form of the most unexpected gift" (*CI*, vii, fn. 1; *CE*, 1, fn. 1). On the closing pages of this work, Esposito revisits the possibility of thinking about community in relation to Nancy's *The Sense of the World* (*CI*, 161, fn. 14; *CE*, 148, fn. 14). Esposito had also engaged in a dialogue with Nancy, which has been published as the foreword the 2001 Italian translation of Nancy's *Being Singular Plural* in Italian, and he wrote the preface to the Italian translation of *The Experience of Freedom*, a gesture reciprocated by Nancy with his foreword to the 2000 French translation *Communitas* "Conloquium" (2010).

In their published correspondence, the two philosophers situate their own writings on community in relation to Heidegger, the Western and metaphysical tradition, and many of the other philosophers discussed in the previous chapters of this book. Most of the discussion is cordial and their interchange covers minute interpretative differences. However, both insist that if there is a major point of contention, it is where each places their emphasis: Nancy focuses on the *cum*, while Esposito the *munus*. Nancy reiterates his Heideggerian goal of not over-determining the relationship between the "with" and the nexus. For Nancy, sharing/division (*partage*) has an existential and symbolic value, which is more ontological than it is political. The *cum*, he claims, has the important task of linking or joining "the *munus* of the *communis*" (2010, 104). Yet he gives little if any significance to the place of the *munus* in his writings. Politics are supposed to serve the purpose of holding open the space that is necessary for us to co-exist. Weak politics, *laissez-passer*, serves as a passageway toward his singular plural ontology. For Esposito, however, the ontology of being-with is immediately formulated in a political and ethical register. That is, the sharing/division (*condivisione*) of the *munus* is ontological, political, and ethical. This shift in emphasis, he claims, has enabled him to carry his earlier ontological formulation of being-with and his critique of *immunitas* into a more biopolitical lexicon (Saidel and Velasco Arias, 2012, 52).

In *Communitas*, community is formulated in relation to ontological and existential philosophy. In the same vein as *The Coming Community*, *Communitas* represents an ontological groundwork, possibly a progenitor, for his later biopolitical writings. He weaves the distinction between *immunitas* and *communitas* into his Heideggerian, or more properly Nancean, analysis of traditional political philosophy. His reading of the political-legal and ethical dimensions of communal duties and obligations is infused with the ontological problem of plurality, which in his subsequent book *Immunitas* is translated into a biomedical and hence a biopolitical analysis. In the following section, I examine his model of a twofold deontological contract, first by examining its *deon*tological aspects, second by its de*onto*logical formulation (with the de- representing an intensive prefix). The order of this section reflects the movement in *Communitas* from the early chapters on contractualism and duty ethics to his later chapters on existentialism, ontology, and nihilism.

## I. Deontology

In the introduction to *Communitas*, "Nothing in Common," Esposito meticulously examines the displacement of community in political philosophy. Community, he argues, "isn't translatable into a political-philosophical lexicon except by completely distorting (or indeed perverting) it" (*CI*, vii; *CE*, 1). Modern political philosophers treat community as if it is a "property," a "thing," a "subject," a "substance," and most concerningly, a "'wider subjectivity'" that "swells the self in the hypertrophic figure of 'the unity of unities.'" What if, he asks, it is not any of these things because that which *draws us together* is nothing?

Esposito argues that we need to wrest community from the social contract model because it conflates the political with the economic such that politics becomes commercialized. What if the communal contract was conceived not in these terms, but as a deontological contract? What would remain were community not reduced to the economic, the political, or political economy in general? Esposito turns to the forgotten etymology of *communitas* for answers. *Com-munus* is a mere contract that draws us together in an improper form of exchange. It is neither a thing itself nor a contract that we enter into in exchange for something in return. All that is exchanged in this contract is *ourselves*. When we are drawn together in the contract of the *munus*, we are expropriated so extensively that we are rendered incapable of appropriating the contract, others, even ourselves.

In this section, I focus on the *deon*tological side of Esposito's communal contract. I examine various implicit references and dimensions in his analysis of the etymology of *communitas*. I situate this work within the broader problematic of wresting community from the trappings of the dispositif of the proper. Esposito begins by deconstructing the modern tradition in political philosophy. The modern tradition, he argues, writes community off by employing a "dubious homology" that confuses community with the res publica (*CI*, xii; *CE*, 5). This confusion raises three immediate problems. First, "public" is an excessively vague term. Second, the *res* connotes that the public is a thing with its own qualities. Third, the public always includes its antipode, the private. These three issues raise a whole series of aporias that confound modern notions of community. In his introduction, Esposito attempts to loosen the connection between community and the public so that he can begin to think about community beyond the tradition of political philosophy and its fidelity to the proper.

Esposito's etymological analysis of the *munus* can be read as an attempt to readdress the classical deontological problem of civic duty. He provides an alternative perspective on the "communitarian turn," which Gerard Delanty cites as the movement "'from contract to community'" (2010, 56).[5] His notion of communal duty represents a heterodox communitarian form of citizenship. It emphasizes duties owed to the community as opposed to the privileges or rights bestowed on individuals in the liberal tradition. The modern social contract, Esposito argues, undermines our "communal bond" when it institutes an "immunitarian" model of citizenship. Individuals are granted immunity from all forms of communal responsibilities.

The modern paradigm of immunity began when Hobbes used the social contract to institute a border between "the originary dimension of common living" and the modern "juridically 'privatistic' and logically 'privative' figure of the contract" (*CI*, xxii; *CE*, 13). When he based our commonality in our "capacity to kill" and "the possibility of being killed" (*CI*, 10; *CE*, 26), Hobbes left us with a stark choice between remaining in a perpetual state of "terror" or converting this destructive element of our relations into a productive model based on "fear." By transposing "originary" and "uncertain" fear into "artificial" and "certain" fear, Hobbes essentially cut us off from our relationships with each other. Esposito calls this "absolute dissociation" in the social contract "the crime of community" (*CI*, 12; *CE*, 27). The social contract erected an artificial barrier that immunizes us from each other.[6] "Subjects," he continues, "have nothing in common since everything is divided between 'mine' and 'yours': division without sharing" (*CI*, 13; *CE*, 28).[7]

When communal duties are formulated within this private political economy, political philosophers are forced to deal with the issue of compensation (*CI*, xiii; *CE*, 6). Here Esposito addresses the problem of the economy of compensation, which is a fundamental aporia in the dispositif of the proper. For all three of our main thinkers, the economy of compensation raises ontological and ethical issues. For Nancy, the common is the incommensurable, which disrupts any mediating or appropriative solutions. For Agamben, the economy of compensation raises the Heideggerian problem of ontological debt, which reorders the relationship between *being* and *having* in such a manner that it is possible to enter into an ontological ethos that disrupts this economy. Agamben, however, stops short of converting this into an ethical ontology, and he uses this formulation to challenge deontological ethics, which I will return to below. At this point, what can be said is that Esposito is also critical of the economy of compensation.

Esposito addresses the economy of compensation through the lens of the classical political problem of *remuneration* for duties performed on behalf of the community (*CI*, xi, 150; *CE*, 4, 139). In *Politics*, for example, Aristotle provided a detailed examination of this problematic (1998). In fact, his formulations still define the parameters that shape how contemporary political theorists such as Esposito broach the problem of remunerating civic duties. If we focus on the rule of the Multitude, leaving aside the rules of the One and the Few, there remain but three solutions. The first solution calls for public duties to be performed without remuneration—a logically sound approach, but hampered by the problem of inequity. Because the multitude is practically excluded from holding public office, this solution results in a politics dominated by the private interests of a small group of oligarchs. The second solution attempts to counterbalance the exclusionary effects of the first by offering all political representatives remuneration. This model too falls short of its goal of being wholly inclusive, because private economic interests still dominate politics. In both, a professional class of political oligarchs holds a monopoly over the political apparatuses who represent, directly or indirectly, the economic interests of the wealthy. Thus, the first two solutions remain trapped in the aporia of the private economy. Each calls for a strict, yet practically impossible, separation between private and public interests.

At stake in this discussion is the political conflation of private interests and public interest. This is a lesson found in Hannah Arendt's detailed analyses of "privation" (1988) and "totalitarianism" (1976), Jürgen Habermas's "refeudalization of the public sphere" (1989), C. Wright Mills's "Power Elite" (1956), and Robert Michel's "iron law of oligarchy" (1962), to name but a few. Not everyone is troubled by this conflation. Liberal pluralists, for example, continue to preach Robert Dahl's position that competition between different interest groups is the driving force of modern democracies (1961). Others, such as neo-Marxists, argue that we have exaggerated this conflation because modern politics is "relatively autonomous" from the economy (Poulantzas, 1978). Communitarians argue that the predominance of private economic interests in modern politics could be curtailed if properly infused with communitarian ethics. Here we find appeals to Alexis de Tocqueville's "civic volunteerism" (2000) or Max Weber's distinction between politicians who "live for politics" and those who "live from politics" (2004). Even radical democrats who claim to be beyond this reductive discourse, such as Ernesto Laclau and Chantal Mouffe (1985), remain trapped within its logic. Neologisms appealing to apolitical, neopolitical, or postpolitical are but empty phrases when conceived within the dispositif of the proper. The core issue is how to move beyond the trap of distinguishing between private economic interests and political public interests.

The third solution is found in the orthodox versions of communism. When property is communalized, private property continues only in the diminutive state of personal possession. Gradually the distinction between public and private interests would disappear, along with the question of remunerating public duties. But is this really a solution, or is the private merely absorbed into the public in this model? Many read *community*, or *communism*, within the Augustinian model of *com-unus*. Here individuals are completely absorbed by a collective subject, which in extreme cases is ascribed its own metaphysical, ontological qualities. Where the proper is appropriated by a com-unity, the multitude is annihilated by the One. Whenever community is conceptualized as a "homogenous totality," argues Esposito, community is subjected to the ethos of modern "nihilism" (*CI*, 159; *CE*, 147). Totalitarianism is so inclusive that it closes off and contains the very division that is necessary to form communal relationships.

This is certainly not an exhaustive list, but I do not want to belabor the issue. What I want to show is how Esposito provides a subtle, yet important and immanent, critique of the third option. Whenever the common is configured within the auspices of the proper, the common is represented as the bearer of the proper. A simple return to the original meaning of the *communitas*, Esposito contends, reveals that on the contrary, the common is "what is *not* proper" because it "begins where the proper ends" (*CI*, x; *CE*, 3). The proper is a derivative of the *proprius* (one's own, particular to itself), which is ultimately the private. The common is thus "improper."

The impropriety of the common is likewise translated into the public/private dichotomy. The public represents the quintessential "other." It is a "voiding, be it partial or whole, of property into its negative" because it removes "what is properly one's own [*depropriazione*]" by "invest[ing] and decenter[ing] the proprietary subject, forcing him to take leave of himself, to alter himself" (*CI*, xiv; *CE*, 7). The public deprives subjects of their property. This does not mean that he is advocating for a simple reversal of the order of possession from private to public property. It is time to rethink the common beyond the public, because the public is too closely aligned with the private and thus both are conceived under the semantics of the proprium. The common, he argues, is neither private nor public.

Esposito's twofold deontological solution begins with a re-evaluation of the role of *interest* in traditional political economy. Interest is always treated in a proprietary sense, as if it is a "compensation for loss" (*inter-esse*). One has an interest in community precisely because the more one gives, the more one can take back for oneself. Robert Putnam's communitarian notion of "social capital" falls within this self-interested model of community (1999). The more one personally invests in one's community, the more social capital one accumulates, which can be used as currency at a later point in the community's "favor bank." If the sense of mutual obligation is truly "generalized"—that is, not based on a simple expectation of a direct exchange of favors— the more the community will be based on social trust and cooperation. This will generate stronger social ties. The problem with this "social exchange" model is that community is treated as if it is a marketplace where individuals invest in it in order to secure future returns. Reciprocity, whether simple or generalized in Putnam's formulation, is ultimately based in self-interest. Putnam himself has not shied away from selling this aspect of his popular theory in his larger study, essays, or many public talks.

Like Nancy, Esposito turns to the etymological construction of interest qua *inter-esse* in search for an opening. The Hobbesian social contract, Esposito notes, sacrifices "not only the *inter* of *esse* but also the *esse* of *inter* in favor of individual interest" (*CI*, 152; *CE*, 141). If we return to the ontological significance of the term *inter-esse*, then it might be possible to separate interest from the dispositif of the proper. Being (*esse*), not property, interests us precisely because being is between (*inter*) us, as

Nancy phrases *interesse* in "Compearance."[8] It is in this realm where the double sense of Esposito's deontological contract operates.

Esposito appeals to the three etymological senses of the *munus* to breach the dispositif of the proper: *onus* (load/burden), *officium* (office), and *donum* (gift) (*CI*, x; *CE*, 4). Each is characterized as a "duty" [*dovere*]. Their deontological connotations are carried through in his subtle play on the contradictory senses in **mei-*, the root of the word *munus*: transformation/opening up (mutable, exchange); lessen (lack, diminish, minus); and binding/closing off (duty, obligation, indebtedness). That is, the *munus* is a deontological contract that opens up and transforms subjects (exchange or *scambio*), diminishes them to the point that they are wholly lacking (expropriation), and binds them to contractual obligations (indebtedness). It is a contract, we could say in a Nancean vein, that is written in the very ex- of their common alteration. Its binding, or obligatory, characteristic is reinforced by the fact that each is commonly exposed to the lack, which Esposito argues is the common. It results in a twofold deontological exchange that opens each to the binding obligation of performing services on behalf of community.

In reference to Marcel Mauss and Émile Benveniste, Esposito argues that the duty characteristic of the *munus* is presented in the form of a "gift." Were one to accept it, one would become obliged "to exchange it in terms of goods or service" (*CI*, xi; *CE*, 4). Contrary to Mauss's notion of gift exchange and Putnam's notion of social capital, this gift exchange does not occur in a give-and-take form of reciprocity; rather, it is an "unrelenting" obligation where "one *must* give . . . because they *cannot not* give." It is also an "unequivocal" exchange that places the receiver in debt to, "'at the disposition of,'" "or more drastically 'at the mercy of' someone else" (*CI*, xii; *CE*, 5). When we are contracted together in the *munus*, the direct "correspondence" of giving and receiving is interrupted. There is no expectation of anything in return. It is, in short, an interruption of the dialectic of alienation and appropriation.[9]

In the same manner as Agamben, Esposito hints at this disruption by making a play on the etymological connection of "debt" and "duty." As discussed in the last chapter, both words derive from *debere* (to owe), which breaks down as *de-habere* or de-having. On the *deon*tological end, debt/duty expropriates subjects. Subjects are placed in an impossible position of not having, holding, or possessing that which is owed. "'I owe *you* something,' but not 'you owe *me* something'" (*CI*, xiii; *CE*, 6). In this de-having, the prospect of the returned favor is radically removed from the relationship. The communal marketplace is thus immediately displaced when each is opened up and exposed to the common. This is a different sense of the common and of debt than is found today in the West. Our debt crisis concerns private financiers who are empowered to repossess private property in exchange for money owed. Communal debt, however, expropriates more than property in the material sense. It also expropriates our "initial property," "of the most proper property, namely," our "very subjectivity" (*CI*, xiv; *CE*, 7).

A deontological community isn't formulated in terms of "having" in the proprietary sense, but by a "debt" that contracts us together (com-) in the gift of the *munus*. Such an "exchange relationship" does not follow the proprietary contractual modalities of "give" [*dare*] and "take" [*prendere*]. We are drawn together into a "transitive act of giving" that has nothing to do with the "stability of a possession and even less the acquisitive dynamic of something earned, but loss, subtraction, transfer" (*CI*, xii; *CE*, 5). We are contractually obliged to give "something that one can *not* keep for oneself and over which, therefore, one is not completely master."

> The fact that the Romans understood by the term *munus* only the gift [*dono*] that was made and never the gift received (which was instead denoted in the word *donum*) signals that it is lacking in "remuneration," and that the breach of a subjective material that it determines remains as such, that is incapable of being made replete, made whole, or healed over; that its opening cannot be closed by any sort of compensation or reparation if it is to continue in fact to remain shared [*condivisa*]. The reason is that in the concept of "sharing with" [*condivisione*], the "with" [*con*] is associated with dividing up [*divisione*]. (*CI*, 150; *CE*, 139)

One might question whether we should replicate a formula found in a Roman notion of community, an imperial power and slave society with a highly stratified notion of citizenship, governed by the few. Further, the elite Roman citizens understood de-having as a *tax* owed. Should community be predicated in these terms? Without further context, this theory could be read as another conservative rendition of communitarianism, moreover a romantic conservative version. This, however, would be an unfair conclusion; Esposito does clarify his political leanings in his discussion with Nancy (2010) and in his subsequent publications. As with the other theorists in this literature, Esposito implores us to differentiate between the spirit of this notion of community and its form. He is also attempting to deconstruct the dispositif of the proper from a clearly left-wing perspective. The political connotations of his theory become clearer in the second part of *Communitas*, which I now discuss.

## II. Ontology

The *munus* radically disrupts the way sharing is articulated in traditional models of community that are based on property, whether it be collectively owned property or by possession of a common identity. With the *munus*, however, members share "an expropriation of their own essence, which," he claims, "isn't limited to their 'having' but one that involves and affects their own 'being subjects'" (*CI*, 148; *CE*, 138). His rendition of *sharing* (*condivisione*) provides a profound challenge to traditional anthropological accounts in political philosophy. It occurs in the "more radical terrain of ontology: that the community isn't joined to an addition but to a subtraction of subjectivity" (ibid.). Here *exposure* plays a formidable role, because in the exposure of *condivisone* individuals are forced open and appear outside themselves.

In the following section, I examine how Esposito complements his *deon*tological communal contract outlined in the first half of *Communitas* with an existential de*onto*logical model of a communal contract in the second half this book. This work is set up in the last two chapters on Heidegger and Bataille, but it only comes to fruition in the appendix "Nihilism and Community."

Esposito's existential strain is grounded in Heidegger's writings on the event of existence, either as the "Call of Being" in *Being and Time* or as the *Ereignis* in his later *Ereignis-Denken*. As I examined in chapter 2, for Heidegger this event prepares us for entering into a modality of being by opening us up and exposing us. Esposito draws from Heidegger's claim that modern humanity remains closed to Being precisely because we treat Being as something that we can *have*. Being is not something that we can identify, hypostatize, and thus appropriate. The *Ereignis* temporarily suspends our appropriative grasps so that being is prioritized over having.

In *Communitas*, Esposito repeatedly criticizes the "affirmative entification" of community in contemporary theories. Like Agamben's use of the term *debt*, Esposito's *munus* performs the function of de-having (debt/duty—*debere*). He differs from Heidegger, however, by trying to rethink this de-having in a plural fashion. Following Nancy's pluralization of existentialism, the event of existence is read in a plural register of being-with. Nancy's revision of this problematic largely concerns the technical problems of rethinking Being as a plural phenomen*a* of beings; Esposito however carries this problematic into a more contentious terrain in Heideggerian scholarship.

Esposito's twofold deontology forces him to deal with the "identity of ethics and ontology" (*CI*, 87; *CE*, 90). Esposito is neither ostentatious nor brazen here. He disputes Levinas's charge that Heidegger "sacrifices the first to the second" and Ricoeur's claim that Heidegger leaves ontology "'on the threshold of ethics.'" He is aware that to venture down this path with Heidegger with a communitarian motive in hand is dangerous. He carefully places some distance between himself and Heidegger by engaging with Heidegger's writings on being-with, belonging, and origination in a critical tone. He then follows this analysis with a chapter on Bataille's reconfiguration of Heideggerian existentialism in a communal fashion. This recourse to Bataille gives Esposito just enough distance to reconfigure Heideggerian existentialism in "Community and Nihilism."

In "Ecstasy," Esposito reiterates the "communitarian" leanings in Heidegger's earlier writings, then he questions Heidegger's uncritical reference to the "*Volk*" and "destiny," and he finishes by challenging Heidegger's misreading of the place of "origin" in Hölderlin's work. According to Esposito, we need to turn to Bataille to right the problem of "the origin and destiny of community"—the subtitle of *Communitas*. Esposito focuses on two dimensions of Bataille's work that enable him to articulate his twofold deontological contract.

Unlike Heidegger's formulation of being-with, Bataille places the *cum* at the end. For Bataille, community is experienced through the horizon of death, which represents the "nullification of every possibility in the expropriating and expropriated dimension of the impossible" for "death is our *common* impossibility of being what we endeavor to remain, namely isolated individuals" (*CI*, 126; *CE*, 121). Esposito reads Heidegger's notion of death as one's most proper (*eigentlichkeit*) possibility literally, so he turns to Bataille for an alternative account. With Bataille, the other's death, or even an act where two people risk their lives, opens us up, exteriorizes us, and places us in communication with each other. This common exposure disrupts our appropriative capacities just enough for communication to occur without pretension. But rather than join Agamben in returning to the problem of language, Esposito remains in the realm of the existential reading of ontology. The experience of a "'common nothingness,'" he claims in a manner similar to Kojève's synthesis of Hegel, Heidegger, and Marx (1980), exposes us to our common and shared incapacity to appropriate what is properly our own: our finitude. Bataille thus figures as a "radical anti-Hobbesian" because his model prioritizes openness and exposure, which are communitarian impulses, as opposed to immunitarian closures and barriers and ultimately the destruction of community in favor of security (*CI*, 128; *CE*, 123–24).[10]

There is also a *deon*tological strain in Bataille's critique of the "restrictive economy" of the Hobbesian social contract tradition (*CI*, 129; *CE*, 124). In its place, Bataille "refers to a 'munificence' purged of any mercantile remnants" (ibid.). Notably, munificence breaks down etymologically as *munus-facere*: to do or perform a *munus*. For Bataille, the "gift," qua sacrifice, to the community is "life." Here Esposito treads back into the tradition that connects the *munus* to the logic of sacrifice. Altruism is traditionally enacted through a sacred duty of giving oneself over as a gift that is owed to *communitas* without any expectation of being remunerated. This is clearly an expropriative act; yet it also resonates with the Hobbesian paradigm of sacrifice.

The relationship between community, contractualism, and existentialism is drawn from Nancy's essay on Bataille's notion of the "unsacrificeable" (*UFP*, *AFT*). Nancy argues, "'finitude' means that existence can't be sacrificed" (cited in *CI*, 133; *CE*, 128). Existence is itself an offering that is, in Esposito's paraphrase, "more originary than every sacrificial scene, but offered to nothing and to no one and therefore not sacrificed" (ibid.). Esposito argues that if the sacrificial logic is replaced by his reading of nihilism, then the "Hobbesian moment" can be surpassed.

Esposito's reading of munificence combines community and contractualism in an existential manner. In his contract, de-having leaves each of us exposed to nothing. This ontological opening exposes us so thoroughly that we are left in a state of incapacitation. Each is forced to face that which one can never be exonerated or immune from and that which one can never appropriate: their finitude. "Finite subjects" are "cut by a limit that cannot be interiorized because it constitutes precisely their 'outside'; the exteriority that they overlook and enters into them into their common non-belonging" (*CI*, xv; *CE*, 7). This side of his argument resonates with Nancy's Heideggerian account of the exposure that occurs when we "compear," that is, appear together. For Esposito, being exposed to our finitude interrupts our appropriative impulses. It extensively disrupts, we might say, *Homo approprians*'s insatiable desire to appropriate everything in its sight, including others, ourselves, and all the items in its wake. When exposed, one experiences "a dizziness, a syncope, a spasm in the continuity of the subject." This exposure is always experienced in a plural manner. Community occurs, claims Esposito, in being exposed to one's "radical impropriety." Community is this "hole into which the common thing continually risks falling" (*CI*, xv; *CE*, 8). It is this risk of "falling" into a "sort of landslide" that constitutes our danger of living together, our finitude, which threatens to penetrate our artificial borders and turn each of us inside-out. Being is always experienced qua being-with. It is this lack, the very lack in our being, which is "configured as an onus." We share this lack that divides us.

Esposito's notion of nihilism is predicated in a nonromantic register. To think about community "in a way that is able to meet the needs of our own time," which is "characterized by a fully realized nihilism," we must revisit the relationship between nihilism and community (*CI*, 147; *CE*, 136). The point where "they cross each other," he contends, is the "no-thing." The *munus* can only take place in the "radical terrain of ontology" where members of community are subtracted and exposed. Identifiable boundaries are forced open such that each appears "as what is 'outside' themselves." Each becomes an "'other'" in "a chain of alterations that cannot ever be fixed in a new identity" (*CI*, 149; *CE*, 138). Esposito's altruistic notion of community is thoroughly defined by alterity or otherness, not by sameness and identity. This procession is not enacted by the other, such as Levinas's second-person philosophy, or by a sacrificial gesture, but by the *munus*, which in his more recent writings has started to occupy the space of the *third* (*TP*).

Community, Esposito argues, is the "*esse* as *inter*, not the relation that shapes being [*essere*] but being itself as the relation" (*CI*, 150; *CE*, 139). It is the "interval of difference, that spacing that brings us into relation with others in a common nonbelonging, in this loss of what is proper that never adds up to a common 'good'" (ibid.). By prioritizing difference over sameness, spacing over place, exposure over safety, risk over security, and so on, he not only reverses the traditional characteristics of community because he also makes a play on the division/sharing that is found in the notion of *condivisione*, like Nancy's *partage*. That is, to be exposed in the division and sharing is to depart from the traditional immunitarian community. Community signifies nothing more than the relationships that occur in a risky situation, in a flight into insecurity, which cannot produce the traditionally understood "effects of commonality, of agreement, and of communion" [*effetti di comunanza, di accomunamento, di comunione*] (*CI*, 150; *CE*, 140). We are not immune to others in this situation. If we refuse to see community in this manner, he contends, then we will continue to find ways to "contain the dangers" [*contenere i pericoli*], "immunize" ourselves, and cut ourselves off from community, such as Hobbes does in his contract (*CI*, 152; *CE*, 141). We will continue to experience community as either a division without sharing (the immunitarian social contract) or a sharing without division (absorption into a grand communal individual).

Fittingly, Esposito concludes by turning to Heidegger first, then Bataille, and finally Nancy. Heidegger demonstrated that relationships only occur across nothingness. If community were something or, worse, everything, then it would represent an annihilation of all relationships. It would result in, recalling the two-fold appropriation, a sheer implosion of unity. Modern nihilism actually abolishes the distance that is necessary for relationships to occur. *Communitas*, on the contrary, is a "unity *in* distance and *of* distance" (*CI*, 157; *CE*, 145). Bataille devised a more concrete way to conceptualize the relationship between community and the no-thing. Much like Nancy's critique of total sense, or Heidegger's critique of sheer immanentism, Bataille defined nihilism not as "the flight of meaning or flight from meaning, but rather meaning's enclosure within a homogenous and complete conception of being" (*CI*, 158; *CE*, 146). Nihilism is a complete enclosure, immanentism, that excludes alterity and difference. Nihilism, in other words, is a product of the dispositif of the proper that directs us to appropriate difference. Difference is thus reduced to sameness, which is precisely how modern notions of community operate. Finally, Nancy "more than anyone else has the merit of clearing a way forward in the closed thought of community" (*CI*, 161; *CE*, 148). Nancy doesn't necessary rejoice in the destructive aspect of nihilism, but he does force us to take issue with the "end of every generalization of sense" and the "emergence of singular meaning that coincides with the absence of meaning" (*CI*, 162; *CE*, 149). It is an opening, or a clearing, to the "nothing held in common that is the world that joins us" (ibid.). Singular plurality, Esposito claims, represents a new path for reconceptualizing community beyond the semantics of the proper and in an existential fashion.

* * *

It is worth returning to Agamben's critique of the economy of compensation for a moment. It is here that we find the core differences between his ontological ethos and Esposito's ethical ontology. For both, debt disrupts the primacy of having over being. Being-in-debt, being-in-the-process-of-de-having we might say, de-propriates and incapacitates *Homo approprians*. This modality prepares that which remains to be an existent. Agamben's philosophy stops here. Across all of his writings he has searched for ways to articulate a modality of being an existent that occurs precisely in the modality that prepares the existent to be-thus, or in his more recent writings, to be a form-of-life. His pinnacle, if we can use such a term, is an ontological *ethos*. Esposito carries this formulation one step further. In addition to preparation and modality, he has sought to think about the other dimension of debt: owing. This is not, as I have demonstrated, a sense of owing something in a proprietary or commercial sense such as paying a tribute or a tax, but an owing that can only be repaid in the sense of a communal duty. Being-in-debt carries the weight of a duty to give back to the *munus*. In exchange for the gift of community, one must give back in the form of a service, duty, or office, and only in the most generous manner (munificence). The ontological and the ethical are not only coterminous in this formulation, because in their intertwinement they open onto a communal or relational model of ethical ontology.

In *The Coming Community*, Agamben appeals to a Heidegger-inspired ontological notion of debt in order to disrupt the economy of compensation. It disrupts the reduction of being to having by exposing and expropriating *Homo approprians*, and thus prepares it to enter into an ontological ethos. In this ethos the self is free to use itself in an inoperative manner. At this stage, however, his reliance on Heidegger's theory of ontological debt still carried a slightly deontological sense because debt is treated as an ontological exigency, as a duty to be. It is only with his more recent distinction between the priestly office and the impoverished monk, in *Opus Dei* and *The Highest Poverty*, that Agamben fully develops his critique of deontology. The former work represents an extensive critique of what he calls the "paradigm of office/duty." From the opening pages, he launches a wide-ranging critique of what we might call "civic duties." This paradigm, he argues, is essentially a managerial, even governmental, paradigm. It is also a Roman paradigm of political action. In addition to *praxis* and *poesis*, with the former being the ideal political action for Aristotle, the Romans introduced a third type of action, "*gerere*," which "originally meant to 'carry'" but in "political-juridical language 'to govern, administer, carry out an office'" (*ODI*, 98; *ODE*, 83). This duty-bound notion of action essentially transforms one into a mere instrument that is deprived of acting and producing because one becomes a simple functionary that merely executes or carries out commands. One's being is defined therefore by one's duty to act. Being and acting become utterly confused because the "ontology of command" is mixed with the "ontology of office." "The official . . . is what he has to do and has to do what he is," thus he is, in short, a "being of command" (*ODI*, *ODE*, 84).[11] One is judged solely on the basis of what one does, not on account of who and how one is.

This paradigm, which converts being into having-to-be (*dovere-essere*), Agamben argues, has come to define the ontology, ethics, and politics of modernity. In his work, he searches for ways that one can be without having to be anything, without being defined by what one does. He does this by addressing the fracture between being and acting, which, he claims in *The Kingdom and The Glory*, represent the "impolitical," "economic-managerial" paradigm of modern economic theology (*RG*, 82; *KG*, 66). Contrary to the ways ethical ontology emphasizes the relationship between ethics and action, which ultimately subordinates actions to simple executions of commands, Agamben searches for a supplemental model of an ontological ethos that is grounded in the relationship between ethos and habitus. His main source for this model is, of course, Aristotle's theory of impotentiality. For Aristotle, habit is "the mode in which a being . . . 'has' a potential"; it is "the point where being crosses over into having" (*ODI*, 109; *ODE*, 93–94). One can only have a potential, however, if one also has an impotentiality (*adynamia*), which is "privation" of habit (a de-having, we could say). This negative side of habit, the habit of privation, is necessary because only with it "can potential endure and have mastery over itself, without always already losing itself in action" (*ODI*, 109–10; *ODE*, 94). If one merely has a potential, then they have no control over it. They would merely execute or carry out their potentiality. But to have "a *hexis* of potential," he claims, "means being able to not exercise it" (ibid.). It is thus necessary to emphasize this inoperative dimension of habit. Instead of making a virtue of exercising one's potentiality to act (the *ergon*), Agamben searches for ways in which one can make a habit into an ethos of the *argos*, where the "ability not to pass into action" is not passed over. He finds such a habit-ethos in the Franciscan monks. There is no point rehashing this formulation here; rather, what must be underlined is that there is a direct relationship between de-having, habitus, and ethos in the impoverished form of life of these monks. Their impoverishment prepares them to enter into a modality of being, an ethos, and thus ultimately an inoperative habitus, that stops short of being converted into duty to act. If we were to properly attend to this dimension of their exemplary way of living, life and form could coincide so completely that they could occur without the normative and legal prescriptions found in deontological formulations, and being would no longer be appropriated by having.

There are at least two questions we have to ask of this formulation that bring us back to Esposito. First, how can such a form-of-life be relational, or communal? He does refer to a communal habitus and common use, but his formulation appears to be more concerned with the liberating sense of this form of life, as an absolution of the **se*, which is often pitched in a negative reading of liberty (freedom from . . . the various dispositifs). As I discuss below, Esposito seeks to conceive of the liberating aspects of the disruption in a more communal manner. If there is a freedom, it can only be a positive freedom. In this sense Esposito is more Italian, whereas Agamben's philosophy of liberation is much more in line with the French tradition. We could even say that he places so much emphasis on the *ex-*, that he leaves himself with little space to think about the *cum*, and when he does it is articulated as a disruption of the *munus*. This brings us to the second question. Does the duty to give back to the *munus* completely absorb the being of the one who owes? Are members of a community merely functionaries of an office, such as a priest who has given his entire life, ultimately sacrificed it, to the cause of the church, or can one be obliged to contribute without losing oneself in the process? There seems to be a zero-sum game in this formulation. Can one belong to a *com-munus* without being wholly othered, altered, or made to be entirely *altruistic* to the point that it would be impossible to distinguish oneself from their community? Agamben is a philosopher of the extremes—priests, monks, planetary petite bourgeoisie, stateless people, *Muselmen*, prisoners at Guantanamo Bay, protestors at Tiananmen Square, etc. Either one remains in a state of abysmal alienation or one uses it as a pathway leading to salvation. But is it realistic to choose between the pathway carved out by ascetic friars and the liturgical life of churchly fathers? Can't we be both singular and plural in the *munus*? This is one of the fundamental tensions in Esposito's philosophy; yet it would be an exaggeration to claim that because one has a duty (de-having), which ultimately de-propriates them, one becomes a mere functionary.

## PART 2. COMMUNITY AFTER *COMMUNITAS*

### III. *Communitas* and *Immunitas*

> If [*communitas*] binds individuals to something that pushes them beyond themselves, then [*immunitas*] reconstructs their identity by protecting them from a risky contiguity with the other, relieving them of every obligation toward the other and enclosing them once again in the shell of their own subjectivity. Whereas *communitas* opens, exposes, and turns individuals inside out, freeing them to their exteriority, *immunitas* returns individuals to themselves, encloses them once again in their own skin. *Immunitas* brings the outside inside, eliminating whatever part of the individual that lies outside. What is immunization if not the preventive interiorization of the outside, its neutralizing appropriation? (*TOP*, 49)

The core distinction between *communitas* and *immunitas* continues to define Esposito's political philosophy. Across all his texts, he argues that community cannot be understood in isolation from immunity. In modernity, community and immunity are connected and juxtaposed, as "object and content of the other" (*IMI*, 12; *IME*, 9). *Communitas* affirms the *munus*, whereas *immunitas* negates it (*TOP*, 58–59).

Generally speaking, *communitas* is a state of being-in-common where each is exposed to each other. In this exposure the exposed are divided and shared out in such a manner that each is compelled to share with others. This is an open and inclusive notion of community that "breaks down the barriers of individual identity" (*CIB*, 85). It is also an antithetical notion of community because it does not form a homogeneous entity whose members share in their common identity. *Communitas* is neither a thing nor a place that is proper to its members. In *communitas* we experience difference precisely because *communitas* occurs in relationships where each is improper. The modern distinction between *ours* and *theirs* is a product of the modern immunitarian dispositif. Unless we can radically rethink community, he argues, we can never achieve an "affirmative bond of common obligation." We will remain in our immunized relationships where the "purely negative right of each individual to exclude all others from using what is proper to him or her" characterizes our commonality (*IMI*, 30; *IME*, 25). *Immunitas* "is the condition of the dispensation from such an obligation and therefore the defense against the expropriating features of *communitas*" (*BBF*, 47; *BBP*, 50).[12]

One of his most succinct statements on the political implications and exigencies of this problematic is found in his essay "Community, Immunity, Biopolitics" (*CIB*). Esposito argues that the contemporary political "task at hand is to overturn in some way—indeed in every way—the balance of power between 'common' and 'immune.'" We must find ways to inaugurate the delicate procedure of separating the "immunitary protection of life from its destruction by means of the common; to conceptualize the function of immune systems in [a] different way, making them into relational filters between inside and outside instead of exclusionary barriers" (ibid., 87–88). This task, he continues, must simultaneously negotiate between "two levels: by disabling [*disattivazione*] the apparatuses of negative immunization, and by enabling [*attivazione*] new spaces of the common."[13] In his biopolitical writings, Esposito characterizes the *enabling* dimensions of his philosophy as affirmative. Affirmative biopolitics dis-activates the immunizing effects of negative biopolitics while simultaneously enabling the affirmative dimensions of the *munus*. In this work, the ethical, political, and ontological dimensions of his philosophy are woven together.

In the continental debate about community, each philosopher argues that traditional notions of community lead to closed and exclusionary notions of the common. This closure is a byproduct of the dispositif of the proper, which reduces the common to the proper. Esposito's emphasis on the role of the immunitary dimension of this dispositif in the traditional configuration of community adds another interpretive layer to this discussion. Immunity is a terminological metaphor with two overlapping vectors: the biomedical vector and the political-legal vector. In his biopolitical trilogy, *Communitas* represents his most extensive analysis of political-legal immunization and its negative effects on community. *Immunitas* shifts its emphasis towards legal and biomedical immunization, whereas *Bíos* represents a historical examination of the proliferation of immunization procedures in modern biopolitics. He continues to examine the combination of these two vectors in his writings on the person, things, and bodies.

Taken from the field of medicine, immunity indicates a function of the body, its capacity to insulate that body from a destructive external environment by identifying what is the body's *own* and eliminating or excluding that which is pathological to it. Biomedical "immunity is the refractoriness of an organism to the danger of contracting a contagious disease" (*IMI*, 9; *IME*, 7). In *Immunitas*, Esposito traces the passage "from natural to acquired immunity" or from "a passive condition to one that is actively induced" (*IMI*, 9–10; *IME*, 7). With the discovery of vaccinations, the modern concept of immunization became inherently reactionary. The main biomedical principle of immunization is "that an attenuated form of infection could protect against a more virulent form of the same type" (*IMI*, 10; *IME*, 7). Put differently, "to vaccinate a patient against a disease, you have to introduce a controlled and tolerable portion of it into the organism" (*TOP*, 61).

Already we have an organic dimension of the proper: what belongs to the body is that which contributes to its internal harmony, balance, and integrity, while what is improper is what breaks down or attacks such integrity. It is, to be sure, a very short step from this "proper" deployment of the concept to its metaphorical extension in politics. Here the Greek notion of the city as the *polis*, whose citizen-members are constituted as a political body (i.e., a *politeuma*) displays the conceptual linkages between the city and its political members as a body, and above all, a proper and "organic" body as natural as that of the biological body itself (see Aristotle, *Politics*, book I). And it is this body, both natural and political, that must be protected from what is external and improper. The immune paradigm is the mechanism through which the political body will be protected in a way analogous to the way the immune function protects the biological body. Meanwhile, according to Esposito's discussion in *Bíos*, what was already a mixed metaphor, that is, already biopolitical, has become explicitly so in the modern era. Building on the analysis provided by Foucault (1981, 2003), Esposito argues that this primarily metaphorical sense of biopolitics has become literal in the application of new techniques of power to the life of populations. In this way it translates politics into a biological (and hence biopolitical) project and thus exaggerates the immunitarian dimensions of the modernity. Today, "immunization of the political body functions similarly" to biomedical immunization as both aim to introduce "a fragment of the same pathogen from which" they seek to "protect [themselves], by blocking and contradicting natural development" (*BBF*, 42; *BBP*, 46).

In political-legal discourse, to be immune is to be freed from the duties and obligations of performing services on behalf of others. It is a form of negative freedom that is quintessential to the modern proprietary subject found in mainstream liberalism. An immunized person is exempt "from the obligation of the *munus*, be it personal, fiscal, or civil" (*IMI*, 8; *IME*, 5). An immunized person is outside of the "social circuit of reciprocal gift-giving [*circuito sociale donazione reciproca*]" (*IME*, 9; *IME*, 6). The immune person is the privative legal person, who receives personal privileges because she is a private proprietor. As she is immune, she is exempt from paying tributes or performing services on behalf of the *munus*. She is outside the "common law" that binds a community together (*TOP*, 58). Immunity thus constitutes the proper subject as a person who is protected and sheltered from being exposed to and thus responsible for the relationships that occur in a community.

Just as the conflation of the biomedical body with the collective, this political-legal notion of individual immunity, the not-divided person, is conflated with the broader community. Members in the immunized community are treated as individuals who hold or possess exclusive rights to their common property, and collective mechanisms are established to protect these rights. Internally, community shelters and protects insiders. Externally, it becomes a hostile and militant fortress. The ever-present threat of alien appropriation invigorates the immunizing apparatuses that create a mythologized notion of unification. "[S] mall, micro-communities, opposed by definition to each other by ethnic, linguistic, and cultural identities" (*CI*, 45; *CE*, 54–55) become obsessed with containing their identities and whatever else "is considered to be properly their own" (*TOP*, 43). Many contemporary social and political theorists have noted that in our globalized era, communities of identity, whether in the Global North, Global South, or transnationally based, have become what Zygmunt Bauman calls "besieged fortresses" (2001). Esposito claims that this "autonimmunization" process is nearly "exasperated" to the point that common existence is no longer conceivable within the confines sketched out by traditional models of community. Today we can no longer distinguish between inside and outside, us and them, because the inside is already marked by what it wants to exclude. This feature gives attempted reassertions of traditional modes of community membership a dangerously xenophobic character. The spiraling fear of "aliens in our midst" seems to necessitate ever stricter criteria of membership, reactivating the worst forms of racist, religious, and ethnic discrimination; we see this today when authorities are empowered to demand citizenship papers from anyone who looks like an "alien."

Esposito insists in all of his writings from *Communitas* onwards that community can only be recognized as an interruption and transformation of immunity. In *Living Thought* he argues that the "burdensome law of the *munus*" provides a challenge to the "state of exception" found in modern individualistic immunization processes (*LT*, 258). A community cannot happen without an immunitary system. The point is to find a balance between community and immunity, for when "they diverge or exceed one another, the consequences can be catastrophic" (*LT*, 261). The task is to refocus the internal mechanisms of the immunitary dispositif. It must "be shifted from a defensive barrier against the outside"—to remove all the "aggressive metaphors, or tropes" and "military jargon" from the biological lexicon of biopolitics—"to a process of differential transformation of the very subjects it identifies" (*LT*, 261). In the closing pages of *Immunitas*, he uses the example of the relationship between the mother and the embryo as a moment of affirmative rather than negative forms of immunity. This relationship challenges the traditional militaristic and exclusionary reading of immunity by establishing a tolerant form of immunity that is open to alteration.[14] This is not a negation of immunity, an anti-immunity, which reproduces the immunization processes, but a "reverse immunity," a "common immunity" (*IMI*, 202; *IME*, 167). It becomes a "filter for contact and communication with the surrounding environment" (*LT*, 261).

## IV. Communitarianism

Esposito argues, quite pointedly, that the "identity-making" communitarians (*CIB*) are at the forefront of the defense of the immunitarian model of community (*CI*, CE). Their model of community is a byproduct of the successive developments of "state sovereignty" and "individual rights," which are both at the forefront of the modern paradigm of immunization (*TOP*, 128). After Hobbes, Locke, and Rousseau, the "regime of the 'common'" was replaced by the regime "of the 'proper.'" In biopolitical terms, each sphere becomes a form of property that must be immunized, often in contradictory ways, from external appropriation. The state and the individual become two privileged spheres, or polarities, against which modern politics are determined. Modern political solutions, Esposito argues, are held by this "vise grip between public and private" (*CIB*). Community withers into the background, is held back and repressed under the weight of the proprietary, sovereign, and hence privileged spheres of the public and the private. The communitarian attempt to foreground the public sphere thus becomes the mirror image of traditional liberal commitment to the priority of the private sphere.

In general terms, three main tenets in the civic republican strains of Anglo-America communitarian thought are important for analyzing Esposito's radical model of republicanism. These three tenets, along with his critique of how the communitarians address each in their philosophy, are not necessarily at the forefront of his deconstruction of the immunitary dispositif. He never explicitly situates his theory in relation to the communitarianism. Rather, he passingly refers to them as mainstream exemplars of the immunized model of community. What makes them interesting, however, is how their critique of liberalism as a tradition that privileges formal democracy over informal democracy, individual rights over the common good, and negative liberty over positive liberty, represents nothing less than the collectivization of individualistic readings of immunity. Whether on an individual or collective scale, the liberals and communitarians reproduce the political-legal vector of immunity.

A core presumption in the liberal approach is that the group is oppressive and individuals must become autonomous agents who are free to determine their own identity (*TP*). Thus, liberalism, despite significant variations, takes as its fundamental value the autonomy of the individual. Isaiah Berlin's now-famous distinction between two competing conceptions of liberty articulates how this autonomy has been conceptualized (1969). The first of these, so-called negative liberty, holds that the necessary conditions of autonomy and freedom have been met when there is no external impingement on individual choice and action. The basic political thrust of negative liberty is to remove impediments to individual actions. The second concept, positive liberty, holds that the mere absence of external impingement is not enough to assure conditions of autonomy and freedom. There are certain capacities, the possession of which is necessary (although perhaps not sufficient), for autonomy to be realized, such as equality of opportunity; this is something that mere formal equality under the law often cannot deliver. Accordingly, we might say that while negative liberty focuses on the formal or procedural conditions of freedom, trying to ensure that all are as free as far as possible from external constraints, positive liberty seeks to stipulate certain kinds of substantive freedoms, the possession of which is needed for freedom and autonomy to prevail. The tension between these two types of liberty is played out in the other two philosophers as well, with Agamben's free use of the self and Nancy's more social appeal to Balibar's concept of equaliberty.

As is evident, and as Berlin argues in his preference for negative liberty, the realization of positive liberty for some often requires a diminishment of the liberty of others. Even though positive liberty might be desirable, it would seem that the only way to secure it would be to impinge on the sphere of freedom and autonomy enjoyed by others; for instance, requiring universal access to education means that some would have to pay higher taxes, so the loss of income restricts their options to some extent. Liberals have difficulty with such choices, since they require a clear criterion for making the necessary claim that some choices or values are more important than others, which would clearly violate the necessary equation of freedom with autonomy of individual choice on which liberalism rests. For this reason, liberals have often been charged by communitarians with espousing an inadequate and abstract concept of the subject and of the good (Taylor, 1985).

Yet, far from being an admission of relativism or failure to reach consensus on the good (McIntyre, 1981), liberalism can be seen as an epistemology containing a moral doctrine. In espousing individual autonomy and the equal value of the autonomy of each person, liberals are not simply giving in to relativism because they also believe—and here is their enlightenment heritage—that in conditions of freedom, the truth will be attained. In other words, the corollary of individual autonomy is that this is the only way to attain an adequate conception of the good. The influence of bad or corrupt institutions that impose an obligation to obey established authority, individuals' dependence on a social order in which benefits are very unevenly distributed, and the undue power of received opinion backed by oppressive custom, are for liberals the great fetter to understanding, let alone attaining, the good. Nineteenth-century liberals, such as Mill, were doubtless far too optimistic in their assumption that the removal of oppressive custom would lead *automatically* to progress, truth, and the good, but were correct in believing that the latter could not be achieved if disagreement as to its nature or form was stifled in advance. Liberals of the classical era could also be faulted for their optimism with respect to the market and capitalism.

There clearly are situations in which no amount of market coordination yields satisfactory results, in which case it will be necessary to appeal to some set of higher-order principles that can be used to make decisions about the overall outcome of social interaction. Whether in the form of Rawls's principle of "justice as fairness" (1971) or some version of religious meta-ethics, liberalism is not in principle incompatible with a communitarian scheme that appeals to tradition, community standards, or even "our way of life" to decide conflicts between actors. But what would unite such communitarian versions of liberalism, or would seek to be compatible with liberalism, is an insistence on proceduralism. This is not to say, *pace* McIntyre, that liberals are fundamentally committed to the right over the good, with the implication that liberals have no sense of the good, but rather, that whatever communitarian values turn out to be appealed to in the case of conflicts between actors, such values must be formalizable in terms of rules. Otherwise, one is stuck with a kind of personal authority to intervene and decide such conflicts, an option that to the liberal mind is far too reminiscent of political theology and the divine right of kings for comfort.

Communitarianism represents a mainstream response to the liberal defense of individualism. Communitarians contend that liberals *privilege* the individual to such an extent that communal bonds are lost. In a liberal democracy, Berlin famously claimed, a free person "should be left to do or be what he is able to do or be, without interference by other persons" (1969). Critics of communitarianism, however, argue that they have an "authoritarian tendency," not unlike the one found in Rousseau's odd brand of republicanism, that is, the "*forced to be free*" dictum (2007). In response, communitarians claim that only their brand of liberty makes sense. Following Rousseau, they argue that the ideal of a pure form of negative liberty could only occur in a mythological state of nature (1987). Because we are social individuals, we can never be freed from external and internal obstacles. In fact, most communitarians attempt to salvage negative liberty by combining it with a social model of positive liberty. Charles Taylor's famous article "What's Wrong with Negative Liberty?" represents the general position held by communitarians on this issue: negative liberty (freedom from) is coextensive with positive liberty (freedom to do and become), that is, establishing "collective control over the common life" (1985, 211). This mixed model of liberty is not unlike Marx and Engel's dictum that "the free development of each is the condition for the free development of all" (1998).

Communitarians also claim that the liberal emphasis on individual rights leads to a strong state and a weak civil society. The proceduralist model of liberalism gives rise to overly active juridical, legislative, and/or executive branches of the state. As an overarching, detached, and value-neutral arbitrator, the liberal state prevents the development of a commonly held value system. The state, in a sense, forces its negative freedom on individuals and communities alike, which is a source of great tension in civil society. All that are left in civil society are rights-bearing, private individuals who pursue their own interests.

Many communitarians thus prefer a weaker model of government and more autonomy for local democracy. In line with the civic republican tradition, they argue that community can only flourish when there is an active, self-governing, and relatively independent civil society. Following other republican thinkers, such as Rousseau (2007) or more recently Arendt (1998), communitarians elevate the role of political activity in the public sphere. Some, such as Robert Putnam (2000), cite Tocqueville's call for a strong and independent public in civil society, held together by voluntary associations; others recognize that the public, meaning the people, has to be closely aligned with the state (Bellah et al., 2008). Cultural communitarians, such as Taylor, reduce community to cultural identity and then transfer this conflation into the political sphere as a national, ethno-cultural property belonging to a political community (1994, 1998).

In generic terms then, most communitarians appeal to positive liberty as an ideal for an active, or participatory, model of citizenship. In a civic republic, citizens are expected to *exercise* political control over their communal lives. Although participating in public life exposes individuals to their community, they stand to benefit more from their public acts than do immunized individuals who live sheltered lives in their own private spheres. Many trumpet the republican ideal of public life as the highest expression of individual life. Some promote civic virtue, such as MacIntyre (1981) and Bellah et al. (2008), while others promote social capital, such as Putnam (2000).

## V. Radical Republicanism

Esposito's work excavates and examines in a singularly powerful way how the dominant Western philosophical-political idealization of an immunized and proper community is becoming increasingly untenable in our current geopolitical circumstances. Esposito's critique is not simply a nihilistic gesture, but is instead a prelude to a perhaps inevitable, but in any case long overdue, rethinking of the basis of political and social relations. From his perspective, community is anything but a common essence or a shared property. The immunized models of community, where members are protected against foreign substances, external threats, and internal contagions, so common in our times, are imploding at a frightening pace. Rather than search for new material to mend the breaches of the communal borders and shield community against the nihilism of expropriation, Esposito searches for the original link between community and expropriation. Community does not shelter, contain, and protect us; rather, community is the very inauguration of an expropriation process. In community, so-called proprietary subjects are mutually exposed and suspended in a common *munus*, which never forms a stable property or furnishes an essential identity. The much-heralded crisis of community today, he contends, is merely the crisis of the project of community conceived under the banner of immunization. Community can no longer be conceived as an archi-original border that shelters the proper from being expropriated in its various senses. If the exigency of community is to be addressed in our times, then we are left with the seemingly impossible task of deconstructing the proper.

This task has not been without its detractors. In the burgeoning English literature on Esposito, a single question is constantly being raised about his work: what kind of politics can come from such an approach? Most recognize that he is coming from somewhere on the Left—his revision of community is grounded in a notion of communism—but his lack of concrete statements, his insistence that he is more committed to deconstructing core categories in modern political thought than to prescribing practical political solutions, and his tendency to present his opinion while working through an interpretation of other theorists, have left many wondering if a concrete politics can be drawn from his political theory.[15]

The question itself is cumbersome. Where is the question coming from and what is being asked of Esposito? Is he expected to appeal to a prefabricated political roadmap, in the manner of Alain Badiou? Bosteels has argued that without such a template, Esposito's notion of the "impolitical" leads into the apolitical terrain of the postpolitical (2010). But is this a fair characterization? Esposito fits within a clear trajectory of critical European political philosophers who prefer to search for new openings for rethinking radical politics by criticizing contemporary political formations, rather than providing ready-made prescriptions. Esposito's theory of community is drawn from the tradition of emancipatory politics. He asks, how can we conceive of an emancipatory community that is no longer proper? To do so, community would have to be understood as improper (with the "im-" standing for both "inside" and "against" the proper).[16] His radical republican solution provides slightly more fodder than Nancy's existential model of democracy and much more than Agamben's contentless community.

Since writing *Communitas*, Esposito has provided hints about his position, more so in recent years. In these writings, two main ideas best highlight his radically deconstructed version of civic republicanism: affirmative freedom and obligations. It is in the combination of affirmative freedom and obligations that the ethical significance, not content, of the *communitas* is found. Moreover, when affirmative freedom becomes affirmative biopolitics, his ontological deontology becomes a biopolitical deontology. In his biopolitical writings, he develops a Deleuzian notion of an "affirmative biopolitics" that affirms *a* life rather than *the* life (*BBF*, 200–215; *BBP*, 182–194; *TP*, 18, 142–151). Affirmative biopolitics, he claims in a different essay, is a "politics no longer *over* life but *of* life" (*TP*, 77).

Esposito's notion of "affirmative freedom/liberty" represents a synthesis of his deconstruction of the proper and his critique of the immunitarian paradigm. How, he asks, can freedom be experienced in a community when our prevailing models of liberty are bound up with a proprietary understanding of our world? This question appears in many of his writings on biopolitics, the legal person, and on community.

Esposito's deconstruction of the mainstream approaches to the relationship between community and liberty begins with a common gesture in his writing—he traces the origins of freedom back to the "semantics of community" (*TOP*, 51). Prior to the modern immunity dispositif, he notes, freedom was conceived as a relational concept with an "affirmative declension." With the Roman *libertas*, for example, freedom was configured "as the external perimeter that delimits what may be done from what should *not* be done" (*TOP*, 52). In *Bíos*, Esposito notes that *libertas* and the English term "freedom" follow from a semantic chain (love and friendship) that held an "affirmative connotation": "the concept of liberty, in its germinal nucleus, alludes to a connective power that grows and develops according to its own internal law, and to an expansion or deployment that unites its members in a shared dimension" (*BBF*, 69; *BBP*, 70). In "Freedom and Immunity," he argues that this communal sense of liberty formed a "connective, aggregating, [and] unifying power" (*TOP*, 52).

The original "constitutive link" between "liberty" and "alterity" (*alteritá*) that was found in the "affirmative" and "relational" notion of liberty was destroyed, he argues in reference to Heidegger, with the modern metaphysical subject (*BBF*, 71; *BBP*, 70). Liberty was translated into an individualistic paradigm, where it became defined as a subject's relationship to itself: "he is free when no obstacle is placed between him and his will—or also between his will and its realization" (*BBF*, 71; *BBP*, 71). Free subjects are those who are the masters of their own wills. As such, modern liberty is inscribed in a "negative horizon of meaning," whereby to be free is to be free from obstacles. In this transformation, freedom as a "mode of being" becomes a "right," "a right to have something as one's own" (*diritto ad avere qualcosa di proprio*) (*BBF*, 71; *BBP*, 72). Individuals are now prioritized over their relation with others. As the modern immunization process progressed, the privileged sense of liberty was gradually translated into a notion of "security." Modern "liberty is that which insures the individual against the interference of others through the voluntary subordination to a more powerful order that guarantees it," whether this be to the sovereign in Hobbes's social contract or the "forced to be free" dictum of Rousseau. The negative inflection of liberty is *immunizing*.

In his essay "Freedom and Immunity," Esposito explicitly states that if we are to solve the problem of thinking about community and freedom, then we must liberate "freedom from liberalism and community from communitarianism" (*TOP*, 55). Mainstream liberal and communitarian models of liberty are derived from the metaphysical model of the subject. Both schools treat freedom as "a quality, a faculty, or a good" that a collective, an individual, or many subjects "must acquire" (*TOP*, 50). The negative declension appeared during the Middle Ages, when freedom began to be conceptualized as a "'particular right': an ensemble of 'privileges,' 'exemptions,' or 'immunity'" (*TOP*, 52). This negative turn gave rise to a notion of liberty that exempts privileged subjects from common obligations and/or juridical responsibilities. Later political theorists, such as Hobbes, Locke, and Rousseau, inherited this model and cemented it as a cornerstone of modern political thought. In the negative model, subjects are expected to engage in a struggle to free themselves from any obstacle that could prevent them from becoming autonomous and proper subjects. Freedom is treated as if it is a *thing* that can be "appropriated" and thus "constituted as a subjective property" (*TOP*, 50). Authentically free subjects must become fully fledged proprietors of themselves, which means that one must become "'proper' and no longer 'common'" (*CIB*, 50). Translated into Esposito's lexicon, the private subject must be immunized from the common. In turn, the common becomes the antisubjective realm that erects communal barriers and demands collective responsibilities, which negate the freedom of the subject. Community, in short, is viewed as the oppressive realm. It presses against the subject and limits her autonomy.

Rather than challenge the predicates supporting the negative model of liberty propagated by liberalism, communitarians make the sloppy mistake of merely translating this individualistic paradigm to the level of communities. "American neo-communitarianism," claims Esposito, mistakenly links "the idea of community to that of belonging, identity and ownership," meaning that community, as we have seen, is treated as a thing that a person identifies with "his/her own ethnic group, land or language" (*TOP*, 48). Instead of creating an immunitarian enclosure around an individual, communitarians construct a perceived enclosure around the community. For them, community is concomitant with the proper. Communitarians treat the common as if it is *"one's own."* Members of the community can only feel secure when their common property is immunized from external appropriation. These communities have built-in immunization mechanisms that are supposed to defend them from alterity. Thus, the negative inflection found in the liberal model of liberty is merely collectivized in this model, which is sometimes exaggerated to frightening degrees. In this move, the need for communal self-preservation inflects the negative element of liberty, privilege becomes security, and affirmative freedom becomes negative immunization (*BBF*, 71; *BPP*, 72). In short, communitarians negate their own efforts to conceptualize a positive model of liberty that occurs within a group setting by reducing liberty to property and hence by reproducing the core logic of the immunitary dispositif.

Esposito's effort to circumvent the closure of community found in the paradigmatic debate between liberals and communitarians begins with a turn away from the proper. Contrary to the communitarians, argues Esposito, community is "what is *not* one's own, or what is unable to be appropriated by someone" (*TOP*, 49). Community can only be experienced as a "loss, removal, or expropriation" because it voids one's identity rather than fulfils it. Community is thus experienced as a radical alteration that disrupts the rigid boundaries that protect an individual's identity. Rather than appeal to an immunizing "enclosure" locking subjects inside themselves, either on an individualistic or collective basis, community is experienced in and through an opening and exposure that "turns individuals inside out, freeing them to their exteriority." His revision of positive liberty as "affirmative liberty" directly addresses this open model of community.

Esposito's relational and affirmative notion of liberty follows from Nancy's "experience of freedom." Esposito ties freedom to the singular plural model of existence. Freedom is not "something that one has," as if it were a thing one could appropriate, but it is merely "something that one is: what frees existence to the possibility to exist as such" (*TOP*, 54). Freedom, following from his work in *Communitas*, is not of the register of *having*, but *being*, or more precisely in *becoming*. Freedom is nothing in particular. In fact, there really is "no freedom" per se, "only liberation"; "one cannot be" free because one "can only *become* free." One becomes free in the practical experience of the "decision of existence."

Without resorting to the evental tradition marking radical philosophical treatises on freedom in the twentieth century, of "freeing freedom" such as Agamben does in his notion of impotentiality, Esposito attempts to "revitalize" the "affirmative power" of freedom by tracing it back to its "common root," where freedom is understood as the "locus of plurality, difference, and alterity" (*TOP*, 55). This is the exact opposite of the modern sense of freedom as the "locus of identity, belonging, and appropriation." For Esposito, this means "freedom is the singular dimension of community" that "sweeps across infinite singularities that *are* plural" (*TOP*, 55). Translated into more practical terms, freedom can only be experienced in an open model of community that "resists immunization." This is a community that internalizes its exteriority while remaining open to difference. In this open and free community, individuals are exposed to alterity, pluralized, and thus prevented from appropriating differences. But if this were all there were to his philosophy of community, we would remain within the realm of the expropriative element of community, which would be closer to Nancy's *cum* than the *munus*. I will end by discussing how he relates the *munus* to the ex, or how he deontologizes the plural and singular force of ontological freedom.

Esposito often refers to Simone Weil to make his argument that communal obligations must replace rights. In *Immunitas*, he echoes the communitarian critique of liberal proceduralism and rights discourse. The "primary goal of law," he claims, "is to immunize the community" (*IMI*, 26; *IME*, 22). The law acts as a mechanism to protect individuals from common life, which exposes them to difference and expropriates them. What occurs here is a confusion between the common and the proper. To defend what it perceives to be the proper of the community, the law actually makes the community less common. Esposito argues that this fundamental mistake is grounded in the privative nature of the notion of proper law or particular law (*ius proprium*). Weil, he argues, formulated a "'law in common,'" which prioritizes "obligations" [*obblighi*] over "rights" [*diritti*]. Obligations (from *obligare*) are binding. In the law in common, we are subjected to "an expropriation of what is proper to us, beginning with the subjective essence" (*IMI*, 27–28; *IME*, 23). The modern legal model of the private person as the bearer of rights, replaces the impersonal subject of *communitas*. Rights that derive from the *ius proprium*, he claims, are always partial because they represent the proper. They distinguish between those who "possess it from the status of those who are deprived" (*IMI*, 29; *IME*, 24). Rights cannot be shared and made common. By elevating the immunizing powers of the *ius proprium*, law "reverses the affirmative bond of common obligation into the purely negative right of each individual to exclude all others from using what is proper to him or her" (IMI, 30; *IME*, 25). Rights are rooted in the proprietary sense of belonging (*appartenenza*). A right "always belongs to someone" (*IMI*, 33; *IME*, 28). In their original meaning, rights were always the fruits of violent appropriative actions. The "root of legal ownership, or what is legally proper," was established through the acts of "taking, grabbing and tearing away" (*capere*, *emere*, and *rapere*) (*IMI*, 33; *IME*, 28). Put in different terms, law represents the deployment of the dialectic of alienation and appropriation, which is incommensurable with the common.[17]

The relationship between rights and the proper is most thoroughly articulated in his notion of the impersonal, which is the main subject of *Third Person* (*TP*). His argument is too complex to cover in detail here, but it is important to mention that in this work he uses the juxtaposition between the person and the impersonal to think about *communitas.*[18] Summarizing this work in *Living Thought*, Esposito argues that the problem with the modern political-legal notion of the person is that it "presupposes the separation from itself as opposed to the unity of the living being" (*LT*, 272–73). As with the modern notion of freedom, the person is drawn from a proprietary model of a subject, where the person is expected to be the owner of her own body.[19] The person is the subject of rights, whereas the impersonal opens the possibility of thinking about obligations. Drawing from Weil, in *Third Person* Esposito notes that rights derive from the "exclusionary dispositif" of immunity; a right is simultaneously "private and privative" (*TP*, 101). Rights are thus particularistic and can only apply to a category of people. The impersonal, on the other hand, is anonymous. It disrupts the immunity mechanisms of the law and opens to justice. The impersonal is singular and plural. It allows for us to think about communal obligations and the *munus*.

One of the most important strains in *Persons and Things* is how persons and things are converted into property in modernity. Western culture, he argues, is characterized by "the absolute primacy of having over being," where "a thing is not first and foremost what it *is* but rather what someone *has*," just as a *persona* was for the Romans "not what one *is*, but what one *has*" (*PT*, 18, 30). More than anyone else, Locke helped solidify the supremacy of having over being when "he made the body into the 'thing' of one's own person" (*PT*, 51). There are two dimensions to this formulation that he takes up in this work: taking and the body.

Esposito returns to the roots of the dispositif of the proper, specifically in its proprietary formulation. This dispositif is rooted in a notion of a hand that takes and seizes things to make them its own. "The hand that grasps and holds is one of the distinguishing features of the human species" (*PT*, 19). "In order for something to become unequivocally one's own," he notes, "it had to be torn from nature or from other people" (*PT*, 22). Ownership is determined at its origin by *taking* with one's hand: "*manu captum*, according to the solemn institution of *mancipium*" (ibid.). The origin of property is appropriation, its "primordial form, property is neither transmitted nor inherited: it is seized" (*PT*, 21). All legal forms of property, whether private or public, refer back to this notion of "original appropriation" (*PT*, 24). Esposito aims to conceive of the common in opposition to public and private property. In Roman law, for instance, public things "are those that belong to the state," versus *communes*, which are "inappropriable" things that "belong to everyone" (2015, 73). Common things are not even the same as *nullius* because this is a mark of things that are "appropriable by whoever first lays hold of them" (ibid.).

Esposito argues that we have to wrest the body from this proprietary model. The body should represent what we might call "the impersonal third dimension" that can neither be reified nor personified. In our biopolitical era, the body can be used to launch a "politics *of* life" to resist and revolt against the "politics *on* life," as Foucault used these phrases (*PT*, 143). The body must be transferred from "the sphere of the proper to that of common," which he contends is happening because it is "eminently common" (*PT*, 105–7). Throughout the texts he evaluates different ways the body has been used in this manner. The existential notion of the body as extensive, for example, "is not what I have, but what I *am*" (*PT*, 119). The body likewise "loses absolute ownership over itself" in prosthetics, he notes in reference to Nancy, because here the "life of the human" and the "life of things" become intertwined (*PT*,

123, 1–27). Today, the politics of the common is best addressed by the body, he concludes, because it is "[f]oreign to both the semantics of the persons and to those of the thing, the living body of increasingly vast multitudes demands a radical renewal of the vocabularies of politics, law, and philosophy" (*PT*, 147).

## Conclusion

In the last chapter, I discussed Campbell's examination of the biopolitical deployments of Heidegger's distinction between proper and improper in *Improper Life*. Campbell claims that Agamben, contrary to his stated goal of diagonalizing the proper/improper, ascribes to a theory of the improper, which opens him up to a thanatopolitical reading of biopolitics. On the other hand, in his affirmative biopolitics, Esposito uses the notion of the impersonal to disrupt the modern dispositif of the person that forces the distinction between the proper and improper. "To be a person," Campbell remarks, "is not to live the separation between proper and improper but rather to be divided so as to make possible the subjugation of one part to another" (2011, 69). The impersonal, he continues, "breaks with the proper and improper" (2011, 78). The radical opening of *communitas* opens onto the impersonal. He even claims that with his reference to Weil's distinction between the justness of impersonal obligations and private personal rights, Esposito "implicitly recalls and extends a form of republicanism" not unlike the work of Michael Sandel. If there is a passage here that connects the impersonal to *communitas*, it is "Esposito's project of 'common law' (or, pace Agamben, a 'common use')" (2011, 80). Unfortunately, these references are found at the end of his analysis of the biopolitical contours of both philosophers' renditions of Heidegger's theory of the proper/improper. Nevertheless, his work demonstrates the Heideggerian, and we have added political and economic, threads in both of their work: the proper.

Esposito's discussion of community represents a radicalization and revitalization of the idea of the common or the communal as it appears etymologically in Latin as *munus*. The *munus* as exposure to otherness and expropriating difference is not merely negative in the sense that the latter would represent a denial of something positive or good.

Rather, nothingness as *munus*, as exposure to difference, is in itself something "positive" because it is how the relation that creates subject positions becomes possible at all. Such negativity, although Esposito shies away from discussing it as anything but a lack—and this might well be a symptom of his insistence on desubstantializing communitarian belonging—in fact implies something of the positive freedom communitarians seek but are inevitably led to reify in terms of the proper and the dialectic of alienation and appropriation.

In any case, what is clear is that, as the *munus* implies, community takes the form of a collective debt that is owed to itself (and therefore anonymously), and it is here that Esposito's work resonates with the republican tradition. That the *munus* is derived from the Roman Republic should be enough to establish Esposito's republican bent. But before one rushes to place at Esposito's door the defects of republicanism as it has been historically constituted, precisely those of which contemporary communitarianism seems most guilty, we must keep in mind that the *munus* is utilized by Esposito to enact a radical deconstruction of every notion of the proper.

Thus Esposito gestures toward and remains in proximity to a radical vision of republicanism. The radical in his theory lies both in the original sense of the term, found in his emphasis on the etymological origins of terms in his political lexicon, and in the contemporary sense of a politics beyond mainstream politics, which he usually defines as "impolitical." For Esposito, the res publica is neither "*la chose publique*," the "common wealth," nor a "common good," because the common is nothing but exposure to common being. The common is not a proprietary and/or moral good around which politics is circumscribed. A politics that is coordinated, mediated, determined, and grounded in things is closed and exclusionary. Politics, he argues in *Communitas*, is ultimately grounded in nothingness. This traversal of the foundational elements of modern politics does not lead us to an abysmal form of absolute nihilism, which is a contradiction of terms; rather, it deconstructs the political terrain so that we are open to rethinking politics and ethics in an ontological manner. Later, he will claim that politics must arise, not necessarily from nothing, but from the disruption of the person and the thing, which are both subsumed by the dispositif of the proper. The impersonal body becomes a new focus for him. Either way, his model of affirmative biopolitics is as much political as it is ethical and communal.

In *Living Thought*, Esposito argues that the extended Italian reflection on *communitas* differentiates it from the French reflections on community. Instead of focusing on "a substance or property," the French (Bataille, Blanchot, and Nancy) take up the theme of "the pure relationship and nothing else" (*LT*, 255–56). Drawing on Derrida's remark in *The Politics of Friendship*, that the French reflections end up as "searchlights without a coast" as their "warnings turn endlessly" (2005, 81), Esposito argues that the *munus* allows the Italian reflections to give a "precise meaning" "to the empty spot around which community takes form" (*LT*, 256). The expropriative aspect of the *munus* means that community "has never really been seen" because community "is nothing but an epistemological threshold," "a critical measure" that is "always resurgent but never intentionally realizable—one that vanishes the moment one seeks to pinpoint it" (*LT*, 257). The exposure, he argues in relation to Agamben and Nancy, calls "into question the subjective logic of presupposition" (*LT*, 256). Only in the combination of affirmative freedom and communal obligations does the division (*divisione*) that defines our relationships open to a notion of community where sharing is not just a sharing out, but also a sharing with (*condivisione*).

In his philosophy there is a direct relationship between his ethical ontology and politics. Politics are not left aside for the future (to come) or made possible in a particular ethos or way of being; instead, his affirmative biopolitics is supplemented by the ethical duty implied by the *munus*. In his republican model, communal duties and obligations, which are ontologically grounded, are prioritized over rights and interests. There is an impolitical opening here that allows for a rethinking of politics and the political.[20] We are drawn or contracted together in an ontological contract that obliges us to give back in response to the gift of community. This is a heterodox deontological contract. The politics that arise here are as much ontological and ethical as they are political. An affirmative biopolitics must affirm life, our ontological relationships, and the gift of community. Contrary to Agamben's modal ontology, which emphasizes the expositional and preparatory characteristics of the event of existence, even Nancy's relational ontology, Esposito has sought to scribe an ethical and political ontology. This is neither a regional ontology nor an ontology of the political, but a grounding of ethics and politics in the realm of first philosophy.

Esposito brings something new to this discussion by re-engaging with the modern Western tradition of political philosophy. Issues such as the validity of metaphysics and pluralizing ontological philosophy or notions of potentiality, communication, and productivity in the Western cannon serve as background materials that guide his examination of the Western tradition. From his most ontological work, *Communitas*, to his subsequent biopolitical writings, Esposito's primary aim has been to traverse this tradition. He forces us to confront the place, or misplacement, of the common in political thought. How does political economy usurp the common, or, more directly, how does this discursive regime empty the common of everything that is proper to it? It is precisely this treatment of the common as something that is proper that he interrogates. The proper has nothing in common with the common. The proper of the common, a phrasing our language forces us to employ, is neither proper nor improper. Modern political economy deceives us into thinking of the common in terms of the proper. But this is a discourse that at its core is privative. It is not suited for thinking about the common, period. In its place, Esposito turns to an ethical economy, which in *Communitas* is more ontological but in his subsequent writings becomes more biopolitical. This ethical economy also addresses the core communist problem of redistribution, not as pieces of property (personal or otherwise) in the first instance, but in terms of an ethical ontology and later ethical-biopolitical notion of sharing (*condivisione*). Esposito radically deconstructs the giving-taking modality of the modern dispositif of the proper. His notion of the *munus* provides more solid grounds, a slightly more practical philosophy at least in relation to this debate, which makes his work stand out.

# Conclusion

We have reached a point where we can no longer ignore the two core issues addressed in this book—the dispositif of the proper and the relationship between ontology, ethics, and politics. At first glance each could be read as yet another waltz around the dance floor with Heidegger, maybe even a last one. But it would be wrong to reduce our main philosophers to being nothing more than Heideggerians because each draws from a number of philosophical and political progenitors that are well beyond the reaches of Heideggerianism. Moreover their engagement with the different so-called "regional ontologies" is not an expropriative gesture. They have each made numerous insights in their particular fields that have shaped how they engage with ontology, politics, and ethics in relation to the dispositif of the proper.

A reconsideration of the dispositif of the proper is long overdue. Today, this dispositif is entangled in a whole series of matters that cannot be solved by reapplying its operations, including the neocolonial or neoimperialist domination of global capital, largely controlled by a small class of elites and their institutions based in the Global North; governmental or immunitarian mechanisms that continuously arrange, order, control, and regulate all aspects of life; global warming, species extinction, rising water levels, environmental racism, environmental destruction, and ecological imperialism; unprecedented flows of refugees and migrants who are abused and exploited at every stage of their dangerous journey; patriarchal movements searching for new ways to maintain the hegemonic position of the masculine; a rising biopolitical economy that converts every form of life into a piece of property; and resurgent ethno-nationalism hell-bent on defending the idiomatic to the point of imploding, which is countered by a politics of demographics. The dispositif of the proper has not only played a significant role in each of these matters, it has guided us to the brink of our ultimate precipice.

Our world is one where *being* is subordinated to *having*. The world of *Homo approprians* is an appropriable world. It already appears as if its work is done, for there is little left to appropriate. But we will continue to dig further into the ground, look deeper into life's hidden structures, produce new synthetic entities, and fly higher into the atmosphere and beyond, all in search of more to appropriate. From pole to pole, outer atmosphere to inner core, boundaries will be fought over, wars will be launched, and borders will be redrawn. But do we want our path into the future to be laid out by an intensification and extenuation of the proper? *Homo approprians* will never be satiated; it will always look for more, even if its last grasp will lead to its end. At what point do we say, "That is enough, you have taken too much, too many have suffered, and you have left us with a world that is so divided and conquered that very little remains that could be considered common"? How can we put an end to this way of being, a disposition that at its core is completely idiotic? Either we follow this thieving idiot to our collective demise or we put an end to its reign.

The question we have to address is how to arrive at a shared world where all its inhabitants are able to live and exist in common. That is, how can we address the ontological exigency of being-in-common? Ultimately, political economy is incapable of fostering a solution to this problem. We must radically rethink how we conceive of *emancipation*. The first step is to expose, render inoperative, and ultimately traverse the dispositif of the proper. Until then, our togetherness will continue to be determined by the violent divisiveness of the proper, and being will continue to be dominated by having. The question today is not how much more can we take, understood in its inequitable distribution, but how much more of our planet, ecosystem, and ultimately life itself can be taken. In place of the invasive modalities of taking and giving of *Homo approprians*, we need to reconceptualize activity as holding and letting go. Being-in-common can only occur through the emancipatory act where each is a part of, not a participant in, the act of letting go of everything that has been held back from the commons. Appropriation negates the commons, yet if we were to learn how to use things without appropriating them and thus converting them into property, the commons could be everywhere. What is called for is neither a grand appropriation of goods, nor a great refusal, nor a rejection, because each replicates the invasive model of property; rather, the commons can be freed through a series of actions that culminate in what we might call, following Agamben, a "great relinquishment."

What is called for here is not a handing over of goods, things, titles, deeds, or patents—a redistribution of the content of the dispositif of the proper, which does not fundamentally dissolve this dispositif. Nothing can be donated, for there are no charitable gifts to give; yet nothing can be taken either. Dis-containment will surely be a pathway filled with confusion, strife, and violence. Those whose hands have been disproportionally empowered to retain their excessive lot are not likely to just let it go. Their dispositions must be exposed, institutions destituated, laws abolished, and hands wrested open. Dis-containment is but a small step along the path to radically transforming how we live together in this world.

Given the hegemonic position that the dispositif of the proper holds in our era, it would be idiotic to toss it aside as yet another Heideggerian neologism. From the beginning, I have demonstrated the centrality of the proper in the modern tradition of political economy. From Proudhon's early critique of the property prejudice, to early formulations of *Homo approprians* in liberalism and communism, the proliferation of proprietary claims in contemporary identity politics and biopolitics, the dispositif of the proper today stands as one of the most potent dispositifs in our world. Whether from a deconstructive or an archaeological approach, each of the three main philosophers covered in this book has sought to expose this dispositif as a critical operation that has shaped our world. I hope that by ending on this note that I can show that despite their shortcomings, their cumulative body of work should inspire much further inspection.

* * *

As a philosopher whose goal is to rethink the Heideggerian problem of being-with, Nancy is quite hesitant to put forth an ontological notion of politics, let alone an ethical ontology. Contemporary political philosophy mistakenly conceives of politics in such a way that it dominates the ontological. Biopolitical philosophy, Nancy contends, mistakenly searches for ways to rethink the relationship between the biopolitical and the ontological, which in the end leads to a biopolitical appropriation of the ontological. On the contrary, Nancy argues, politics must be kept separate from the ontological.

Under the auspices of the problem of ontological difference and the modern symbolic economy, modern political theology leads us to conceive of the political as the transcendental sphere that symbolically represents the whole. The political task in this formulation is to appropriate the symbolic in order to render the collective proper and complete. This political gesture leads to a closure not only of community but of being. In our globalized world, the political-theological dream of transcendence has been completely immanentized; the political is now so far-reaching that everything, including the social, has become political; politics are formal and totalitarian; and there is no outside that can be used to distinguish between the authentic and inauthentic representations of the whole. In short, there is no form upon which our symbolic unity can be projected.

This retreat of the symbolic representation of our relations provides an opening for rethinking the relationship between the ontological and the ontic (including politics and ethics). It also gives us pause to re-examine not only the traditional formulation of ontological difference as the difference between beings and Being, but also its incorporation in Western political theology. It is in this combined reflection that Nancy's philosophy reaches its pinnacle—he argues that we need to rethink ontology as an ontology of sharing and division. Being shares and divides us up, and we are shared and divided in being. The ontological problematic, in other words, should no longer be one of ontological difference, representing the identity and difference between two, but of being-with, co-existence, compearance, and so on. Ontology is immediately stripped of its onto-theological bifurcation, of its revelatory and thus representational structure, and is placed firmly in the world without foundations. Being-with becomes a matter of first philosophy.

This seismic shift—it really cannot be called a Copernican revolution—shatters the political-theological foundations of political philosophy. Politics can no longer be tasked with representing the symbolic unity of the group. At most, politics have to be given a lesser role of holding open the space that is necessary for us to coexist in-common. In coexistence we are shared and shared out. This is an incommensurable space beyond politics, a space where politics has no business being in the first place. Contemporary ecotechnical politics, in other words, must be severely weakened. This is the proper meaning of the symbol. There really are no ethical prescriptions here, but an *ethos* of coexistence. In short, there is a relationship between ontology and politics, but he advises against interweaving them. There is still a place in our world for politics, but politics ought to let us be and not dominate every aspect of our lives, especially our being-in-common. Whether this is a sufficient formulation given our current biopolitical era is a separate question. What we can say is that for Nancy, the philosopher is not entitled to make political prescriptions, especially those that concern the democratic space of the in-common.

It is difficult to pin down Nancy's position on the dispositif of the proper. He is clearly critical of the model of *Homo approprians* and the political-economic sense of appropriation. When it comes to his own prescriptions, however, he is more ambiguous. If we were to venture an interpretation, we might argue that he attempts to formulate a scaled-back notion of the proper. We would have to turn to his deconstruction of the symbolic economy to piece this together. Contrary to the juxtaposition of the authentic and inauthentic, appearance and reality, Nancy searches for an alternative notion of the proper that cannot be appropriated in either a perceptual or manual sense (neither *percipere* nor *mancipare*). His solution is to turn to a hidden dimension in the proper itself, which is the proper as that which is most near and proximate (*prope*, **pro*). On the one hand, the proper is never presented but only presencing. He thus emphasizes the movement and flow of towards-being, being-there, or being-towards (*prae-esse*), all of which occur only in the *ex-*. In this manner, the proper can only be tangentially sensed, but never seized or appropriated. On the other hand, since the proper signals nearness and proximity, the proper is relational. This relation, however, only occurs in the dispersal and disposition that simultaneously joins and distances the parts. It is a symbolic relationship, precisely in the sense of the sym-bol (put-with) where parts share in, are shared out, and share through division. Thus, if we were to advance this reading, we could make the claim that the proper represents both the *ex-* and the *co-* of coexistence. The parts are dispersed and disposed in an open relation where they exist near and proximate to each other. But this reading is likely a forced one as his reflections on the proper are much too divergent to summarize in a simple formula.

* * *

Of the three main philosophers covered in this book, Agamben is the most apprehensive about the prospects of rethinking the relationship between ontology and politics or ethics. There are many parallels between Agamben and Nancy on this account. For example, Nancy's notion of eco-techniques performs a function similar to that of biopolitics for Agamben. Both lead to an appropriation and ultimately closure of being. For Nancy, politics must be given the weakened task of holding open the space that will let us be-in-common. Letting in his formulation is more akin to a loosening, widening, opening, or, in short, holding open an unobstructed passageway (*laxus*). Politics thus is tasked with letting existents coexist without meddling in their ways of being. This is probably a step too far for Agamben, who argues that given that politics today are biopolitical, it is not possible to ask a government to refrain from meddling in its populations' lives, nor could we even try to recalibrate the operations of government to function as mechanisms that hold open the space that will let us be-in-common. For modern governmental machines have been calibrated in such way that, at their core, their operations appropriate ways of living and convert all forms of life into biopolitical dispositions. This subordination of being is so comprehensive and acute that he often advocates exemplary ways of being that are largely impolitical. At certain points, it even appears as if his fear of contaminating his ideal ontological modality by bringing it into relation with the biopolitical machinery of modern governments leads him to appeal to exemplary ways of being that are so impolitical, so loose, and so passive, that he appears to scribe a philosophy of submission rather than one of admission, as in Nancy's case of weak politics.

If there is a positive role for modern governmental machinery in his philosophy, it can only be their production of abject and impolitical dispositions, which he argues actually create openings for establishing an ontological modality of being that is disruptive of their biopolitical operations. Rather than attempting to overcome alienation (*zoē*, bare life, depoliticization, poverty, resident aliens, etc.) by appropriating the apparatuses that have put one in their position in the first place, being alienated provides an opportunity. In his earlier work, he tended to fetishize the abjectness of such a position. In his more recent work, he has switched his attention to more intentional forms of estrangement. From the Franciscan friars, to the protests of 1968, to Occupy Wall Street, he has sought to find a form of living that is defiant in its core. Instead of celebrating being improper, which is a negative disposition, the form-of-life he advocates defies and ultimately traverses the dialectic of the proper and improper. In place of action, he appeals to a form of habit that is inoperative. And in place of property, he promotes a notion of common use. Together, the use and habits of bodies represent a challenge to the biopolitical mechanisms of modern states. They do not directly confront, seize, and take control of these apparatuses; rather, in their form-of-life, ontological ethos, they form a destituent kind of power. This carries a double meaning. On the one side, it is a destitute, abandoned, and forsaken position, all understood in the sense of de-having, deprivation, and impoverishment. But *destiuere* in Latin also means to fix or set a position. That is, it means to firmly entrench oneself in a position contrary to the forces of the dispositifs, especially the dispositif of the proper. When inhabiting this form of form-of-life, one is liberated and free to use one's body however one chooses. Destituent power undoes and renders inoperative the biopolitical dispositifs, at least temporarily. This is an exemplary form-of-life whose very modality of being fundamentally and radically challenges the standing political order at its core.

If we were to advance a fair reading, we could conclude that, in the same fashion as Nancy, Agamben seeks to deconstruct the proprietary, moral, and authentic articulations of the proper to arrive at a sense of the proper that has been covered over by the modern dispositif of the proper. He "diagonalizes" the dialectic of the proper and the improper to disclose a more original etymological sense: **se-ethos*. From his early essays right up to his recent publications, we could say, he has consistently sought to resurrect the forgotten sense of Heraclitus's testimony "*ēthos anthrōpō daímōn*": "For man, *ethos*, the dwelling in the 'self' that is what is most proper and habitual for him, is what lacerates and divides [*daímōn*], the principle and place of a fracture" (*PI*, 171; *PE*, 118). Modern forms of impropriety provide an opening to diagonalize the distinction between proper and improper forms of life. The more improper one is, the closer one is to disclosing this truth. To render the improper proper thus does not mean that improper life is proper in the modern senses of the term; rather, being improper opens up the possibility of becoming proper in a radical manner that cannot be captured by the modern dispositif of the proper. Only by abandoning the proper, by becoming properly improper, can we enter into an ontological ethos where we are free to be our most proper being.

* * *

Contrary to Nancy and Agamben, Esposito argues that in our biopolitical order we have no choice other than to reconfigure the relationship between ontology, ethics, and politics. At their core, modern governments are immunizing machines. Life and government are so thoroughly intertwined that it is not possible to recalibrate the immunizing apparatuses to turn away from life. Not only do politics target life, but economics do as well. In our biopolitical economy, the dispositif of the proper and the immunizing apparatuses are so thoroughly enmeshed, almost to the point of being consubstantial and thus identical, that there is no way to escape or avoid them. We have no choice but to engage with this biopolitical economy in its own terms. We must find ways to weaken the immunizing apparatuses, to loosen them up, so that they are no longer capable of establishing rigid borders between lives, either of those living within them or those held outside. Only through conflict and strife can we find a politics that affirms our common life in *communitas*. And only in this manner is it possible to find an equilibrium between *immunitas* and *communitas*. This is a problem that is simultaneously ontological, ethical, and political.

Esposito's political and ethical notion of *communitas* unfolds in an ontology where being is no longer dominated by having. The first thing that must be accomplished is a traversal of *Homo approprians* and its immunizing apparatuses. In *Communitas*, this is accomplished by the ontological duty that forces open, exposes, and depropriates the subject. His *communitas* divides and shares out subjects in such a manner that they are obliged to give back to the *munus*. The *munus* must be shared. The deontological economy of *communitas* replaces the political economy of property with a notion that each has a duty, ontological and communal, to contribute to the *munus*. His radically deconstructed model of republicanism prioritizes positive liberty over negative liberty, obligations over rights, and informal politics over formal politics. In his subsequent writings, this ethical ontology is gradually translated into an affirmative model of biopolitics that seeks to affirm the vitality of lives, contrary to the devitalizing aspects of immunity. A politics *of* life must replace our current politics *on* life. In all of these writings he searches for ways to conceive of *communitas*, or more generally the common, in manners that disrupt the dispositif of the proper.

In his writings on the person and the thing, for example, he argues that we have to defend the impersonal and/or the body against the intrusion of this dispositif. The body today is starting to be subjected to this regime. There are now many examples of people, corporations, even governments that are claiming a right to own the body or body parts. If we are to continue to slip into this discourse, the body will be incorporated into the regime of the proper, and it will no longer serve as a potential site of liberation. The body is now key to this struggle, because the body has served as the primarily instrument, specifically in the Lockean metaphor of the hand that takes and appropriates, that constitutes a thing as property. But we have to ask what use it will be to turn the body into a piece of property when the regime of property ultimately leads to inequities and exploitation? So many bodies that are disposed by the proper are devitalized, commodified, depoliticized, and ultimately configured as bare and unworthy life (*zoē*). Whether these are the abducted bodies of indigenous women, the exploited bodies of sweatshop workers, the "disabled" bodies that are structurally excluded from basic facets of everyday lives, the bashed and beaten bodies of queer youth, or the bodies of refugees washing up on the shores of Europe, these and too many other bodies to list here are treated as disposable. The dispositif of the proper will continue to find new disposable bodies. What if the body were to be freed from this appropriative apparatus? What if a body were incommensurably singular but also common, which could be used without being possessed and thus exploited? Bodies could be put to common use, to contribute to the *munus*. When stated within the sensibility of the dispositif of the proper, such a formulation sounds highly precarious and it is open to a whole series of exploitive connotations. But Esposito implores us to think about the ramifications of this broader problem, before it is too late and the body has been subjected to the laws of the proper, the regime of rights, and ultimately immunized from the *munus*. What we have here is an intrinsic connection between ontology, ethics, and politics. For him, there is no other way.

Esposito takes a stronger position on the dispositif of the proper than Agamben and Nancy, who seek to deconstruct the proprietary, moral, and authentic articulations in search of a hidden dimension. Esposito is clear on this account. The proper is private and exclusive. Neither public nor communal property is suitable for thinking about the commons because both are derivatives of private property. Not even rendering the proper improper will work, because if we are to dis-contain the commons from the dispositif of the proper, the dialectic of alienation and appropriation must be traversed.

* * *

If we are to live in a shared world where the common is no longer constituted by the divisiveness of the proper and being is no longer determined by having, we must expose and ultimately render inoperative the dispositif of the proper. There are no reversals available here. The appropriative disposition of *Homo approprians* must be disrupted, incapacitated, and, in the long run, dismantled so that we can develop new forms of resistance that traverse the dialectic of alienation and appropriation. Agamben, Esposito, and Nancy, are but three of the many contemporary philosophers who have sought to resurrect and contemporize this long-standing radical critique. This philosophical critique continues to be grounded in the material, political, economic, and environment, but it addresses more than a way of living and being in common, because in our world it now addresses the ultimate exigency – the ontological exigency.

# Abbreviations

Works that are cited frequently have been abbreviated as follows.

Giorgio Agamben

*AP* *Altissima povertà. Regole monastiche e forma di vita* (Milano: Neri Pozza, 2011).

*CC* *The Coming Community*, trans. Michael Hardt (Minneapolis: University of Minnesota Press, 1993).

*CCD* *Che cos'è un dispositivo?* (Roma: Nottetempo, 2006).

*CV* *La comunità che viene* (Torino: Bollati Boringhieri, 2001).

*DP* "What Is a Destituent Power?" In *Environment and Planning D: Society and Space* 32 (2014): 65–74.

*HS* *Homo Sacer: Sovereign Power and Bare Life*, trans. Daniel Heller-Roazen (Stanford, CA: Stanford University Press, 1998).

*HP* *The Highest Poverty: Monastic Rules and Form-of-Life*, trans. Adam Kotsko (Stanford, CA: Stanford University Press, 2013).

*KG* *The Kingdom and the Glory: For a Theological Genealogy of Economy and Government*, trans. Lorenzo Chiesa (Stanford, CA: Stanford University Press, 2011).

*LO* *L'aperto: L'uomo e l'animale* (Torino: Bollati Boringhieri, 2002).

*ODE* *Opus Dei: An Archaeology of Duty*, trans. Adam Kotsko (Stanford, CA: Stanford University Press, 2013).

*ODI* Agamben, Giorgio. *Opus Dei. Archeologia dell'ufficio* (Torino: Bollati Boringhieri, 2012).

*PE* *Potentialities: Collected Essays in Philosophy*, trans. Daniel Heller-Roazen (Stanford, CA: Stanford University Press, 1999).

*PI* *La potenza del pensiero* (Vicenza: Neri Pozza, 2005).

*MSF* *Mezzi Senza Fine* (Torino: Bollati Boringhieri, 2013, 2nd printing).

*MWE* *Means without End: Notes on Politics*, trans. Cesare Carino and Vincenzo Binetti (Minneapolis: University of Minnesota Press, 2000).

*RA* *Remnants of Auschwitz: The Witness and the Archive*, trans. Daniel Heller-Roazen (New York: Zone Books, 2002).

*RG* *Il Regno e la Gloria. Per una genealogia teologica dell'economia e del governo* (Vicenza: Neri Pozza, 2007).

*SE* *State of Exception*, trans. Kevin Attell (Chicago: University of Chicago Press, 2005).

*SLE* *The Sacrament of Language: An Archaeology of the Oath*, trans. Adam Kotsko (Stanford, CA: Stanford University Press, 2011).

*SLI* *Il sacramento del linguaggio. Archeologia del giuramento* (Roma: Gius, Laterza and Figli, 2008).

*ST* *Stasis. La guerra civile come paradigma politico* (Torino: Bollati Boringhieri, 2015).

*TO* *The Open: Man and Animal*, trans. Kevin Attell (Stanford, CA: Stanford University Press, 2004).

*WA* *What Is an Apparatus? And Other Essays*, trans. David Kishik and Stefan Pedatella (Stanford, CA: Stanford University Press, 2009).

*WM* "The Work of Man," trans. Kevin Attell in *Giorgio Agamben: Sovereignty and Life*, eds. Matthew Calarco and Steven DeCaroli (Stanford, CA: Stanford University Press, 2007): 1–10.

## Maurice Blanchot

*CU* *La communauté inavouable*. (Paris: Les Éditions de Minuit, 1983).

*UC* *The Unavowable Community*, trans. Pierre Joris. (Barrytown, NY: Station Hill, 1988).

## Roberto Esposito

*BBF* *Bíos: Biopolitica e filosofia* (Torino: Einaudi, 2004).

*BBP* *Bíos: Biopolitics and Philosophy*, trans. Timothy C. Campbell (Minneapolis: University of Minnesota Press, 2008).

*CE* *Communitas: The Origin and Destiny of Community*, trans. Timothy C. Campbell (Stanford, CA: Stanford University Press, 2010).

*CI* *Communitas: Origine e destino della comunità* (Torino: Einaudi, 1998).

*CIB* "Community, Immunity, Biopolitics," trans. Zakiya Hanafi. *Angelaki* 18, no. 3 (2013), 83–90.

*IME* *Immunitas: The Protection and Negation of Life*, trans. Zakiya Hanafi (Cambridge, UK: Polity, 2011).

*IMI* *Immunitas: Protezione e negazione della vita* (Torino, Einaudi, 2002).

*LT* *Living Thought: The Origins and Actuality of Italian Philosophy*, trans. Zakiya Hanafi (Stanford, CA: Stanford University Press, 2012).

*PT* *Persons and Things*, trans. Zakiya Hanafi (Cambridge, UK: Polity, 2015).

*TOP* *Terms of the Political: Community, Immunity, Biopolitics*, trans. Rhiannon Neol Welch (New York: Fordham University Press, 2013).

*TP* *Third Person: Politics of Life and Philosophy of the Impersonal*, trans. Zakiya Hanafi. Cambridge, UK: Polity, 2012).

## Martin Heidegger

*BT* *Being and Time*, trans. John Macquarrie and Edward Robinson (New York: Harper & Row, 1962).

*BW* *Martin Heidegger: Basic Writings*, trans. Frank A. Capuzzi and J. Glen Gray (New York: Harper Collins Publishers, 1993).

*ID* "The Principle of Identity," in *Identity and Difference*, trans. Joan Stambaugh (Chicago: University of Chicago Press, 2002).

*SI* "Der Satz der Identität," in *Identity and Difference* (Chicago: University of Chicago Press, 2002).

*TB* *On Time and Being*, trans. Joan Stambaugh (New York: Harper & Row, 1972).

*ZSD* *Zur Sache des Denkens* (Tübingen: Max Niemeyer, 1969).

## Jean-Luc Nancy

*AFT* *A Finite Thinking*, ed. Simon Sparks (Stanford, CA: Stanford University Press, 1993).

*BP* *The Birth to Presence*, trans. Brian Holmes (Stanford, CA: Stanford University Press, 1993).

*BSP* *Being Singular Plural*, trans. Anne O'Byrne and Robert Richardson (Stanford, CA: Stanford University Press, 2000).

*CD* *La Communauté désoeuvrée* (Paris: Christian Bourgois Editeur, 1986).

*CWM* *La Creation du monde, ou, la mondialisation* (Paris: Galilée, 2002).
*CWG* *The Creation of the World, or Globalization*, trans. David Pettigrew and François Raffoul (Albany, NY: SUNY Press, 2007).
*EF* *The Experience of Freedom*, trans. Bridget McDonald (Stanford, CA: Stanford University Press, 1993).
*ESP* *Être singulier pluriel* (Paris: Galilée, 1996).
*IO* *The Inoperative Community*, trans. Peter Connor (Minneapolis: University of Minnesota Press, 1991).
*LC* *La Comparution: politique à venir* (Paris: Christian Bourgois Editeur, 1991).
*LCD* *La Communauté désavouée* (Paris: Galilée, 2014).
*RP* *Retreating the Political*, ed., Simon Sparks (New York: Routledge, 1997).
*SM* *Le Sens du monde* (Paris: Galilée, 1993).
*SW* *The Sense of the World*, trans. Jeffrey S. Librett (Minneapolis: Minnesota University Press, 1997)
*TD* *The Truth of Democracy*, trans. Pascale-Anne Brault and Michael Naas (New York: Fordham University Press, 2010).
*TC* "The Compearance: from the Existence of 'Communism' to the Community of 'Existence,'" trans. Tracy B. Strong. In *Political Theory* 20:3 (1992): 371–98.
*UPF* *Une pensée finie*. Paris: Galilée, 1990).

Pierre-Joseph Proudhon

*QP* *Qu'est-ce que la propriété?* (Paris: Libraire Internationale, 1867).
*WP* *What Is Property*? trans. Donald R. Kelly and Bonnie G. Smith (New York: Cambridge University Press, 2005).

# Notes

## Introduction

1. There is now a substantial debate about the meaning and the application of the term *dispositif* in contemporary biopolitical theory, especially in the Italian strains. Drawing from Michel Foucault in *Commonwealth*, Michael Hardt and Antonio Negri characterize a dispositif as a "network of heterogeneous elements oriented by a strategic purpose" and as "the material, social, affective, and cognitive mechanisms active in the production of subjectivity" (2009, 126). This is a slightly different definition than the one given by Agamben in "What Is an Apparatus?" where he likens a dispositif to an *oikonomia*. A dispositif, he contends, is "a set of practices, bodies of knowledge, measures, and institutions that aim to manage, govern, control, and orient—in a way that purports to be useful—the behaviours, gestures, and thoughts of human beings" (*WA*, 12; *CCD*, 20). Later he defines a dispositif as "anything that has in some way the capacity to capture, orient, determine, intercept, model, control, or secure the gestures, behaviours, opinions, or discourses of living beings" (*WA*, 14; *CCD*, 22).

In this book, I use the term in its widest possible sense. I examine the various nuances in the ways the term has been employed, especially in the writings of Agamben and Esposito. For now, it is necessary to point out that in addition to the characterizations listed already, I draw from Foucault and Gilles Deleuze. Foucault popularized the term in the mid-1970s. In the first volume of *The History of Sexuality*, for example, he addresses the "*dispositif* (or apparatus) of sexuality" (1981). His clearest definition is found in an interview called "The Confession of the Flesh" where he defines a dispositif as "a thoroughly heterogeneous ensemble consisting of discourses, institutions, architectural forms, regulatory decisions, laws, administrative measures, scientific statements, philosophical, moral and philanthropic propositions—in short, the said as much as the unsaid" (1980, 194). In the same text he notes that a dispositif is strategic. "It manipulates relations of forces," either by "developing them in a particular direction, blocking them, stabilising them, utilizing them, etc." It is thus embedded in power/knowledge relations: "the apparatus consists in," he contends, "strategies of relations of forces supporting, and supported by, types of knowledge" (1980, 194.). In "What Is a *Dispositif*?" Deleuze argues that dispositifs "are machines which make one see and speak" (1992, 160). A dispositif is composed of fractured and criss-crossing lines of force that determine what can and cannot be seen, what and how something can be said, and what forms of subjectivity are possible. The disjointed and often contradictory elements of the dispositif are discursive and nondiscursive. I would like to thank Mihnea Panu for bringing this wider literature to my attention. He exams this work in his forthcoming book *Enjoyment and Submission in Modern Fantasy* (2016) and in his first book *Contextualizing Family Planning* (2009).

## Chapter 1. Political Economy and the Proper

Earlier drafts of parts one and three appeared in my dissertation, while an earlier draft of part two can be found in Bird 2013.

1. With the recent publication of the *Schwarzen Hefte* finally putting an end to speculation about his racism and anti-Semitism, this line of attack will only increase. Heidegger was a romantic conservative. Although there are moments in his writings and lectures where his nationalist and racist beliefs shine through, it was in his personal conduct that his real political leanings were exposed. One needs no further proof than his betrayal of Husserl. From taking over the chair, to his opening address, to his ignominious dedication in *Being and Time*, Heidegger conducted himself not only as an unscrupulous and arrogant careerist (the kindest reading possible), but as an egomaniacal reprobate and racist schmuck. The same can be said for Proudhon, whose own diaries reveal an equally intolerant man who was as anti-Semitic as he was misogynistic. That said, it would be wrong to side with those like Pierre Bourdieu in *The Political Ontology of Martin Heidegger* (1991) or Richard Wolin in *The Heidegger Controversy* (1990), who advise us to reject the totality of Heidegger's thought. Rather than enter into philosophical navel-gazing, I believe we should listen to Brian Singer's précis of this problem: "we cannot simply reduce Heidegger's theory to the 'syllogism'" because the "problem . . . lies not just with Heidegger himself but with his influence, the latter being so extensive as to have inspired, directly or indirectly, generations of thinkers," including those "whose politics are

often very hostile to those of Heidegger" (1993, 540). We must accept, he concludes, that "Heidegger was both a Nazi *and* a great philosopher." After all, claims Badiou in the first sentence of *Being and Event*, "Heidegger is the last universally recognized philosopher" (2005, 1). For an overview of Heidegger's influence on the debate concerning community, see Bird, 2008; Bernasconi, 1993; Critchley, 1999; Gratton, 2004; James, 2006; Norris, 2011; and Raffoul, 1999.

2. Three representative texts are Bosteels, 2010; Elliot, 2011; and Norris, 2011.

3. See C. B. Macpherson's work on the "possessive individual," 1962, 1975, and 1978. Also see Vandana Shiva's critique of the Western property prejudice in *Biopiracy* (1997).

4. For a broader discussion of this history, see Armitage, 2004, and Pateman, 2007.

5. There is a contradiction in Locke's theory. Although his naturalized theory of private property could represent a strong argument against slavery, an emancipatory theory, Locke was employed as the secretary to the Lords Proprietors of Carolina. It is surmised that he helped to draft the 1682 Constitution of Carolina, *The Fundamental Constitutions of Carolina*, which provided a legal rationale for slave ownership. Further, this document was probably drafted during the same period that he wrote his chapter on property, "Of Property," in the *Second Treatise* (see Armitage, 2004). Not all humans, in other words, were entitled to become proprietary subjects, just European men.

6. This is a direct quote from the German edition; the English one reads "*propriété*—property (Eigentum) and characteristic feature (Eigenschaft)" and "property—possession (Eigentum) and peculiarity (Eigentümlichkeit)." The English translator has added possession as one of the two sense of *Eigentum*, which was not present in the German version.

7. One can find a similar line of argument in the "old" Marx. For example, in the opening pages of the first volume of *Capital*, Marx discusses the enigmatic character, that is, false semblance, of exchange relationships. He argues that capitalism is partially sustained in and through the mistaken identification of the personal with property. At this stage, "characters" appear as the "personifications of the economic relations that exist between them" (1974, 60). Commodification is the common measure of exchange relations.

8. "*la propriété de la propriété d'être la propriétaire.*"

9. "*Mais enfin, qu'est-ce que la souveraineté? C'est, dit-on, le «pouvoir de faire des lois». Autre absurdité, renouvelée du despotisme.*" This quote is from Charles Bonaventure Marie Toullier. Arendt says something similar when

she defines "sovereignty" as "the ideal of uncompromising self-sufficiency and mastership," which, she claims, "is contradictory to the very condition of plurality" (1998, 234). Underlines are used throughout to indicate that a foreign term has been italicized in the original.

10. "*il désigne la qualité par laquelle une chose est ce qu'elle est, la vertu qui lui est propre. . . . Il exprime le droit dominal d'un être intelligent et libre sur une chose.*"

11. I shall not carry this argument to its end because Proudhon's metaphysical claims are based on dated nineteenth-century philosophy. Further, he treated the subject as irrational, for which he then attempts to compensate by appealing to the "rule" of "rational law." One must therefore be selective with Proudhon. For a thorough discussion on how we can salvage classical anti-authoritarian theory, without reproducing some of its contradictory and antiquated axioms, see Newman 2001 and May 1994.

12. The contract was also incapable of curbing the corruptive forces of *amour propre* (selfishness) and returning humans to their more natural sense of *amour-de-soi* (love of self, self-preservation). Rousseau was one of the first critics of the dispositif of the proper and *Homo approprians*.

13. The definite article betrays his Judaeophobia.

14. "*[V]oleur est celle d'un homme qui cache, emporte, distrait une chose qui ne lui appartient pas, de quelque manière que ce soit.*" The English text translates "*appartient*" as "belong," but I have used "appertain" because "to belong" and "*appartenir*" have different etymologies.

15. Most French etymologists claim that "thief" (*voleur*) stems from "to fly" (*voler*). To steal something is to make it fly, that is, as if it was a magic trick. As in most of his work, including his translation of the Hebrew phrase, he does not provide sufficient evidence to back up his narrative. I merely employ him for figurative purposes here.

16. There is an interesting parallel here with Arendt. She does refer to him over the course of *The Human Condition* (1998, 67, 91). Their political perspectives are obviously different, but both are critical of the framing of property as invasive. Arendt favors exclusion, while Proudhon argues that property must be dropped altogether.

17. A more popular example is found in Herbert Marcuse's second chapter in *One-Dimensional Man* called "The Closing of the Political Universe" (1966). He notably entitles the subsection that focuses on Marx's *Grundrisse* as "Prospects of Containment" (1966, 34–48). I say this not to infer that Marcuse subscribed to the thesis of "technological determinism," as critics such as Perry Anderson argued in *Considerations of Western Marxism*, but to highlight how prominent this thesis was in the New Left.

18. Balibar also notes that "Individuals are 'proprietors of themselves' (or 'their own Person') only if they reappropriate their labor power and its

complete use, and thus labor itself. But the only 'subject' of this process is the collective social relationship" (ibid.). He is careful to point out that this "subject" is not the "society in the person."

19. Ricoeur also notes that Marx was not clear about this distinction in his early works, and he only clarified it in his later writings. This is evident with even a cursory reading of Marx's essay on alienation and estrangement.

20. "*Was beide Sachen zueinander gehören läßt, was beide Sachen nicht nur in ihr Eigenes bringt, sondern in ihr Zusammengehören verwahrt und darin hält, der Verhalt beider Sachen, der Sach-Verhalt, ist das Ereignis*" (1969, 20). The standard English translation reads: "What lets two matters belong together, what brings the two into their own and, even more, maintains and holds them in their belonging together—the way two matters stand, the matter at stake—is Appropriation." I have chosen not to stick with the Standard English translation for three reasons. First, it renders the "*Ereignis*" as the "Event of Appropriation," which for reasons I outline in the following chapter is a misreading. Second, the Standard English translation renders "*Eigenes*" as "own," which I have translated as "properness." Third, the Standard English translation misses Heidegger's play on the notions of "holding" and "things"/"matter" in such terms as "*Sach*," "*Verhalt*," and "*Sach-Verhalt*" (matter/thing, held, and fact of the matter).

21. See Taminiaux, 1997.

22. For a clear demonstration of Heidegger's hermeneutical method, see his lectures in *Hegel's Phenomenology of Spirit* (1988).

23. "*auf den Weg zu achten, weniger auf den Inhalt. Beim Inhalt recht zu weilen, verweht uns schon der Fortgang des Vortrages*."

24. Epoch or the phenomenological *epochē* derives from *epekhein*, "to pause, hold up a position" (*epi-* ["on"] + *ekhein* ["to hold"]). It translates as "*an sich halten*," claims Heidegger (*TB*, 9).

25. Of course, there is a reference here to Derrida's (1992) reading of Walter Benjamin's "Critique of Violence" (1978). Benjamin argues that "mythical violence is lawmaking" and "divine violence is law-destroying" (1978, 297). The "former is bloody, the latter is lethal without spilling blood"; the former is "bloody power over mere life for its own sake," while the latter is "pure power over all life for the sake of the living" (ibid.). Agamben uses this formulation in his own eschatological musings on the coming community. I mention this distinction to highlight, not the relationship between violence and politics, but that between violence and evidence, which remains a phenomenological and theological problem. Nancy is interesting on this front because he engages with the turn to negative theology in continental theory, yet he strives to dissolve the theistic strains. For him, "negativity" is not a "mystical negativity" (*ESP*, 195; *BSP*, 169).

26. B. C. Hutchens argues that Nancy's "textual strategy" examines a

"multi-stranded knot . . . whose ends are enclosed by the strands in such a way that to pull on any strand is merely to tighten the knot itself" (2005, 9). Alexander the Great's cutting of the Gordian knot is not a solution. "The Gordian knot is a perplexity: on the one hand, the strand of meaning is meaningful only once the knot is unraveled; yet, on the other, the meaning of the knot itself (tied, untied, or cut) is determined by the role the notion of meaning plays in the process of untying itself" (2005, 9).

## Chapter 2. Ontology and the Proper

The materials in this chapter were first formulated in a very crude form in the first chapter of my dissertation.

1. I have elected to set aside Esposito's interpretation of Heidegger and raise it in chapter 5 instead. Esposito has largely inherited the Heideggerian tradition from Nancy and Bataille. Of the three main philosophers, his theory of the proper is most engaged with the tradition of political economy, which is why he figured more prominently in chapter 1. Agamben's and Nancy's readings of the proper and ontology, on the other hand, are much more embedded with Heidegger's philosophy.

2. In the English Heideggerian literature, "ownership" and "authenticity" tend to be the most popular translations. For the former, see Boedeker, Jr., 2001; Dreyfus, 1991, 1994. For the latter, see Olafson, 1994, 1998 as well as Vogel, 1994. More recently, François Raffoul has argued that the *Ereignis* should be translated as "enowning" in "Rethinking Selfhood: From Enowning" (2007). These are but a few examples; the issue of interpreting *das Eigen* continues to be one of the most contentious topics in Heideggerian scholarship.

3. Heideggerian scholars who argue that he did account for the possibility of Being-with in an *eigentlich* manner cite this passage as proof. Lawrence Vogel, for example, refers to this as an "ethical" passage (see 1994). Given Heidegger's past and his reluctance to think through being-with, it is hard to read this passage as anything other than a moral dictum instructing us on how to become a more *eigentlich* individual.

4. For a discussion of this reception, see Armstrong, 2000, 1-67.

5. See Jean-Luc Nancy, "'What Is to Be Done?'" *Retreating the Political*, trans. Leslie Hill (New York: Routledge, 1996), 157–58. Also see Lysaker's two articles published in 1999.

6. One of the most popular Heideggerian motifs is idiomatic wordplay. His lecture on identity lives up to this reputation. In fact, there is a *Wortspiel, in idiomatischem Deutsch*, in the title of his lecture "*Der Satz der Identität.*" As this lecture unfolds, he traverses the metaphysical framework, which

is figuratively represented by turning the "principle of identity" into the "leap of identity." It becomes a "leap," "in the sense of a spring," away from the trappings of metaphysics. This transformation, he suggests, is so disruptive that a metaphysician is rendered incapable of grasping what has happened (*ID*, 32; *SI*, 96). It is a transversal that springs beyond the grounds of metaphysics, that is, *Abgrund*. Moreover, *Der Satz* has multiple uses in German, all of which are implicated at different points in this lecture. It can be translated as "principle," "theorem," "proposition," "sentence," "game," and in this instance, a "leap." It does not have the same etymology as the English word "*principle*," which derives from *princeps*, *primus* + *capere*, literally the "first taker."

7. Most of these connotations have been translated out of the English text, which even leaves out two of the most pointed and idiomatic German sentences that precede this thought.

8. "Conservative" is a political loanword that entered German from French, so we cannot make an immediate etymological connection between *Konservativer* and *Diener*. Chateaubriand first coined the political sense of this term in title of his journal *Le Conservateur* in 1819. The journal was dedicated to Edmund Burke, the Romantic critique of the Enlightenment, and the restoration of the monarchy in France. The ideal model of political conservatism is to have the collective personally serve the person of authority.

9. In this passage, Heidegger also makes a subtle play on the etymologies of *Gleichheit* (sameness/likeness) and *zusammen* (together), which is less evident in English. *Gleichheit* can be translated as sameness, equality, identity, likeness, and uniformity. "Like" derives from "*gelic*" (Old English), which has the same Proto-Germanic roots as *Gleichheit: *galikaz*. It is broken down as "having the same form with a corresponding body," from **ga-* ("with, together") **likan* ("body," such as *Leiche*—corpse in modern German). "Same," on the other hand, stems from *same/sama* (Old Norse). Like "*zusammen*," it is rooted in the Proto-Germanic term **samon*, which connotes a process that gathers things together. The gathered-together appear as if they are the same. *Gleichheit* (sameness/likeness) is therefore the result of an activity that gathers (*sammelt*) to-gether (*zu-sammen*). In German, *Sammlung zusammen* is an obvious tautology—gathering toward the gathering—and it is less commonly used than its English equivalent "gathering together." But unlike its English counterpart, it clearly emphasizes how sameness is synthetically produced.

10. It is quite plausible that one of the main references in this text is the Christian doctrine of the *communicatio idiomatum in concreto* or the doctrine of the genus of appropriation. One might argue that Heidegger was trying

to formulate the *Ereignis* as a nonappropriative, unidentifiable, and anhypostatic event of trans-propriation (*communicatio idiomatum in abstracto*). It would be interesting to compare this formulation with Agamben's more recent attempts to disrupt the economic theology that he claims was produced by the Church Fathers to salvage their Christological formulations of the Trinity. Both Agamben and Heidegger, one might argue (employing Karl Barth), seek to subvert the enhypostatic logic of appropriation and replace it with an anhypostatic formulation.

11. The English text translates *Ereignis* as "Event of Appropriation," *Übereignen* as "appropriation," *Vereignen* as "ownership," and *Zueignen* as "appropriation."

12. "*Das Zusammengehören von Mensch und Sein in der Weise der wechselseitigen Herausforderung bringt uns bestürzend näher, daß und wie der Mensch dem Sein vereignet, das Sein aber dem Menschenwesen zugeeignet ist*" (emphasis in original, ibid.). Both the "*zugeeignet*" and the "*vereignet*" are past participles tied to the "*ist*," which refer to the *belonging*-together.

13. *Grimms Deutsches Wörterbuch*. The first reads, "*aus eignem besitze in einen fremden geben*," and the second reads, "*proprium dare durch (ver) verstärkt, welches deutlich den übergang in fremden*." I have used the same work to examine "*Zueignen*."

14. "*Es gilt, dieses Eignen, worin Mensch und Sein einander ge-eignet sind, schlicht zu erfahren, d. h. einzukehren in das, was wir das Ereignis nennen*."

15. "*Il verbo solvo, da cui deriva il participio assoluto, si lascia, infatti, analizzare in se-luo e indica l'operazione sciogliere, di liberare (luo) che conduce (o riconduce) qualcosa al proprio *se*." The English text, correctly translates the seemingly insignificant clause "*si lascia . . . analizzare*" as "can be analysed," however, in doing so it fails to convey another sense of *solvo*—to permit something requires self-abandonment or letting oneself go.

16. Nancy refers to Agamben's interpretation in a footnote in the same passage.

17. In most of my quotes of Nancy, I have made slight modifications to the standard English translations of particular phrases or key words. I want to ensure that the orientative sense of his words and not just their significant sense is evident. In these instances, I have elected to use words that stem from similar etymologies or resonate with the broader strains he is trying to elaborate. Nancy is quite playful with language and his word selection creates multilayered texts. This cannot be directly translated into English, especially across an entire text. One does have more liberty, when translating short little passages, than a translator does who is often faced with the unenviable decision to choose between form or meaning. If the translation is to be readable, the translator often has to sacrifice the

literal for the idiomatic. From here on, I will not insert the cumbersome and ostentatious phrase "modified" when citing Nancy.

18. Nancy, on the other hand, seeks a "deconstruction of Christianity," which he defines as "the bringing to light of that which will have been the agent of Christianity as the very form of the West, much more deeply than all religion and even as the self-deconstruction of religion, that is, the accomplishment of philosophy by Judeo-Platonism and Latinity, ontotheology as its own end, the 'death of God' and the birth of the sense of the world as the abandonment without return and without *Aufhebung* of all 'christ,' that is, of all hypostasis of sense" (*SW*, 55, fn. 50; *SM*, 91, fn. 1).

19. "*où il se tient, se tenant et se saisissant lui-même, en ce lieu ou en cet avoir-lieu archi-originaire, comme la différence ouvert de sa mêmeté d'être*."

## Chapter 3. The Existential Community

1. Crowley's main critical references come from Simon Critchley and Oliver Marchart.

2. The term has recently been employed by Frédéric Neyrat in *Le communisme existential de Jean-Luc Nancy* (2013). Existential communism represents a second generation of radical French existential theory. Many books have been written on the first generation of thinkers that we have come to call "Existential Marxism." Besides Sartre's works, Maurice Merleau-Ponty wrote *Humanism and Terror* (1969) and *Adventures of the Dialectic* (1973). There are also numerous accounts of this largely post-war movement, including Mark Poster's comprehensive account of this movement in *Existential Marxism in Postwar France: From Sartre to Althusser* (1975) and *Sartre's Marxism* (1982), as well as Thomas R. Flynn's *Sartre and Marxist Existentialism* (1986).

3. *La communauté désavouée* (2014). Since this work has not been translated into English yet, all translations from this text are my own.

4. Nancy in Esposito and Nancy, "Dialogue on the Philosophy to Come" (2010). This exchange first appeared as the introduction to Davide Tarizzo's Italian translation of *Être singulier pluriel*, "Dialogo sulla filosofia a venire" in *Essere Singolare Plurale* (2001).

5. I thank Anne O'Byrne for pointing out to me the continuity in Nancy's thought a few years back. This insight has helped me tremendously. Besides O'Byrne's own *Natality and Finitude* (2010) and Eposito and Agamben's interpretations of Nancy, there are a few additional English studies on Nancy that have influenced my own thinking: Hutchens, 2005; Armstrong, 2009; James, 2005; and Morin, 2012.

6. In a footnote, Lacoue-Labarthe identifies his politics with the French

autonomous Marxist group *Socialisme ou Barbarie* and Nancy with the New Left literary magazine *Esprit*.

7. I examined his debate with Blanchot in Bird, 2008. For other accounts of this debate see Bernasconi, 1993; James, 2010; Hole, 2013; and Morin, 2012.

8. In "Myth Interrupted" he argues that foundational myths represent an attempt to appropriate the origins, which results in a closure of community. To overcome mythological thinking, we must carefully examine the resources that myths rely on. This is precisely what he does when he examines the horizons behind us and how community has been conceptualized in modernity (*CD*, 107–74; *IO*, 41–70).

9. See Bellah et al., 2008; Etzioni, 1994; MacIntyre, 1981; *Putnam, 1999; and of course* Tocqueville, 2000.

10. "Social capital" is a popular term Anglo-American sociologists use to "measure" group cohesiveness and reciprocity. Robert Putnam defines social capital as "*connections* among individuals—*social networks* and the *norms* of *reciprocity* and *trustworthiness* that arise from them. In that sense social capital is closely related to what some have called '*civic virtue*.' The difference is that 'social capital' calls attention to the fact that civic virtue is most powerful when *embedded* in a *dense network of reciprocal social relations*. A society of many virtuous but isolated individuals is not necessarily rich in social capital" (1999, 19).

Other famous definitions include James Coleman's: "Social capital is defined by its function. It is not a single entity, but a variety of different entities having two characteristics in common: They all consist of some aspect of social structure, and they facilitate certain actions of individuals who are within the structure" (1988, S98).

And Pierre Bourdieu's: "the aggregate of the actual or potential resources which are linked to possession of a durable network of more or less institutionalized relationships of mutual acquaintance or recognition" (1986, 248). Social capital is "made up of social obligations ('connections'), which is convertible, in certain conditions, into economic capital and may be institutionalized in the form of a title of nobility" (1986, 243).

Also see Granovettor, 1973; Isaksen, Sambasivan, and Hochschild, 2008; Portes, 1998; Putnam, 1995a, 1995b; Wellman, 1979; and Wellman and Wortley, 1990.

11. During this period, he appeals to a notion of "literary communism"; see his essay "Literary Communism" (*CD*, 175–98; *IO*, 71–81).

12. I am grateful Giovanbattista Tusa for pointing this out to me. Tusa has written a few important articles on Derrida's influence on Nancy, see 2011 and 2013.

13. *«Pour autant, toute espèce de phénoménologie, voire*

*d'outre-phénoménologie, n'ouvre pas encore assez à la venue du sens, ou au sens en tant que venue, ni immanente, ni transcendante. Cette venue est infiniment présupposée: on ne s'y laisse pas prendre, emporter, mettre à bout»*.

14. Nancy does concede, however, that even this third way is present in phenomenology. Phenomenology does, after all, seek to "preserve this presupposition," "as a protection against or a holding at a distance [*tenue à distance*] from that (the sense) which exceeds the phenomenon in the phenomenon itself" (*LSW*, 34–35; *TSW*, 17).

15. This is a concept of great importance in his political theory, which he continues to use in his writings. Ecotechnics represents the theoretical combination of Heidegger's critique of technology, the post-Marxist critique of the reproductive apparatuses in capitalism, and a critique of capitalist political economy. In short, it represents how the symbolic economy of modern capitalism enframes the world. Hutchens defines "ecotechnics" as the "circulation of capital and all its equipollences" (2005, 167). It is "the deleterious effects of the circulation of capital on the circulation of sense" (ibid., 141). Morin points out that Nancy uses this term to describe how the global economy works, where means and ends are confused, and politics becomes concerned with the "management of production, exchange, and growth," that is, the political becomes economical in contemporary political economy (2012; 103–5).

16. In *Networks of the Political*, Armstrong provides an excellent discussion of Nancy's critique of contemporary theories of citizenship, the subtle references, and how this passage connects to his original political issue of the retreat of the political (see 2009, 98–115).

17. This is a theme Nancy returns to in his recently translated essay "Fraternity" (2013).

18. Besides Anderson, 1991; see Balibar, 2004; Bauman, 2001; Delanty, 2010; Joseph, 2002; and Lingis, 1994.

19. For an excellent discussion of Nancy's deconstruction of the "symbolic," see O'Byrne, *Natality and Finitude*, 123–27. O'Byrne claims that Nancy's ontology is an "ontology of symbolic being." She notes that "the *sumbolon* has a material existence; specifically, it has a surface and edges that will be set alongside and touch the edge of its companion piece. It functions through touch as much as sight, allowing Nancy to make a shift away not from the ocular metaphor as such but from the assumption that what is primary is the singular seeing eye/I seeing an object that is understood as not itself seeing" (2010, 125). This reading has fundamentally influenced the one I have advanced in this chapter.

20. What is less well known is that Weber borrowed this theme from Tönnies (see Oexle, 1992; Cahnman, 1976).

21. For an excellent discussion of this passage, see François Raffoul, 1999.

22. This is nearly an impossible sentence to translate into English due to his wordplay. The original French reads: ". . . *mais non pas au sens extrinsèque du «partage»: il faut qu'ils se le partagent, il faut qu'ils se le «symbolisent». . . .*"

23. Daniela Calabrò has written an important work in Italian that thoroughly examines this motif across Nancy's oeuvre: *Dis-piegamenti: Soggetto, corpo e comunità in Jean-Luc Nancy* (2006). "*Dis-piegamenti*" refers simultaneously to Nancy's philosophical efforts to conceive of the sense of the world in a distributed, exposed, and open fashion; that is, *partagé.*

24. Nancy develops the notion of abandonment in "Abandoned Being" (*BP*, 36–47). "To *abandon*," Nancy argues, "is to remit, entrust, or turn over to such a sovereign power, and to remit, entrust, or turn over to its *ban*, that is, to its proclaiming, to its convening, and to its sentencing. . . . The law of abandonment requires that the law be applied through its withdrawal. The law of abandonment is the other of the law, which constitutes the law" (*BP*, 44).

25. How to conceive of the democracy in an open yet inclusive, existential yet postphenomenological, and communal yet postidentitarian fashion has remained one of the fundamental problems in Nancy's political philosophy. The distinction between the *formal* and ecstatic, which is not a direct negation of formality qua informality, notions of democracy has always remained at the forefront of his meditations on the topic. For example, in "Finite and Infinite Democracy" he juxtaposes the formal seizure of power and the model of a permanent revolution, or the insurrection and the installation of power (2009, 57; 2011, 64).

## Chapter 4: The Community Without Content

1. This is my translation of a discussion Agamben had with Alain Badiou about *The Coming Community*. The original reads: «*Pour moi, le problème est d'essayer de diagonaliser le propre et l'impropre, de penser, aussi bien en logique qu'en politique, une langue qui soit au-delà du propre et de l'impropre, c'est pourquoi je me heurte au pb* [*problème*] *de l'appartenance*». See Alain Badiou, "Intervention dans le cadre du Collège international de philosophie sur le livre de Giorgio Agamben: 'La communauté qui vient, théorie de la singularité quelconque,'" accessed on January 29, 2012. http://www.entretemps.asso.fr/Badiou/Agamben.htm).

2. In a short but poignant essay on friendship in philosophy, Agamben re-articulates how Nancy's existential reading of *partage* (*condivisione* in Italian) and community draws parallels with the Aristotelian model of friendship (*WA*, 25–37). Of all the writings I cite in this chapter, this one comes the closest to demonstrating his fidelity to Nancy's philosophy.

3. For an overview of this reading see Whyte, 2010; Edkins, 2007; and Elliot, 2011. For a defense of Agamben on this account, see Salzani, 2012.

4. For example, there is plenty of overlap between *Means Without End* and his other writings in the early 1990s. In fact, large portions of it contain verbatim passages found in *The Coming Community* (in part II) and *Homo Sacer* (in part I).

5. Exceptions to this rule are the three aforementioned articles as well as Acosta, 2011, and Durantyae, 2009.

6. My translation from Badiou "Intervention": «*Au fond, moi, j'essaie d'esquisser une théorie de l'événement dans le langage, à savoir l'être dit dans le langage, nom linguistique comme une espèce d'archi-événement, comme une espèce d'acte transcendantal, qui conditionne dans le langage tous les types d'événements. C'est peut-être une tâche impossible et pas très claire dans le livre. Mais l'idée était de penser le langage non plus comme une grammaire, non plus comme une langue avec des propriétés linguistiques, mais comme événement. L'idée était que ce qui est la langue propre de l'événement est événement dans le langage. L'être dans le langage est cet événement qui n'est ni propre ni impropre ni appartenance ni inappartenance. . . .* ». For an extensive discussion of this text see Acosta, 2011.

7. Durantaye argues that Agamben addresses the proper within "the realm of language" (2009, 181). Campbell also points out that the same gesture can be found in Agamben's distinction between the *Muselmann* and the speaking being in *Remnants of Auschwitz* (2011, 39).

8. The Italian version reads "*la situazione del logos nell'arkhē.*"

9. "*Per questo, nel libro, la domanda decisiva non è 'che fare?,' ma 'come fare,' e l'essere è meno importante del così.*"

10. Although Durantaye leaves out a discussion of Hannah Arendt, he provides an excellent overview of these concepts (see 2009, 18–20).

11. Agamben plays extensively with two distinctions in this essay: *ergon* (labor, work) and *argos* (from *a-ergon*, not working, idle, lazy, being without work); as well as *ergeia* (being-at-work) and *dunamis* (potentiality). For a detailed account of how he employs these terms in his theory of community, see Acosta, 2011.

12. "*l'opera dell'uomo*" and "*l'opera dell'uomo in quanto uomo.*"

13. The Italian edition of "On Potentiality," "*La potenza del pensiero,*" was published after the English version, and it has been significantly updated, so it does not directly correspond to the English one. I will only refer to the Italian text when necessary to elucidate a key concept.

14. In *Homo Sacer*, Agamben revisits this notion of transition in relation to Nancy, Bataille, Heidegger, and Kojève. "Everything depends on what is meant by 'inoperativeness.' It can be neither the simple absence of work nor (as in Bataille) a sovereign and useless form of negativity. The only coherent

way to understand inoperativeness is to think of it as a generic mode of potentiality that is not exhausted (like individual action or collective action understood as the sum of individual actions) in a *transitus de potentia ad actum*" (*HS*, 61–62).

15. I do not intend to provide a critical introduction of Agamben's political philosophy. Of the extensive literature on Agamben, Leland de la Durantaye's *Giorgio Agamben* (2009) stands out as a comprehensive account of Agamben's philosophy. Besides this book, I also draw heavily from Timothy Campbell's detailed study of Agamben's and Esposito's biopolitical renditions of the proper in *Improper Life* (2011). For situating Agamben's thought within the broader trajectory of contemporary "Italian Theory" (used in English in Italy), see Dario Gentili's chapter on Agamben in *Italian Theory: Dall'operaismo alla biopolitica* (2012).

16. In Badiou's "Intervention," he stated that, "if there is a second edition of this book, I am going to remove that definition of the planetary petite bourgeoisie" («*s'il y a une réédition de ce livre, je vais enlever cette définition de la petite bourgeoisie planétaire*»).

17. Agamben employs this derogatory term instead of "*romani*" to emphasize how the proper refers to those who are improper.

18. This is a controversial reading of the protests in Tiananmen Square. He is too quick to brush aside the "generic" call for "democracy" and "freedom," in order to advance his claim that the protestors' "demands" (*rivendicazione*) were marked by their "relative absence of determinate contents" (*CV*, 67; *CC*, 85).

19. In the *Means Without End* version of this sentence, he includes *Gattungwesen* in the parentheses: "(i.e., language as *Gattungwesen*)" (*MSF,* 69; *MWE,* 84).

20. He notes that this appendix should be read as a "commentary on section 9 of Martin Heidegger's *Being and Time* and proposition 6.44 of Ludwig Wittgenstein's *Tractus*" (*CV*, 71; *CC*, 89). In other words, a commentary on the relationship between essence, existence, and the *logos* qua discourse/speech (*Rede*) in Heidegger's existential analytical and Wittgenstein's mysterious, possibly theological statement that "It is not how things are in the world that is mystical, but *that* it exists."

21. "*[L]'unica esperienza etica . . . è di essere la (proprio) potenza, di esistere la (proprio) possibilità; di esporre, cioè, in ogni forma la propria amorfia e in ogni atto la propria inattualità.*"

22. Agamben claims this "expositive relationship" "is not a relationship of identity (the same thing, *idem*), but of ipseity (the same thing *ipsum*)" (*CV*, 79; *CC*, 96). Recalling the confusion between *idem* and the *auto* raised by Heidegger, Agamben claims in this text that many "misunderstandings in

philosophy have arisen" in their confusion. "The thing of thought is not the identity"—i.e., it, that one (*id-dem*)—"but the thing *itself*" (*la cosa stessa*). The "thing itself" is neither "another thing towards which the thing tends," nor "simply the same thing"; rather, "the thing here transcends toward *itself*, toward its own being such as it is" (*CV*, 79; *CC*, 96).

23. In *The Kingdom and the Glory* Agamben points out that when examining the "semantic history" of a term, we must distinguish between the "sense" and the "denotation" of the word. The former remains relatively the same, while the latter changes over time (*RG*, 34–35; *KG*, 20–21).

24. There are six main texts in this strain: *The Kingdom of the Glory* (*KG*), *The Sacrament of Language* (*SL*), *The Highest Poverty* (*HP*), *Opus Dei* (*OD*), *Stasis* (*ST*), and *L'uso dei corpi* (2014). Unfortunately, the last two texts were not yet available in English while I was writing the final draft of this chapter in the summer of 2015. I have included *Stasis* in this chapter, but not *L'uso dei corpi*. Given its length, range of topics, and difficulty level, it would have taken too long for me to work through this text with my functional reading level of Italian. At this stage in his writing, however, his core problems, solutions, and references have been repeated, and I believe that it is still possible to make many tentative conclusions regarding his ethics and politics without this text.

25. *The Open*, *What Is an Apparatus*, and "What Is a Destituent Power?"

26. Thanos Zartaloudis notes that within this providential machine "government is only possible" if these two levels are correlated (2010, 75). The kingdom represents the mystical and religious sphere of *auctoritas*, which grants—or legitimizes—authority to power. The government represents *potestas*, the actual exercise or execution of power.

27. He defines *oikonomia* as "a set of practices, bodies of knowledge, measures, and institutions that aim to manage, govern, control, and orient—in a way that purports to be useful—the behaviours, gestures, and thoughts of human beings" (*WA*, 12; *CCD*, 20).

28. This section was written in the summer of 2015, prior to the expected English translation of this work. All the translations are my own.

29. A note on the gender pronouns: since I am working with the English text which translates all the possessive pronouns into the masculine form, and since the subjects of these texts are men (monks and priests), I use the masculine form in this section.

30. *The Use of Bodies* is purported to be his most prescriptive text in this series. But, as I show in this section, he formulates a theory of the use of bodies in this text.

31. It would be interesting to conduct a more thorough account of how Agamben diverges from Foucault on this account. In *Discipline and Punish*,

Foucault repeatedly cites ascetictic practices as precursory forms of disciplinary techniques that converted the human body into an obedient, useful, and ultimately mechanical instrument—especially in the chapter on "docile bodies" (1995). I imagine such a study will be possible when his *Use of Bodies* has been published.

32. Of note, the English title for this book uses the hyphenated "form-of-life," whereas the Italian version uses "*forma di vita*." Agamben is very clear that his ideal is to think of a form-of-life where life and form completely coincide.

## Chapter 5: The Deontological Community

1. As with most of the main texts I have used in this book, periodically I have slightly modified the translations.

2. This chapter represents a combination of a number of publications. Part 1 represents an updated version of parts 2 and 3 from Bird, 2013. Part 2 represents an updated selection of pieces that I cowrote with Jon Short (Bird and Short, 2013). I am a grateful to Jon for allowing me to use this material in this chapter. All of these materials have been updated to fit with the broader trajectory of this book and several new paragraphs have been added.

3. For a discussion about *Communitas*'s place in the debate about community, and more particularly the debate on Nancy's theory, see Acosta, 2013; Calabrò, 2012; Hole, 2013; and Short, 2013.

4. My translation from "*La differenza rispetto a Nancy, Blanchot e Bataille, e in particolare a Nancy, che pure, per un periodo, ha avuto una certa influenza sul mio lavoro, sta nel fatto che, rispetto all'idea di comunità, egli punta tutta l'attenzione sull'elemento del cum, dell'avec, del mit, lavorando ad un'ontologia del con-esserci, che si rifà da un lato a Heidegger e dall'altro a Bataille*" (Saidel and Velasco Arias, 52).

5. Gerard Delanty is referring to the title of a collection of essays on communitarianism edited by Fred Dallmayr in 1978.

6. In *Bíos*, he claims that this immunizing function of Hobbes's social contract "not only places the problem of the *conservation vitae* at the centre of his own thought, but conditions it to the subordination of a constitutive power that is external to it, namely to a sovereign power," which is the basic foundation of the immunitary dispositif of modern biopolitics (*BBF*, 42; *BBP*, 46).

7. "*Sudditi . . . sono precisamente coloro che non hanno nulla in comune dal momento che tutto è stato diviso tra il 'mio' e il 'tuo': divisione senza condivisione.*"

8. "Finite existence is necessarily divided/shared [*partagée*]. 'Politics' must designate what *interests* us in the 'common.' The stakes are the interest (that which matters) of *inter-esse* (simultaneously: 'to be between,' 'to be separated,' 'to differ,' 'to be amongst,' 'to participate')" (*LC*, 94; *TC*, 390).

9. For a detailed examination of Esposito's relationship to the problem of the gift in continental philosophy and Maussian anthropology, see Weir, 2013. This is a problem he returns to in *Persons and Things*, which I will return to further below.

10. Of course, Bataille serves as the third person in the debate between Blanchot and Nancy, and peripherally in Agamben. Esposito's placement of this chapter at the end of this book is significant in this regard, which he signals by placing a reference to Blanchot's *Unavowable Community* in the first footnote of this chapter.

11. "*L'ufficiale . . . è ciò che deve e deve ciò è: è, cioè, un essere di comando.*"

12. This dichotomy has been well covered in the literature on Esposito. See Calabrò, 2012; Campbell, 2006; Gentile, 2012; and Short, 2014.

13. "*Si tratta, in qualche modo ed anzi in ogni modo, di rovesciare i rapporti di forza tra 'comune' ed 'immune.' Di separare, attraverso il comune, la protezione immunitaria dalla distruzione della vita. Di pensare diversamente la funzione di sistemi immunitari, facendone più che barriere escludenti, dei filtri di relazione tra interno ed esterno. Come? A partire da quali presupposti? Con quali strumenti? Il problema va affrontato a doppio livello. Quello della disattivazione degli apparati di immunizzazione negativa e quello dell'attivazione di nuovi spazi del comune*" (author's personal copy).

14. This reading has received both positive (Deutscher, 2010, 2013) and negative reactions (Chiesa, 2010; O'Byne, 2013).

15. The place of politics in Esposito's theory has been raised from different perspectives by Bosteels, 2010; Campbell, 2012; and Neyrat, 2010. The framing of the question is also the subject of the discussion Esposito has with Jean-Luc Nancy in "Dialogue on the Philosophy to Come" (2010).

16. For an excellent discussion of Esposito's use of "im-" in his writings on the "impolitical" as both a position internal to politics and against politics, see Bosteels, 2010. Esposito uses this double sense when writing about the improper. It is a spacing, a gap, even a hole inscribed within the very dispositif of the proper that is essential to its core functions. To appropriate and close it off is to put an end to politics, which, Esposito claims, results in "totalitarianism" (*BBF*, *BBP*). Esposito seeks to exploit this space to circumvent and traverse it. He employs this deconstructive motif across most of his writings. For a detailed account of how Esposito's notion of the impolitical serves as a radical deconstruction of the political, see "*Il pensiero dell'impolitico di Roberto Esposito*" (Gentile, 2012: 155–65).

17. For an examination of Esposito's treatment of property rights in contemporary biopolitical formulations, see Stone, 2014.

18. Besides *Third Person* and *Living Thought*, English translations of Esposito's theory of the impersonal can be found in "The *Dispositif* of the Person" (2012), "For a Philosophy of the Impersonal" (2010), and in *Two* (forthcoming). For a discussion of the person/impersonal in Esposito's recent writings, see Barkan, 2012; Bosteels, 2010; Campbell, 2011, 2012; Goodrich, 2012; and Russell, 2014.

19. "The maximum expansion of individual freedom. Only that this freedom comes by way of a potential reduction of the body to an appropriated thing. The point of suture between these opposites is always relative to the definition of person. To be the owner of a body, the person cannot be coextensive with it; in fact, the person is specifically defined by the distance that separates it from the body. If you look at the bioethics developed as part of the liberal tradition, you find, in its ultimate form, the ancient Roman separation" (*TP*, 13).

20. There is now a debate regarding the place of the impolitical in Esposito's thought in the English literature. For a positive account of the relation between his thinking of the impolitical, the *munus*, and the possibilities they present for affirmative biopolitics, see Acosta, 2013. For a negative account see Bosteels, 2010. Of course, the main work in question here is his now-classic text *Categories of the Impolitical* (2015), which although originally written in 1988 has just been translated into English.

# Bibliography

Acosta, María del Rosario. "A Tiny Displacement of the World: On Giorgio Agamben's Coming Community." *Epoché: A Journal for the History of Philosophy* 16(1) (Fall 2011), 93–112.

———. "Hegel on *Communitas*: An Unexplored Relationship Between Hegel and Esposito." *Angelaki* 18(3) (2013), 13–31.

Agamben, Giorgio. *The Coming Community*, trans. Michael Hardt. Minneapolis: University of Minnesota Press, 1993. *La comunità che viene*. Torino, Italy: Bollati Boringhieri, 2001.

———. *Infancy and History: The Destruction of Experience*, trans. Liz Heron. New York: Verso, 1993.

———. *Homo Sacer: Sovereign Power and Bare Life*, trans. Daniel Heller-Roazen. Stanford, CA: Stanford University Press, 1998.

———. *Potentialities: Collected Essays in Philosophy*, trans. Daniel Heller-Roazen. Stanford, CA: Stanford University Press, 1999. *La potenza del pensiero*. Vicenza, Italy: Neri Pozza, 2005.

———. *Means Without End: Notes on Politics*, trans. Cesare Carino and Vincenzo Binetti. Minneapolis: University of Minnesota Press, 2000). *Mezzi Senza Fine*. Torino, Italy: Bollati Boringhieri, 2013, 2nd printing.

———. "The Work of Man," trans. Kevin Attell. In *Giorgio Agamben: Sovereignty and Life*, ed. Matthew Calarco and Steven DeCaroli, 1–10. Stanford, CA: Stanford University Press, 2007). "*L'opera dell'uomo*." In *La potenza del pensiero*, 372–84. Vicenza, Italy: Neri Pozza, 2005).

———. *Remnants of Auschwitz: The Witness and the Archive*, trans. Daniel Heller-Roazen. New York: Zone Books, 2002.

———. *The Open: Man and Animal*, trans. Kevin Attell. Stanford, CA: Stanford University Press, 2004. *L'aperto: L'uomo e l'animale*. Torino, Italy: Bollati Boringhieri, 2002.

———. *State of Exception*, trans. Kevin Attell. Chicago: University of Chicago Press, 2005.

———. *What Is an Apparatus? And Other Essays*, trans. David Kishik and Stefan Pedatella. Stanford, CA: Stanford University Press, 2009. *Che cos'è un dispositivo?* Roma: Nottetempo, 2006.

———. *The Kingdom and the Glory: For a Theological Genealogy of Economy and Government*, trans. Lorenzo Chiesa. Stanford, CA: Stanford University Press, 2011. *Il Regno e la Gloria. Per una genealogia teologica dell'economia e del governo.* Vicenza, Italy: Neri Pozza, 2007.

———. *The Sacrament of Language: An Archaeology of the Oath*, trans. Adam Kotsko. Stanford, CA: Stanford University Press, 2011. *Il sacramento del linguaggio. Archeologia del giuramento.* Roma: Gius, Laterza and Figli, 2008.

———. *The Highest Poverty: Monastic Rules and Form-of-Life*, trans. Adam Kotsko. Stanford, CA: Stanford University Press, 2013. *Altissima povertà. Regole monastiche e forma di vita.* Milano, Italy: Neri Pozza, 2011.

———. *Opus Dei: An Archaeology of Duty*, trans. Adam Kotsko. Stanford, CA: Stanford University Press, 2013. *Opus Dei. Archeologia dell'ufficio.* Torino, Italy: Bollati Boringhieri, 2012.

———. "What Is a Destituent Power?" *Environment and Planning D: Society and Space* 32 (2014), 65–74.

———. *Stasis. La guerra civile come paradigma politico.* Torino, Italy: Bollati Boringhieri, 2015.

Anderson, Benedict. *Imagined Communities: Reflections on the Origin and Spread of Nationalism.* London: Verso, 1991.

Anderson, Perry. *Considerations of Western Marxism.* London: New Left Books, 1976.

Arendt, Hannah. *The Origins of Totalitarianism.* New York: Harcourt, 1976.

———. *The Human Condition.* Chicago: University of Chicago Press, 1998.

Aristotle. *Politics*, trans. C. D. C. Reeve. Indianapolis: Hackett Publishing Company, 1998.

Armitage, David. "John Locke, Carolina, and the *Two Treatises of Government.*" *Political Theory* 32(5) (2004), 602–27.

Armstrong, Philip. *Reticulations: Jean-Luc Nancy and the Networks of the Political.* Minneapolis: Minnesota University Press, 2009.

Badiou, Alain. 2005. *Being and Event*, trans. Oliver Feltham. New York: Continuum, 2005.

———. "Intervention dans le cadre du Collège international de philosophie sur le livre de Giorgio Agamben: 'La communauté qui vient,' théorie de la singularité quelconque." Accessed on January 29, 2012. http://www.entretemps.asso.fr/Badiou/Agamben.htm.

Balibar, Étienne. "'Possessive Individualism' Reversed: From Locke to Derrida." *Constellations* 9(3) (2002), 299–317.

———. *We, the People of Europe? Reflections on Transnational Citizenship*, trans. James Swenson. Princeton, NJ: Princeton University Press, 2004.

Barkan, Joshua. "Roberto Esposito's Political Biology and Corporate Forms of Life." *Law, Culture and the Humanities* 8(1)(2012), 84–104.

Bauman, Zygmunt. *Community: Seeking Safety in an Insecure World*. Cambridge, UK: Cambridge University Press, 2001.

Bellah, Robert N., et al. *Habits of the Heart: Individualism and Commitment in American Life*. Berkeley: University of California Press, 2008.

Benjamin, Walter. "Critique of Violence." In *Reflections: Essays, Aphorisms, Autobiographical Writings*, trans. Edmund Jephcott. New York, Shocken Books, 1982.

Berlin, Isaiah. "Two Concepts of Liberty." In *Four Essays on Liberty*, 118–72. Oxford, UK: Oxford University Press, 1969.

Bernasconi, Robert. "On Deconstructing Nostalgia for Community within the West: The Debate between Nancy and Blanchot." *Research in Phenomenology* 23 (1993), 3–21.

Bird, Greg. "Community beyond Hypostasis: Nancy Responds to Blanchot." *Angelaki* 13(1) (2008), 3–26.

———. "Roberto Esposito's Deontological Communal Contract." *Angelaki* 18(3) (2013), 33–48.

———. "Ripensare il proprio da Agamben a Esposito." In *Differenze Italiane: politica e filosofia: mappe e sconfinamenti*, ed. D. Gentili and E. Stimilli, 213–225. Roma: DeriveAprondi, 2015.

Bird, Greg, and Jon Short. "Community, Immunity, and the Proper: An Introduction to the Political Theory of Roberto Esposito." *Angelaki* 18(3) (2013), 1–12.

Blanchot, Maurice. *The Unavowable Community*, trans. Pierre Joris. Barrytown, NY: Station Hill, 1988. *La communauté inavouable*. Paris: Les Éditions de Minuit, 1983.

Boedeker, Jr., Edgar C. "Individual and Community in Early Heidegger: Situating das Man, and Self-ownership in Dasein's Ontological Structure." *Inquiry* 44 (2001), 63–100.

Bonito-Oliva, Rosella. "From the Immune Community to the Communitarian Immunity: On the Recent Reflections of Roberto Esposito," trans. Timothy Campbell. *Diacritics* 36(2) (2006), 70–82.

Bosteels, Bruno. "Politics, Infrapolitics, and the Impolitical: Notes on the Thought of Roberto Esposito and Alberto Moreiras." *The New Centennial Review* 10(2) (2010), 205–38.

Bourdieu, Pierre. "The Forms of Capital." In *Handbook of Theory and Research for the Sociology of Education*, 241–58. New York: Greenwood, 1986.

———. *The Political Ontology of Martin Heidegger*, trans. Peter Collier. Stanford, CA: Stanford University Press, 1991.

———. *Pascalian Meditations*, trans. Richard Nice. Stanford, CA: Stanford University Press, 2000.

Cahnman, Werner Jacob. "Tönnies, Durkheim and Weber." *Social Science Information* 15(6) (1976), 839–53.

Calabrò, Daniela. *Dis-piegamenti: Soggetto, corpo e comunità in Jean-Luc Nancy*. Milano, Italy: Mimesis, 2006.

———. *Les détous d'une pensée vivante: transitions et changements de paradigm dans la reflexion de Roberto Esposito*. Paris: Mimesis, 2012.

Campbell, Timothy. "Bios, Immunity, Life: The Thought of Roberto Esposito." *diacritics* 36(2) (2006), 2–22.

———. *Improper Life: Technology and Biopolitics from Heidegger to Agamben*. Minneapolis: University of Minnesota Press, 2011.

———. "'Enough of a Self': Esposito's Impersonal Biopolitics." *Law, Culture and the Humanities* 8(1) (2012), 31–46.

Caputo, John D. *Demythologizing Heidegger*. Indianapolis: Indiana University Press, 1993.

Chiesa, Lorenzo. "The Bio-Theo-Politics of Birth." *Angelaki* 16(3) (2011), 101–15.

Coleman, James S. "Social Capital in the Creation of Human Capital." *American Journal of Sociology* 94 (1988), 95–120.

Critchley, Simon. "With Being-With? Notes on Jean-Luc Nancy's Rewriting of Being and Time." *Studies in Practical Philosophy* 1(1) (1999), 53–67.

Crowley, Martin. "Being Beyond Politics, with Jean-Luc Nancy." *Qui Parle: Critical Humanities and Social Sciences* 22(2) (2014), 123–45.

Dahl, Robert A. *Who Governs? Democracy and Power in an American City*. New Haven, CT: Yale University Press, 1961.

De la Durantaye, Leland. *Giorgio Agamben: A Critical Introduction*. Stanford, CA: Stanford University Press, 2009.

Delanty, Gerard. *Community*, 2nd ed. New York: Routledge, 2010.

Deleuze, Gilles. "What Is a *Dispositif?*" In *Michel Foucault: Philosopher: Essays Translated from the French and German*, ed. T. J. Armstrong, 159–68. London: Harvester Wheatsheaf, 1992.

Derrida, Jacques. *Margins of Philosophy*, trans. Alan Bass. Chicago: University of Chicago Press, 1982.

———. *Of Spirit*, trans. Geoffrey Bennington and Rachel Bowlby. Chicago: University of Chicago Press, 1989.

———. "Force of Law: The 'Mystical Foundation of Authority.'" In

*Deconstruction and the Possibility of Justice*, ed. Drucilla Cornell. New York: Routledge, 1992.

———. *Specters of Marx*, trans. Peggy Kamuf. New York: Routledge, 1994.

———. *Positions*, trans. by Alan Bass.. London: Continuum, 2002.

———. *Sovereignties in Question: The Poetics of Paul Celan*, trans. Thomas Dutoit. New York: Fordham University Press, 2005.

———. *The Politics of Friendship*, trans. George Collins. New York: Verso, 2005.

Deutscher, Penelope. "Reproductive Politics, Biopolitics and Auto-immunity: From Foucault to Esposito." *Bioethical Inquiry* 7 (2010), 217–26.

———. "The Membrane and the Diaphragm: Derrida and Esposito on Immunity, Community, and Birth." *Angelaki* 18(3) (2013), 49–68.

Dreyfus, Hubert. *Being-in-the-World: A Commentary on Heidegger's Being and Time*, Division 1. Cambridge, MA: MIT Press, 1991.

———. "Interpreting Heidegger on Das Man." *Inquiry* 38 (1994), 423–30.

Durkheim, Emile. *The Division of Labor in Society*, trans. W. D. Halls. New York: The Free Press, 1984.

Edkins, Jenny. "Whatever Politics." In *Giorgio Agamben: Sovereignty and Life*, ed. Matthew Calarco and Steven DeCaroli, 70–91. Stanford, CA: Stanford University Press, 2007.

Elliot, Brian. "Community and Resistance in Heidegger, Nancy, and Agamben." *Philosophy and Social Criticism* 37(3) (2011), 259–71.

Esposito, Roberto. *Bíos: Biopolitics and Philosophy*, trans. Timothy C. Campbell. Minneapolis: University of Minnesota Press, 2008. *Bíos: Biopolitica e filosofia*. Torino, Italy: Einaudi, 2004.

———. *Communitas: The Origin and Destiny of Community*, trans. Timothy C. Campbell. Stanford, CA: Stanford University Press, 2010. *Communitas: Origine e destino della comunità*. Torino, Italy: Einaudi, 1998.

———. "For a Philosophy of the Impersonal," trans. Timothy Campbell. *The New Centennial Review* 10(2) (2010), 121–34.

———. *Immunitas: The Protection and Negation of Life*, trans. Zakiya Hanafi. Cambridge, UK: Polity, 2011. *Immunitas: Protezione e negazione della vita*. Torino, Einaudi, 2002.

———. *Third Person: Politics of Life and Philosophy of the Impersonal*, trans. Zakiya Hanafi. Cambridge, UK: Polity, 2012.

———. "The *Dispositif* of the Person." *Law, Culture and the Humanities* 8(1) (2012), 17–30.

———. *Living Thought: The Origins and Actuality of Italian Philosophy*, trans. Zakiya Hanafi. Stanford, CA: Stanford University Press, 2012.

———. *Terms of the Political: Community, Immunity, Biopolitics*, trans. Rhiannon Noel Welch. New York: Fordham University Press, 2013.

———. "Community, Immunity, Biopolitics," trans. Zakiya Hanafi. *Angelaki* 18(3) (2013), 83–90.

———. *Due: La macchina della teologia politica e il posto del pensiero.*. Turin: Einaudi, 2013. Included as English need to fix when it comes out in Winter 2015.

———. "German Philosophy, French Theory, Italian Thought." In *Differenze Italiane: politica e filosofia: mappe e sconfinamenti,* ed. D. Gentili and E. Stimilli, 9 –20. Roma: DeriveAprondi, 2015.

———. *Categories of the Impolitical,* trans. Connal Parsley. New York: Fordham University Press, 2015.

———. *Persons and Things,* trans. Zakiya Hanafi. Cambridge, UK: Polity Press, 2015.

Esposito, Roberto, and Jean-Luc Nancy, "Dialogue on the Philosophy to Come," trans. Timothy Campbell. *The Minnesota Review* 75 (2010), 71–88. "Dialogo sulla filosofia a venire." In *Essere Singolare Plurale,* trans. Davide Tarizzo, vii–xxix. Torino: Einaudi: 2001.

Etzioni, Amitai. *The Spirit of Community: The Reinvention of American Society.* New York: Simon, 1994.

Flynn, Thomas R. *Sartre and Marxist Existentialism.* Chicago: University of Chicago Press, 1986.

Foucault, Michel. "The Confession of the Flesh." In *Power/Knowledge: Selected Interviews and Other Writings 1972-1977,* ed. C. Gordon, 194–228. New York: Pantheon Books, 1980.

———. *The History of Sexuality I,* trans. Robert Hurley. London: Penguin, 1981.

———. *Discipline and Punish: The Birth of the Prison,* trans. A. Sheridan Smith. New York: Vintage Books, 1995.

———. *Society Must Be Defended: Lectures at the Collège de France 1975–1976,* trans. David Macey. New York: Picador, 2003.

Fraser, Nancy. "The French Derrideans: Politicizing Deconstruction or Deconstructing the Political?" *New German Critique* 33 (Autumn 1984), 127–54.

Gadamer, Hans-Georg. *Truth and Method,* trans. Joel Weinsheimer. New York: Continuum, 2004.

Gentili, Dario. *Italian Theory: Dall'operaismo alla biopolitica.* Bologna: Mulino, 2012.

Goodrich, Peter. "The Theatre of Emblems: On the Optical Apparatus and the Investiture of Persons." *Law, Culture and the Humanities* 8(1) (2012), 47–67.

Granovettor, Mark. "The Strength of Weak Ties." *American Journal of Sociology* 78 (1973), 1360–80.

Gratton, Peter. "Mitsein and Sharing: Heidegger and Nancy on the Political Community." *Review Journal of Political Philosophy* 2(1–2) (2004), 33–58.

Habermas, Jürgen. *The Structural Transformation of the Public Sphere: An Inquiry into a Category of Bourgeois Society*, trans. Thomas Burger. Cambridge, MA: MIT Press, 1989.

———. *Being and Time*, trans. John Macquarrie and Edward Robinson. New York: Harper & Row, 1962.

———. "Time and Being." In *On Time and Being*, trans. Joan Stambaugh. New York: Harper & Row, 1972. *Zur Sache des Denkens*. Tübingen, Germany: Max Niemeyer, 1969.

———. "The Self-Assertion of the German University," trans. Karston Harries. *Review of Metaphysics* 38 (March 1985), 467–502.

———. *Hegel's Phenomenology of Spirit*, trans. Parvis Emad and Kenneth Maly. Bloomington: Indiana University Press, 1998.

———. *Martin Heidegger: Basic Writings*, trans. Frank A. Capuzzi and J. Glen Gray. New York: Harper Collins, 1993.

———. "The Principle of Identity." In *Identity and Difference*, trans. Joan Stambaugh. Chicago: University of Chicago Press, 2002. "Der Satz der Identität." In *Identity and Difference*, trans. Joan Stambaugh. Chicago: University of Chicago Press, 2002.

Hole, Kristin. "The Ethics of Community: Nancy, Blanchot, Esposito." *Angelaki* 18(3) (2013), 103–18.

Husserl, Edmund. *The Crisis of the European Sciences and Transcendental Phenomenology: An Introduction to Phenomenological Philosophy*, trans. D. Carr. Evanston, IL: Northwestern University Press, 1970.

———. *Cartesian Meditations: An Introduction to Phenomenology*, trans. Dorion Cairns. The Hague, Netherlands: Martinus Nijhoff, 1973.

———. *Logical Investigations*. Vol. 1, trans. J. N. Finley. New York: Routledge, 2001.

Hutchens, B. C. *Jean-Luc Nancy and the Future of Philosophy*. Montreal: McGill-Queens University Press, 2005.

Isaksen, Lise Widding; Sambasivan Uma Devi; and Arlie Russell Hochschild. "Global Care Crisis: A Problem of Capital, Care Chain, or Commons?" *American Behavioral Scientist* 52:3 (2008), 405–25.

James, Ian. *The Fragmentary Demand: An Introduction to the Philosophy of Jean-Luc Nancy*. Stanford, CA: Stanford University Press, 2006.

———. "Naming the Nothing: Nancy and Blanchot on Community." *Culture, Theory and Critique* 51(2) (2010), 171–87.

Joseph, Miranda. *Against the Romance of Community*. Minneapolis: University of Minnesota Press, 2002.

Kojève, Alexandre. "In Place of an Introduction." In *Introduction to the Reading of Hegel: Lectures on the Phenomenology of Spirit*, ed. Allan

Bloom, trans. James H. Nichols, Jr. Ithaca, NY: Cornell University Press, 1980.

Laclau, Ernesto, and Chantal Mouffe. *Hegemony and Socialist Strategy: Towards a Radical Democratic Politics*. London: Verso: 1985.

Lefort, Claude. "The Permanence of the Theological-Political." In *Democracy and Political Theory*, trans. David Macey, 213–55. Cambridge, UK: Polity Press, 1988.

Lévinas, Emmanuel. "Meaning and Sense." In *Emannuel Lévinas: Basic Philosophical Writings*, ed. Adriann T. Peperzak et al. Indianapolis: Indiana University Press, 1996.

Levinson, Brett. "Biopolitics in Balance: Esposito's Response to Foucault." *The New Centennial Review* 10(2) (2010), 239–62.

Lingis, Alphonso. *The Community of Those Who Have Nothing in Common*. Bloomington: Indiana University Press, 1994.

Lysaker, John T. "Lenin, Nancy, and the Politics of Total War." *Philosophy Today* 43 (1999), 186–95.

———. "On What Is to Be Done with What Is Always Already Arriving." *Studies in Practical Philosophy* 1(1) (1999), 86–113.

Locke, John. *Second Treatise on Government*, ed. C. B. Macpherson. Indianapolis, IN: Hackett Publishing Company, 1980).

MacIntyre, Alasdair. *After Virtue*. Notre Dame, IN: University of Notre Dame Press, 1981.

Macpherson, C. B. *The Political Theory of Possessive Individualism: Hobbes to Locke*. London: Oxford University Press, 1962.

———. "Liberalism and the Political Theory of Property." In *Domination*, ed. Alkis Kontos, 89–100. Toronto: University of Toronto Press, 1975.

———. "The Meaning of Property." *Property: Mainstream and Critical Positions*, 1–13. Toronto: University of Toronto Press, 1978.

Marcuse, Herbert. *One-Dimensional Man*. Boston: Beacon Press, 1966.

Marx, Karl. *Capital*. Vol. 1, trans. Eden and Cedar Paul. New York: Everyman's Library, 1974.

———. "Estranged Labour. " In *The Economic and Philosophical Manuscripts of 1844*, trans. Martin Milligan, 69–84. Amherst, NY: Prometheus Books, 1998.

Marx, Karl, and Frederick Engels. *The German Ideology*. Amherst, NY: Prometheus Books, 1998. "Die deutsche Ideologie." In *Karl Marx und Frederich Engels: Werke, Band 3*, 9–521. Berlin: Institut für Marximus-Leninismus, 1954.

———. "The Communist Manifesto." In *The Economic and Philosophical Manuscripts of 1844*, trans. Martin Milligan, 203–43. Amherst, NY: Prometheus Books, 1998.

May, Todd. *The Political Philosophy of Poststructuralist Anarchism*. University Park: Pennsylvania State University Press, 1994.

Merleau-Ponty, Maurice. *Humanism and Terror: An Essay on the Communist Problem*, trans. John O'Neill. Boston: Beacon Press, 1969.

———. *Adventures of the Dialectic*, trans. Joseph Bien. Evanston, IL: Northwestern University Press, 1973.

Michels, Robert. *Political Parties: A Sociological Study of the Oligarchical Tendencies of Modern Democracy*, trans. Eden and Cedar Paul. New York: Free Press, 1962.

Mills, Catherine. "Agamben's Messianic Politics: Biopolitics, Abandonment and Happy Life," *Contretemps* 5 (2005).

Mills, C. Wright. *The Power Elite*. New York: Oxford University Press, 1956.

Morin, Marie-Eve. *Jean-Luc Nancy*. Malden, MA: Polity, 2012.

Nancy, Jean-Luc. *The Experience of Freedom*, trans. Bridget McDonald. Stanford, CA: Stanford University Press, 1988.

———. *The Inoperative Community*, trans. Peter Connor. Minneapolis: University of Minnesota Press, 1991. *La communauté désoeuvrée*. Paris: Christian Bourgois Editeur, 1986.

———. "The Compearance: From the Existence of 'Communism' to the Community of 'Existence,'" trans. Tracy B. Strong. *Political Theory* 20(3) (1992), 371–98. "La comparution." *La comparution: politique à venir*, eds. Jean-Luc Nancy and Jean-Christophe Bailly. Paris: Christian Bourgois Editeur, 1991.

———. *The Birth to Presence*, trans. Brian Holmes. Stanford, CA: Stanford University Press, 1993.

———. *The Sense of the World*, trans. Jeffrey S. Librett. Minneapolis: University of Minnesota Press, 1997. *Le sens du monde*. Paris: Galilée, 1993.

———. *Being Singular Plural*, trans. Anne E. O'Bryne and Robert D. Richardson. Stanford: Stanford University Press, 2000. *Être singulier pluriel*. Paris: Galilée, 1996.

———. *La Communauté affrontée*. Paris: Galilée, 2001.

———. *A Finite Thinking*, ed. Simon Sparks. Stanford, CA: Stanford University Press, 2003. *Une pensée finie*. Paris: Galilée, 1990.

———. 2003. "'Our World,' an Interview," trans. Emma Campbell. *Angelaki* 8 (2) (2003), 43–54.

———. *The Creation of the World or Globalization*, trans. François Raffoul and David Pettigrew. Albany: State University of New York Press, 2007. *La creation du monde, ou, la mondialisation*. Paris: Galilée, 2002.

———. *Dis-Enclosure: The Deconstruction of Christianity*, trans. Bettina Bergo et al. New York: Fordham University Press, 2008.

———. "Conloquium," trans. Janell Watson. *Minnesota Review* 75 (2010), 101–8.

———. "Finite and Infinite Democracy," trans. William McCuaig. In *Democracy in What State*, 58–75. New York: Columbia University Press, 2011."Démocratie finie et infinite." In *Démocratie dans quell état?*, 53–65. Montréal: Les Éditions Écosociété, 2009.

———. *The Truth of Democracy*, trans. Pascale-Anne Brault and Michael Naas. New York: Fordham University Press, 2010.

———. "Fraternity," trans. Sarah Clift. *Angelaki* 18(3) (2013), 119–23.

———. *Adoration: The Deconstruction of Christianity II*, trans. John McKeane. New York: Fordham Press, 2013.

———. *La communauté désavouée*. Paris: Galilée, 2014.

Nancy, Jean-Luc, and Philippe Lacoue-Labarthe. *Retreating the Political*, ed. Simon Sparks. New York: Routledge, 1997.

Negri, Antonio. 2012. "The Sacred Dilemma of Inoperosity. On Giorgio Agamben's *Opus Dei*." Accessed on August 1, 2015. http://www.uninomade.org/negri-on-agamben-opus-dei/.

Negri, Antonio, and Michael Hardt. *Empire*. Cambridge, MA: Harvard University Press, 2000.

———. *Commonwealth*. Cambridge, MA: Harvard University Press, 2009.

Newman, Saul. "Derrida's Deconstruction of Authority." *Philosophy & Social Criticism* 27(3) (2001), 1–20.

Neyrat, Frédéric. "The Birth of Immunopolitics," trans. Arne De Boever. *Parrhesia* 10 (2010): 31–38.

———. *Le communisme existential de Jean-Luc Nancy*. Paris: Éditions Lignes, 2013.

Norris, Andrew. "Jean-Luc Nancy on the Political after Heidegger and Schmitt." *Philosophy and Social Criticism* 37(8) (2011), 899–913.

O'Byrne, Anne. *Natality and Finitude*. Indianapolis: Indiana University Press, 2010.

———. "*Communitas* and the Problem of Women." *Angelaki* 18(3) (2013), 125–38.

Oexle, Otto Gerhard. "Les groups sociaux du moyen age et les débuts de la sociologie contemporaine," trans. Florence Chaix. *Annales ESC* 3 (1992), 751–65.

Olafson, Frederick A. "Individualism, Subjectivity, and Presence: A Response to Taylor Carman" *Inquiry* 37 (1994), 331–37.

———. *Heidegger and the Ground of Ethics: A Study of Mitsein*. New York: Cambridge University Press, 1998.

Panu, Mihnea. *Contextualizing Family Planning: Truth, Subject, and the Other in US Governing*. New York: Palgrave, 2009.

———. *Enjoyment and Submission in Modern Fantasy*. New York: Palgrave, 2016.

Pateman, Carole. "The Settler Contract." In *Contract and Domination*, ed. Carole Pateman and Charles W. Mills, 35–78. Cambridge, UK: Polity, 2007.

Pitkin, Fenichel. *The Attack of the Blob: Hannah Arendt's Concept of the Social*. Chicago: University of Chicago Press, 1998.

Portes, Alejandro. "Social Capital: Its Origins and Applications in Modern Sociology." *Annual Review of Sociology* 24 (1998), 1–24.

Poster, Mark. *Existential Marxism in Postwar France: From Sartre to Althusser*. Princeton, NJ: Princeton University Press, 1975.

———. *Sartre's Marxism*. New York: Cambridge University Press, 1982.

Poulantzas, Nicos. *Political Power and Social Classes*. London: New Left Books, 1978.

Proudhon, Pierre-Joseph. *What Is Property*?, trans. Donald R. Kelly and Bonnie G. Smith. New York: Cambridge University Press, 2005. *Qu'est-ce que la propriété?* Paris: Libraire Internationale, 1867.

Putnam, Robert. "Bowling Alone: America's Declining Social Capital." *Journal of Democracy*, 6(1) (1995a), 65–78.

———. "Tuning In, Tuning Out: The Strange Disappearance of Social Capital in America." *Political Science & Politics* 28 (1995b), 664–83.

———. *Bowling Alone*. New York: Simon, 1999.

Raffoul, François. "The Logic of the With: On Nancy's Etre Singulier Pluriel." *Studies in Practical Philosophy* 1(1) (1999), 36–52.

———. "Rethinking Selfhood: From Enowning." *Research in Phenomenology* 37 (2007), 75–94.

———. *The Origins of Responsibility*. Bloomington: Indiana University Press, 2010.

Rawls, John. *A Theory of Justice*. Cambridge, MA: Belknap Press of Harvard University Press, 1971.

Ricoeur, Paul. *Hermeneutics and the Human Sciences*, trans. John B. Thompson. Cambridge, UK: Cambridge University Press, 1981.

———. *Lectures on Ideology and Utopia*, ed. George H. Taylor. New York: Columbia University Press, 1986.

———. *Oneself as Another*, trans. Kathleen Blamey. Chicago: University of Chicago Press, 1992.

Rousseau, Jean-Jacques. "Discourse on the Origin of Inequality among Men." In *Basic Political Writings*, trans. Donald A. Cress, 23–109. Indianapolis: Hackett, 1987.

———. *The Social Contract*, trans. Maurice Cranston. New York: Penguin, 2007.

Russell, Matheson. "The Politics of the Third Person: Esposito's *Third Person* and Rancière's *Disagreement.*" *Critical Horizons* 15(3) (2014), 211–30.

Saidel, Matías L., and Gonzalo Velasco Arias. *Roberto Esposito. Dall'impolitico all'impersonale: Conversazioni filosofiche.* Milan, Italy: Mimesis, 2012.

Salzani, Carlo. "*Quodlibet*: Giorgio Agamben's Anti-Utopia." *Utopian Studies* 23(1) (2012), 212–37.

Sartre, Jean-Paul. *Being and Nothingness: A Phenomenological Essay on Ontology*, trans. Hazel E. Barnes. New York: Washington Square Press, 1984.

———. *Critique of Dialectical Reason.* Vol. 1, trans. Alan Sheridan-Smith. New York: Verso, 1991.

Shiva, Vandana. *Biopiracy: The Plunder of Nature and Knowledge.* Boston: South End Press, 1997.

Short, Jon. "On an Obligatory Nothing: Situating the Political in Post-metaphysical Community." *Angelaki* 18(3) (2013), 139–54.

———. "Esposito, Foucault, and the Commons." *Theory and Event* 17(3) (2014).

Singer, Brian. "The 'Heidegger Affair': Philosophy, Politics, and the 'Political.'" *Theory and Society*, 22(4) (1993), 539–68.

Stone, Matthew. "Roberto Esposito and the Biopolitics of Property Rights." *Social & Legal Studies*, 24(3) (2015), 381–98.

Taminiaux, Jacques. *The Thracian Maid and the Professional Thinker: Arendt & Heidegger*, trans. Michael Gendre. Albany, NY: SUNY Press, 1997.

Taylor, Charles. "What's Wrong with Negative Liberty?" In *Philosophical Papers: Philosophy and the Human Sciences.* Vol. 2, 211–29. Cambridge, UK: Cambridge University Press, 1985.

———. "The Politics of Recognition." In *Multiculturalism: Examining the Politics of Recognition*, ed. A. Gutman, 25–73. Princeton: Princeton University Press, 1994.

———. "The Dynamics of Democratic Exclusion." In *Journal of Democracy* 9(4) (1998), 143–56.

Tocqueville, Alexis de. *Democracy in America.* Vols. 1 & 2, trans. Henry Reeve. Toronto: Bantam, 2000.

Tönnies, Ferdinand. *Community and Society*, trans. C. P. Loomis. New York: Harper Torchbooks, 1957.

———. "The Individual and the World in the Modern Age." In *Ferdinand Tönnies on Sociology: Pure, Applied, and Empirical. Selected Writing*, eds. W. J. Cahnman and R. Heberle. Chicago: University of Chicago Press, 1971.

Tusa, Giovanbattista. "La questione ultima: il tema del sacrificio tra Derrida e Nancy." In *Intorno a Jean-Luc Nancy*, ed. Ugo Perone, 117–22. Torino, Italy: Rosenberg & Sellier, 2011.

———. "Senza Riserva." *Epèkeina* 3(2) (2013), 261–83.

Vogel, Lawrence. *The Fragile "We": Ethical Implications of Heidegger's "Being and Time."* Evanston, IL: Northwestern University Press, 1994.

Weber, Max. *Economy and Society.* 2 vols., trans. G. Roth and C. Wittich. Los Angeles: University of California Press, 1978.

———. *Max Weber: The Vocation Lectures*, trans. R. Livingston. Indianapolis: Hackett Publishing Company, 2004.

Weir, Lorna. "Roberto Esposito's Political Philosophy of the Gift." *Angelaki* 18(3) (2013), 155–67.

Wellman, Barry. "The Community Question." *American Journal of Sociology* 84 (March 1979), 1201–31.

——— and Scot Wortley."Different Strokes from Different Folks: Community Ties and Social Support." *American Journal of Sociology* 96(3) (1990), 558–88.

Whyte, Jessica. "'A New Use of the Self': Giorgio Agamben on the Coming Community." *Theory and Event* 13(1) (2010).

Wolin, Richard. *The Heidegger Controversy: A Critical Reader.* Cambridge, MA: MIT Press, 1993.

Zartaloudis, Thanos. *Giorgio Agamben: Power, Law and the Uses of Criticism.* London: Routledge, 2010.

# Index